Governing and Managing
Knowledge in Asia

Series in Innovation and Knowledge Management

Series Editor: Suliman Hawamdeh   **ISSN: 1793-1533**
                  (University of Oklahoma)

Vol. 1   Managing Strategic Enterprise Systems and e-Goverment Initiatives in Asia: A Casebook
edited by Pan Shan-Ling *(National University of Singapore)*

Vol. 2   Knowledge Management: Through the Technology Glass
by Meliha Handzic *(University of New South Wales)*

Vol. 3   Governing and Managing Knowledge in Asia
edited by Thomas Menkhoff *(Singapore Management University)*,
Hans-Dieter Evers *(Bonn University)* and Yue Wah Chay *(Nanyang Technological University)*

Series on Innovation and Knowledge Management – Vol. 3

Governing and Managing Knowledge in Asia

Editors

Thomas Menkhoff

Hans-Dieter Evers

Yue Wah Chay

World Scientific

NEW JERSEY · LONDON · SINGAPORE · BEIJING · SHANGHAI · HONG KONG · TAIPEI · CHENNAI

Published by

World Scientific Publishing Co. Pte. Ltd.

5 Toh Tuck Link, Singapore 596224

USA office: 27 Warren Street, Suite 401-402, Hackensack, NJ 07601

UK office: 57 Shelton Street, Covent Garden, London WC2H 9HE

Library of Congress Cataloging-in-Publication Data
Governing and managing knowledge in Asia / editors, Thomas Menkhoff, Hans-Dieter
  Evers, Yue Wah Chay.
    p. cm.
  Includes bibliographical references and index.
  ISBN 981-256-193-5 (pbk. : alk. paper) ISSN 1793-1533
    1. Knowledge management--Asia. I. Menkhoff, Thomas. II. Evers, Hans-Dieter. III.
  Chay, Yue Wah.

  HD30.2.G685 2005
  658.4'038--dc22

                         2005043820

British Library Cataloguing-in-Publication Data
A catalogue record for this book is available from the British Library.

Typeset by Stallion Press
Email: enquiries@stallionpress.com

Printed in Singapore by B & JO Enterprise

Contents

Part V   Focus on K-sharing Behavior in Organizations

Contributors

Yue Wah **CHAY** is Associate Professor of Psychology, School of Humanities & Social Sciences, Nanyang Technological University (NTU), Singapore. Prior to joining NTU, he was a faculty member of the School of Business, Singapore Management University (SMU) and the National University of Singapore (NUS). His current research interests include knowledge systems, citizenship behavior, work commitment, assessment and executive careers.

Ho-Beng **CHIA** is Assistant Professor at the Department of Management and Organization, National University of Singapore. His current research interests include motivating and encouraging organization citizenship behavior; knowledge sharing and creative problem solving; cross cultural negotiations and mediation as well as topics in human resource management.

Hans-Dieter **EVERS** is Professor and Senior Fellow, Center for Development Research, University of Bonn, Germany. He has taught at Bielefeld University, Monash University, Yale University, National University of Singapore and Gadjah Mada University and was several times a Visiting Professor of Management at the Singapore Management University and a Distinguished Visiting Professor of Sociology, National University of Singapore. He has published widely on development planning, knowledge governance and urbanisation in South-east Asia.

Solvay **GERKE** is Professor of South-east Asian Studies and Director, Center for Development Research, University of Bonn, Germany. She was a Visiting Fellow at the Institute of Malay Civilization, National University of Malaysia and at other South-east Asian universities. She has carried out extensive research on family planning, migration, life styles and social stratification in Indonesia and Malaysia. With Thomas Menkhoff she has edited a book *Chinese Entrepreneurship and Asian Business Networks* (London, 2002; 2004).

Dishan **KAMDAR** is Assistant Professor in Management at the Indian School of Business. He received his PhD from the National University of Singapore in 2004. His primary research interest is contextual work performance and extra-role behaviors. His research interest in extra role behavior includes both "promotive" and "prohibitive" behaviors like organizational citizenship behaviors (OCB), knowledge sharing, voice and whistle blowing.

Patrick **LAMBE** is founder of Straits Knowledge, a research and consulting firm in Singapore. He is also an Associate Adjunct Professor at Nanyang Technological University, and Adjunct Professor at Hong Kong Polytechnic University. His research interests are on taxonomies and on tacit knowledge transfer.

Lionel Meng Huat **LIM** was a Research Assistant at the Singapore Management University where he obtained a Bachelor of Business Administration degree (Summa cum Laude) with a concentration in Finance. He is currently working as an Analyst in a bank.

Benjamin **LOH** is Research Associate at the Institute of Southeast Asian Studies, Singapore. He holds an honours degree in Sociology from the National University of Singapore and was a Tun Dato Sir Cheng-Loke Tan scholar at the University of Warwick where he obtained an MA in Sociology in 2004. His research interests include organizational change management, knowledge sharing and management, industrial cluster policies in South-east Asia, and economic sociology.

RaviShankar **MAYASANDRA N**. is a Doctoral Student and Teaching Assistant in the Department of Information Systems, School of Computing, National University of Singapore. As part of his doctoral study, he has been involved in intensive field work at Infosys Technologies, Wipro Technologies, and Satyam Computer Services — three of India's top IT organizations. His research interests include global IT outsourcing, IT in developing nations, identity issues in organizations, knowledge management, and qualitative research methods.

Thomas **MENKHOFF** is Practice Associate Professor of Management in the Lee Kong Chian School of Business, Singapore Management University (SMU). He has formerly taught in the National University of Singapore, the University of Cologne and the University of Bielefeld in Germany. His current research interest is concentrated on knowledge management, change leadership and on Chinese business networks, on which he edited a book together with Solvay Gerke entitled *Chinese Entrepreneurship and Asian Business Networks* (2002; 2004).

Marshall W. **MEYER** is the Richard A. Sapp Professor of Management and Sociology at the Wharton Business School, University of Pennsylvania, USA. Previous appointments include the University of California, Irvine; University of California, Riverside; Cornell University and Harvard University. Marshall's research interests comprise organizational theory and design, organizational change, organizational performance and not-for-profit organizations.

Glenn J. **NOSWORTHY** is Adjunct Associate Professor at the Department of Management and Organization, National University of Singapore. Now an independent consultant, he has been a lecturer and department head at NUS, has worked as an organizational psychologist with several public sector organizations in Canada and Singapore, and has been a regional vice president for an international consultancy, SHL. His research interests are in the areas of organizational citizenship, knowledge sharing and applicant reactions to assessment.

Shan Ling **PAN** is Assistant Professor and the Coordinator of the Knowledge Management Laboratory in the Department of Information Systems of the School of Computing at the National University of Singapore. His primary research focuses on the recursive interaction of organizations and information technology (enterprise systems), with particular emphasis on issues related to work practices, cultures and structures from a knowledge perspective.

Thomas B. **RILEY** is the Chair and Executive Director of the Commonwealth Centre for e-Governance based in Ottawa, Canada. His work is focused on the development of e-Governance practices and readiness assessments for governments in the developing world. He has a thirty-two-year background in information and policy issues as they relate to good governance and good government.

Ai Chee **TANG** is Associate Director and currently the head of the Center for Academic Computing (CAC), the research IT support arm for Faculty Research and Schools at Singapore Management University. A pioneer of SMU since 1999, she helped to set up the IT Infrastructure in SMU, overseeing the implementation of critical network, servers and IT application systems. A business graduate from NUS, Ai Chee has more than 15 years of IT experience of which 10 is in the education industry. She is also a certified IT Project Manager (CITPM).

Milan **ZELENY** is Professor of Management Systems at Fordham University, New York, USA. Prior to his appointment at Fordham, he was Professor at the European Institute for Advanced Studies in Management (E.I.A.S.M.), Brussels; Associate Professor, Graduate School of Business, Columbia University; and Assistant Professor, CBA, University of South Carolina. Milan is Editor-in-Chief of *Human Systems Management*. His research interests/specializations include knowledge management, high technology management and multiple criteria decision making.

List of Figures

List of Tables

Acknowledgments

The editors gratefully acknowledge the support they received from the Singapore Management University (SMU) with regard to the set-up and scholarly activities of the research interest group "The Knowledge Force" as well as the generous funding of two SMU research projects which inspired the production of this monograph: (i) *Benchmarking Organizational Knowledge: A Study of Singapore and German Organizations* (Chay Yue Wah, Thomas Menkhoff, and Hans-Dieter Evers); and (ii) *Building an Intelligent Organization: A Knowledge Management Framework for the Singapore Management University (SMU)* (Thomas Menkhoff, Chay Yue Wah and Hans-Dieter Evers). Special thanks are due to Professor Tan Chin Tiong, SMU's Provost; Associate Professor Tsui Kai Chong, Founding Dean, Lee Kong Chian School of Business, SMU; Practice Professor Augustine Tan, School of Economics and Social Sciences, SMU, and Vice Provost for Research (2001–2), SMU; Professor Roberto Mariano, Dean of SMU's School of Economics and Social Sciences, Vice Provost for Research and Deputy Director of the Wharton-SMU Research Centre; Professor David Montgomery, Dean of SMU's Lee Kong Chian School of Business; Professor Lim Kian Guan, Associate Dean, Lee Kong Chian School of Business, SMU; Associate Professor Annie Koh, Associate Dean, Lee Kong Chian School of Business and Dean, Executive Education, SMU; Ms. Kuo Pey Juan (and her team), Assistant Director, Office of Executive Education, SMU; Associate Professor Francis Koh, Associate Dean, Lee Kong Chian School of Business; Juliet Lee, Senior Editor, World Scientific Publishing; and Ang Pheng Huat, Department of Information Systems, NUS, for financial, managerial, administrative, editorial and other inputs, as well as the various contributors and interviewees.

The editors are especially indebted to the Ministry of Foreign Affairs, Singapore and Mr. M Jasimuddin, Chief Programme Officer, Governance and Institutional Development Division (GIDD), Commonwealth Secretariat, for their visionary "Singapore-Commonwealth Third Country Training Programme — Knowledge Management Programme" initiative which motivated us to compile this monograph.

Introduction

Governing and Managing Knowledge in Asia

Thomas Menkhoff, Hans-Dieter Evers and Yue Wah Chay

Why This Book?

In an era of rapid global market expansion, continuous innovations in information and communication technologies, intensified competition and the great digital divide, the capability to secure timely access to *actionable knowledge*, i.e., the ability to create, organize, leverage and protect intellectual capital resources and to achieve value creation outputs represents a core competency of policy makers, government officials, business leaders and managers (Sveiby, 1997; Steward, 1997; Chan and Mauborgne, 1997; Li-Hua, 2004; Truch, 2004).

At the national level, one of the challenges is to *govern* knowledge effectively by providing governmental support for the development of a knowledge infrastructure via a conducive legal framework, re-organizing the educational system and setting up institutions to support research and development activities.

A by now famous example is cited in the World Development Report of 1998/99. Ghana and the Republic of Korea started off with almost the same GNP/cap in 1960. Thirty years later the Korean GNP/cap had risen more than six times, the Ghanaian was still hovering at the same level (in 1985 prices). Half the gap could be explained in terms of the "traditional" factor inputs, the other half, according to World Bank experts, was attributed to 'knowledge' as a factor of production (World Bank, 1999).

Knowledge has since been identified as one of the major factors, if not THE crucial factor of development. The idea is, indeed, fascinating. If natural resources are scarce, if foreign direct investment (FDI) does

1

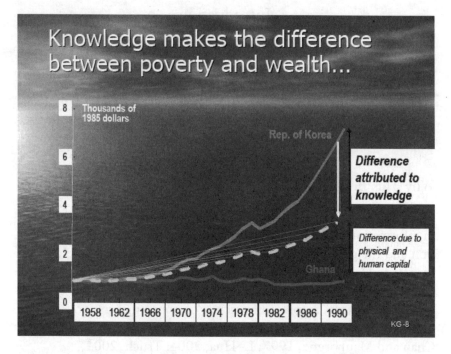

Fig. 0.1. Knowledge and development.
Source: *World Development Report 1998/99*, World Bank (1999).

not flow into the country as expected, if land is not fertile or scarce, knowledge can be introduced and put to effective use. In the almost poetic words of the World Bank, "knowledge is like light. Weightless and tangible it can easily travel the world, enlightening the lives of people everywhere" (World Bank, 1999:1).

Knowledge governance (Kaufmann *et al.*, 1999; Evers and Menkhoff, 2004; Stehr, 2004) is both an administrative process and a structure of authority relations; it involves the channelling of resources in building up knowledge management capabilities and improving the competitive advantage of a country in the world market by utilizing knowledge as a factor of production. How can this be achieved? What are the issues and hurdles? Where are the Asian role models? What are the chances of success for latecomers? We hope that this book provides some tentative answers to these questions.

At the organizational level, the effective governance and management of both tangible and intangible knowledge resources (in short: *knowledge management*)[1] such as experience-based knowledge about customers' spending habits and consumer preferences or employees' competencies and successful problem-solving approaches in specific projects requires leadership support, a culture of knowledge sharing, suitable technology solutions such as shareware systems and people with a particular mindset and orientation to work and peers (Grant, 1996; Hansen, 1999; Nahapiet and Ghoshal, 1998; Liebowitz, 2000; Szulanski, 2000; Alavi and Leidner, 2001; Chay, Menkhoff, Loh and Evers, 2005). According to knowledge management (KM) experts, the management of knowledge should be business driven and strategic in outlook so as to maximize return on (intellectual) capital and to sustain business success in an era of turbulent markets and global market expansion (Liebowitz, 2000).

During the past few years, many Asian countries have proactively embraced the knowledge governance agenda aimed at catching-up with fully-developed economies in Europe and North-America so as to enhance their global economic relevancy and to improve service delivery, e.g. by leveraging on "new-age E-governance" frameworks (Misra, Hariharan and Khaneja, 2003:47). We believe that it is time to document and review some of the experiences and lessons learned by Asian policy-makers, KM practitioners and researchers with regard to the governance and management of knowledge and to disseminate these to other interested parties in order to reduce the tension between local concerns for "common digital ground" and the realities of an increasingly competitive, global knowledge market. In each society there is a unique interplay between local and global knowledge. Local knowledge is increasingly destroyed rather then preserved (Evers, 2003; 2004). If it seems unlikely that the knowledge gap between the developing and developed world will be closed completely, at least narrowing the

---

[1] KM refers to the totality of organizational strategies aimed at creating a smart organization, which is able to leverage upon its various IC assets, to learn from past experiences, whether successful or unsuccessful, and to create new value through knowledge. At the people level, KM puts emphasis on the competencies, education and learning abilities of organizational members. At the organizational level, KM is concerned about the creation, utilization and development of the collective intelligence of an organization. Technologically, effective KM requires the efficient organization of a suitable communication and information infrastructure (e.g. intranet) based on relevant taxonomies and knowledge repositories.

gap at the lower end should be targeted (e.g. through human capital development initiatives or connectivity programmes). We argue that global knowledge has to be localized and that more local knowledge should be used in developing a knowledge society to obtain a sustainable knowledge-based economy.

A fully functioning Asian knowledge society will have successfully translated global knowledge into relevant local knowledge based on the development of a distinct Asian epistemic culture that contributes to the production of new unique knowledge (e.g. in form of locally produced vaccines for the Asian bird flu). It has been argued that the "free" development of ideas is the lifeblood of effective knowledge societies. While early industrialization was successfully carried out in many cases with the help of authoritarian governments, knowledge societies that are able to produce new knowledge and to create a productive economy through innovations arguably need a somewhat different socio-political system so as to stimulate a culture of entrepreneurship and innovation. The diverse cultural heritage of Asian societies could be an ideal basis for developing a vibrant knowledge society if the political conditions are "right".

As far as ASEAN is concerned, Singapore and Malaysia have achieved considerable progress in attaining the vision of a "knowledge society". Both countries are on their way to becoming knowledge societies driven to a large extent by persistent government policies, the vision and blueprints of strategic knowledge elites (Evers, 1974; 1988) and the competencies of experienced knowledge workers and experts. Furthermore, they are geographically far enough from the center of the economic power of North America and the European Union to be marginalized, but close enough to the upcoming economic power of China (and India). China's economic growth has already created a vast demand for knowledge, e.g. in the form of consultancy services. This will also stimulate the production of a new "Asian" knowledge in Malaysia, Singapore and Thailand and thus further the development of a knowledge society in these countries.

The Asian crisis has certainly been a setback for Malaysia and Singapore, but we believe it is not a decisive one (Menkhoff and Gerke, 2002; 2004). There are a few homegrown problems such as the relatively small number of local biotechnology experts in Singapore or the difficulties of Malaysia to bring home highly trained scientists and engineers from abroad — but these are problems and policy issues that have been addressed and will be tackled in the mid term. What is much more difficult is the establishment of an appropriate and vibrant (epistemic) culture of innovative knowledge production rather than knowledge consumption (Evers and Menkhoff, 2004).

The rise of the Asian knowledge society has not gone unnoticed by the Governments of other emerging markets and developing countries who are keen to learn from "model countries" such as Singapore and its "intelligent island vision". The China-Singapore Suzhou Industrial Park is a classic example in this respect (Pereira, 2003).

Singapore's so-called "Third Country Training Programme" provides an effective mechanism for development cooperation and k-transfer initiatives, e.g. in the area of human capital development or knowledge management. During the past few years, the authors of this book (as founding members of the community of interest "The Knowledge Force": http//www.research.smu.edu.sg/faculty/km/) have been proactively involved in such measures, e.g. by conducting training programs on knowledge governance and KM. In 2002, they led the development of a course proposal/outline for a new executive program on "Knowledge Management in an Era of Globalization — Implications for Management and Governance" for SMU's Office of Executive Education which won a respective tender by the *Commonwealth Secretariat* (UK) and the *Ministry of Foreign Affairs* (Singapore). The program has been taught several times since 2002[2] and represents

---

[2]The 1st training program was held at SMU from May 20–24, 2002 and attended by altogether 20 senior government officials and policy-makers from various African countries, South Asia, the Caribbean Islands, Malaysia, Malta and Cyprus. Faculty comprised Prof Hans-Dieter Evers, Center for Development Research, Bonn, FRG; Prof T. Riley, Executive Director, Commonwealth Centre for e-Governance, Ottawa, Canada; Practice Associate Professor Thomas Menkhoff, SMU (Course Director) and several KM practitioners and software specialists. The 2nd run took place between September 15–19, 2003, at SMU. It was attended by 20 senior civil servants from African countries, South Asia, the Caribbean Islands, Samoa, Solomon Islands, Tuvalu and Malta. It was led by Practice Associate Professor Thomas Menkhoff (Course Director, SMU), Professor Hans-Dieter Evers (University of Bonn) and Mr. M. Jasimuddin, Commonwealth Secretariat, Chief Programme Officer (Asia Region), Governance and Institutional Development Division. The 3rd round of the training measure was conducted from May 10–14, 2004, and the 4th KM course is planned for May 2005.

(due to the lack of suitable teachware) a key push factor for putting this monograph together. Typical course participants comprise senior public sector officials from various Commonwealth countries who are sponsored by the Commonwealth Secretariat (UK) and the Ministry of Foreign Affairs (Singapore). The 1-week program explores the ongoing shift towards a knowledge society/economy, its theoretical and empirical origins, the tension between the global knowledge market and *local* knowledge needs, K-economy related manpower development issues, definitions, domains, enablers and best practices of knowledge management as well as the strategic architecture of sustainable national K-economy infrastructures. The core question of the program initiative is as follows: What kind of knowledge governance and management systems can enable individuals, organizations and nations to transform learning and innovative capabilities into key value added competencies?

This monograph is aimed at discussing the issues raised above and providing some tentative answers to the questions posed. It features 14 timely and authoritative essays on governing and managing knowledge written by renowned scholars and practitioners from the USA, Canada, Germany, United Kingdom, India and Singapore.

The book:

- provides useful and operational definitions of KM-related terms (e.g. "knowledge" which we define in line with Milan Zeleny's conceptualization in Chapter 1 as *manifest ability of purposeful coordination of action*;
- analyzes some of the socio-cultural preconditions as well as consequences in reaching the stage of a knowledge society by contrasting the experiences of selected Asian and European countries based on the proposition that respective successes are contingent upon effective knowledge governance structures, organizational and managerial know how, human capital, vibrant epistemic cultures, global development trajectories, etc.;
- highlights the strategic role of professional knowledge elites (strategic groups) in reaching K-economy status such as politicians,

experts, consultants, engineers, planners, civil servants or university professors;

- illustrates KM challenges and good knowledge management practices in both private and public sector organizations based on case studies; and
- delivers the critical information business leaders and managers need to "incenticize" knowledge sharing and knowledge combination processes which are so crucial for effective organizational performance, knowledge creation and innovation.

We hope that the monograph will help readers to:

- appreciate the ongoing rise of the knowledge society/economy and respective change drivers as well as socio-economic/managerial consequences;
- understand the challenges of creating and disseminating knowledge for *local* needs in a global and increasingly competitive knowledge market place;
- know some of the requirements and key elements of a national information infrastructure as well as governance implications aimed at supporting the shift towards a globally competitive knowledge society/economy;
- learn about the concept and origins of knowledge management as well as its implications for individuals, public and private sector organizations, nations and policy-makers;
- differentiate the various building blocks of smart organizations in terms of leadership, technology, people, culture, etc. and to appreciate the role of technological KM enablers such as intranets;
- realize that the knowledge revolution is transforming conventional workplaces into "smart" workplaces and to appreciate respective human capital development/organizational behavior concepts such as knowledge sharing culture or organizational citizenship behavior (OCB); and
- benchmark (emerging) KM practices prevalent in readers' own country/organization with good ideas and practices elsewhere.

Contents

The book comprises five parts. Part 1 (What is Knowledge?) provides the reader with an operational definition of "knowledge" and
other KM-related terms. Part 2 (The Rise of Asian Knowledge Society) scrutinizes the socio-cultural enablers and outcomes of a fully-
developed knowledge society based on a comparison of selected Asian
and European countries. Part 3 (Strategic Groups as K-Economy
Drivers) portrays and assesses the important role of professional knowledge elites in achieving K-economy status such as development consultants, civil servants, science and technology experts, planners or
university professors. Part 4 (KM Applications and Challenges) illustrates the challenges and benefits of implementing effective knowledge
management practices in both private and public sector organizations based on case study material. Part 5 (Focus on K-Sharing in
Organizations) outlines what needs to be done to incenticize knowledge sharing and knowledge combination processes which are so critical for effective organizational performance, innovation and value
creation.

What is Knowledge?

In Chapter 1, **"Knowledge of Enterprise: Knowledge Management
or Knowledge Technology?"**, Milan Zeleny outlines why knowledge
technology (KT) is an important new development, extending and
ultimately replacing IT. Meaningful and substantial knowledge management is crucially dependent on a useful and operational definition of
knowledge. Such a notion of knowledge must be clearly differentiated
from so-called "explicit (or codified) knowledge", i.e., from information. Information, in any form or shape, is not knowledge. While information is a symbolic description of action, knowledge is action itself.
Milan Zeleny defines knowledge as the "manifest ability of purposeful
coordination of action". He redefines the purpose of KM as turning
information (description) into knowledge (action) and not vice versa.
According to him, there can be an information overload but never

any "knowledge overload". As the author elaborates, the understanding that "knowing is doing and doing is knowing" comes from the Western *philosophical* tradition of pragmatism, exemplified by Dewey, Lewis and Polanyi. *Sociological* contributions to a theory of knowledge form the subject of the next chapter.

The Rise of Asian Knowledge Society

The 2nd chapter " **'Knowledge' and the Sociology of Science"** by Hans-Dieter Evers provides a short exposition of some earlier debates within the sociology of knowledge, especially the ideas of Karl Mannheim. It is pointed out that the discussion on knowledge governance and management has its roots in the classical literature of the sociology of knowledge. Two important thoughts stand out in this debate: (i) that "rational" scientific knowledge, available in the writings of researchers and experts, is only one form of knowledge; and (ii) that the production and use of knowledge is embedded in social, cultural and political relations. The current distinctions between knowledge and experience, tacit and explicit knowledge, local or indigenous and global knowledge owe much to the earlier debates as outlined by the author.

The production, dissemination and utilization of knowledge in conjunction with the introduction and development of information and communication technology (ICT) are key preconditions for developing a knowledge society. However, as argued by Hans-Dieter Evers in Chapter 3, **"The Knowledge Gap and the Digital Divide"**, countries, regions and populations are divided in terms of access to ICT. Socio-economic indicators on Brazil, Korea, Malaysia, Singapore, the Netherlands and Germany are used to show that the existing global digital divide and the knowledge gap are widening between developing countries and the industrial countries and within individual nations. The moral and cultural issues of the digital divide and the knowledge gap are identified. For Hans-Dieter Evers, access to primary education and the acquisition of reading and writing skills is a basic human right, and an internal digital divide between those that have access to further knowledge and others without access is unjust and not acceptable. Some countries have embarked on an ambitious plan to close the digital divide and to use knowledge as a base for economic development, by-passing earlier stages of industrialization. Some commentators have, in contrast, asserted that it is doubtful that closing the digital divide will let developing countries leapfrog to higher levels of development as the knowledge economy will deepen the digital divide between regions and populations and actually expand the gap between rich and poor. The author discusses this controversy, arguing that global knowledge has to be localized and that minimal standards of "basic digital needs" should be formulated so as to tackle the knowledge gap.

The tension between global and local knowledge is also a major theme of the Chapter 4, **"Local and Global Knowledge: Social Science Research on South-east Asia"** by Solvay Gerke and Hans-Dieter Evers which traces the development of social science research on South-east Asia and its increasing localization. A model is developed to summarize the output of interpretative schemes and published documents. Statistical data on the global absorption of locally produced knowledge are used to measure the way towards a knowledge society. Singapore, Brunei, Malaysia and the Philippines have relatively high local social science output, whereas Indonesia, Cambodia, Vietnam, Myanmar and Laos have low output rates. The authors diagnose four different paths from 1970 to 2000: Indonesia shows a stable high level of dependence; Malaysia and the Philippines are increasing local output but also increasing dependence; Singapore, however, is increasing output while decreasing dependence on global social science knowledge. The results are surprising as the data indicate that there is indeed an increasing production of local knowledge (on SEA) in globally recognized journals. The analysis suggests that South-east Asian scientists play an increasing role in interpreting their own societies, a clear indication of "reflexive modernization" and the growth of knowledge societies.

In Chapter 5, **"Transition Towards a Knowledge Society: Malaysia and Indonesia in Global Perspective"**, Hans-Dieter Evers systematically examines the progress of Malaysia and Indonesia with regard to their aspirations of developing into knowledge societies. The paper outlines the basic features of a knowledge society and analyzes some of the social and cultural preconditions as well as consequences in reaching the stage of a knowledge society. How far have Malaysia and Indonesia advanced towards the stage of a knowledge society in comparison to other European and Asian countries? Indonesia's political leadership only vaguely circumscribes the characteristics of this new stage of development. Malaysia's political elite has, however, developed a vision when and how to reach the stage of a fully developed industrialized nation with a knowledge-based economy. The essay underlines the importance of effective knowledge governance and the development of a vibrant, epistemic culture of knowledge production driven by strategic knowledge elites such as transformational leaders, forward-looking civil servants, experts, diverse knowledge workers etc. in line with *glocal* development requirements and aspirations.

Strategic Groups as K-economy Drivers

In Chapter 6, **"Knowledge Management: An Essential Tool for the Public Sector"**, Thomas B. Riley explores the role and potentials of knowledge management and knowledge sharing, particularly as they relate to knowledge-intensive organizations in the public sector. Research and interviews on this subject area were conducted in Canada, the United States and the United Kingdom. As stressed by the author, the subject matter is crucial to understand when assessing and developing tools to transform governments into effective public sector organizations in the new global information technology infrastructure. However, the principles of knowledge management are not just about information technology. More important, this evolving discipline is all about capturing knowledge to better improve public administration principles, e.g. with the help of story-telling or communities of practice. As Thomas B. Riley argues, these principles can be of intrinsic value to both developed and developing countries. It is hoped that Thomas B. Riley's chapter and the case descriptions (featuring selected KM activities of the World Bank and several KM initiatives of the Canadian Federal Government) will serve as a useful guide to any public sector organization that wants to take up the challenge of promoting and implementing knowledge governance and knowledge management systems.

Chapter 7, **"Expert Knowledge and the Role of Consultants in an Emerging Knowledge-based Economy"** by Hans-Dieter Evers and Thomas Menkhoff pays tribute to a particular (strategic) group of professionals in the emerging globalized knowledge society/economy, namely experts and consultants. The essay discusses the following issues: Who are these experts and consultants? Why is this group of knowledge workers strategically important and why is their importance — socially in terms of number of persons and economically in terms of output or turnover — growing? How can we explain the increasing professionalization of consultants? How do they gain their expertise and which role does academic knowledge play in professional attainment? How do consultants package and apply expert knowledge? What are the challenges experts and consultants are facing in the new economy? Data on local consultancy firms are used to construct a profile of the Singapore consulting industry, their staff and their professional organizations. The analysis suggests that international consultants are more aggressive in advertising and selling their expertise than local consultants. They tend to distance themselves from academics as the producers of innovative knowledge, but stress their own (actionable) experience and knowledge resources. Finally, the authors discuss the new situation under which consultants have to operate in the *new* economy.

Chapter 8, **"Building Vibrant Science and Technology Parks with Knowledge Management: Trends in Singapore"** by Thomas Menkhoff, Hans-Dieter Evers, Marshall W. Meyer and Lionel Lim analyzes the role of Science and Technology Parks as K-economy catalysts. For Singapore's policy makers, knowledge creation through research and development (R&D) represents a prime mover in restructuring the economy to improve the city-state's competitiveness in an era of accelerated change, technological innovation and global market expansion.

The first part of the chapter sheds light on the knowledge governance process initiated by the Singapore government some time ago which resulted in building up substantial human capital assets as well as knowledge creation capabilities as evidenced by the rapid development progress of the island republic. The second part of the essay focuses on an important catalyst of the envisaged evolution of Singapore into a fully developed knowledge-based economy: the Singapore Science Park, its basic structure, policy objectives, tenants, etc. How does it contribute to the desired creation of a vibrant milieu for innovation via research and development activities in line with the state-driven movement towards enhanced competitiveness? To provide a tentative answer to that question the third part of the paper portrays the activities of its developer and manager, Ascendas Pte. Ltd., an organization that provides several value-added services for tenants in form of high quality (e.g. networking) space and facilities. A key proposition of this chapter is that the implementation of KM frameworks in science and technology parks (exemplified with the help of the Singapore Science Park and the governance activities of its developer Ascendas Pte. Ltd.) can help to create a smart park milieu with a vibrant epistemic culture of R&D works and innovation as well as synergistic collaboration between tenant firms. Respective challenges and research implications are outlined, too.

In Chapter **9**, **"Applying Knowledge Management in University Research"**, Benjamin Loh, Ai-Chee Tang, Thomas Menkhoff, Yue Wah Chay and Hans-Dieter Evers reflect on the dramatic changes universities are encountering in the knowledge-based economy. University missions and functions are "pragmatized" in a K-economy because of emerging new players and competing markets for knowledge production (e.g. consulting houses or think tanks), the availability of higher education to a wider range of social classes and age groups, as well as the assimilation of information technology into the university environment. The dynamics and conduct of university research, in particular, has correspondingly become more sensitive to industry collaboration opportunities, commercial exploitation, and is increasingly transdisciplinary. One of the key arguments of this chapter is that knowledge management (KM) practices and tools can support universities in addressing these demands. Institutions of higher education can benefit from KM by creating and maintaining relevant knowledge repositories, improving knowledge access, enhancing the knowledge environment, and valuing knowledge. This is illustrated with reference to the Singapore Management University (SMU) where KM is increasingly being applied in research and other areas.

KM Applications and Challenges

Chapter 10, **"Notes from an 'Intelligent Island': Towards Strategic Knowledge Management in Singapore's Small Business Sector"** by Thomas Menkhoff, Chay Yue Wah and Benjamin Loh outlines the benefits and challenges of implementing strategic knowledge management systems in small and medium-sized enterprises (SMEs) with reference to Singapore. Since the 1980s, Singapore's Government has implemented several policy measures to realize the vision of an "intelligent island" aimed at remaining relevant in the global knowledge-based economy. The article addresses following research questions: Why has knowledge management become an issue? How can SMEs benefit from strategic KM? What are the potential pitfalls of KM applications in small firms? What are the strategic imperatives of using KM in SMEs? Do small and large firms require different KM systems? What are the critical success factors which have to be considered during implementation? How do smart and KM-enabled SMEs look like in reality? Some of these questions are answered based on the case of a small intelligent pest control firm in Singapore whose owners made effective use of development grants provided by government agencies tasked with the transformation of Singapore's small business sector in line with official IT-related development blueprints.

Based on indepth survey research, Patrick Lambe's case study in Chapter 11, **"Collaboration and Competition: The Knowledge Research Institute of Singapore as a Model KM System"**, highlights KM implementation challenges in a (fictive) research organization aimed at helping managers and others anticipate and address common, repeated, and damaging but often unacknowledged pitfalls in rolling out a KM project, for instance, poor strategic alignment, project resourcing or knowledge sharing difficulties. The case was constructed in the form of a learning activity known as *decision game* which is a form of presentation pitched somewhere between a case study and a simulation. Like a problem-based case study, it presents readers with a well-defined initial context, events which cannot be modified, and a central dilemma to reflect on. Like simulations, decision games unfold sequentially and invite response and interpretations as the reader proceeds through them. Unlike case studies, they more closely mirror the complex, uncertain and ambiguous unfolding of events in the real world. Unlike simulations, the reader does not get the chance to systematically explore different, well-defined option routes. The expert *analysis* of key issues in the case (presented after the main case study) is aimed at facilitating the readers'/learners' reflection.

In Chapter 12, "**Creating a KM Platform for Strategic Success: A Case Study of Wipro Technologies, India**", RaviShankar Mayasandra N. and Shan Ling Pan attempt to understand the vital issues emerging in IT outsourcing vendor organizations' on-going efforts to create an organization-wide strategic KM infrastructure. In their study, they consider the challenges surrounding the creation of a strategic KM platform (called KNet) at Wipro Technologies, one of India's premier Information Technology (IT) outsourcing vendor organizations. By using social organizational identity theory, the authors address two research questions: 1) How are KM strategies implemented in an IT outsourcing organization?; and 2) What are the unique challenges faced by an IT outsourcing organization during the creation of a strategic KM platform? They argue that the response of the organizational constituents to the expectations of organization-wide KM depend on unique embedded structural and socio-cultural contexts in the various organizational units. Particularly so, in the case of organizations which have grown into highly decentralized multiple organizational units leading to organizational members closely identifying with various local entities such as work groups, department, project teams, business units and so on, thereby finding it difficult to appreciate the strategic relevance of organizational interventions like KM. It follows that effective KM implementations ought to have inbuilt organizational mechanisms to handle the likely conflicts arising out of localized differences.

Focus on K-sharing Behavior in Organizations

The study by Yue Wah Chay, Thomas Menkhoff, Benjamin Loh and Hans-Dieter Evers in Chapter 13, **"What Makes Knowledge Sharing in Organizations Tick? — An Empirical Study"**, aims to understand the social and organizational factors that influence knowledge transfer which is critical for knowledge reuse and innovation. A model of knowledge management and knowledge sharing was developed inspired by the work of Nonaka, Nahapiet and Ghoshal and others. Data on demographics and various social capital measures were collected from a sample of 262 members of a tertiary educational institution in Singapore. Reward and recognition, open-mindedness and cost concerns of knowledge hoarding turned out to be the strongest predictors of knowledge sharing rather than pro-social motives or organizational concern. Individuals who are highly competent in their work abilities are less likely to share what they know when they perceive that there are few rewards or when sharing is not recognized by the organization. The findings provide evidence for the importance of a conducive organizational climate and state-of-the art performance management system in high-performing organizations where knowledge sharing represents a key enabler of improved business performance and value innovation.

The final Chapter 14 on **"The Moderating Effects of Friendship Ties and Dispositional Factors on Inducement and Knowledge Sharing among Employees"** by Ho-Beng Chia, Dishan Kamdar, Glenn J. Nosworthy, and Yue Wah Chay examines the effect of performance appraisal on the sharing of knowledge among employees. 295 oil refinery employees in an India-based organization responded to three vignettes that described opportunities to share information with co-workers that would result in greater productivity. In addition, the employees were given different information about the company's appraisal system (i.e., whether knowledge sharing was formally recognized or not). Including knowledge sharing in the appraisal system had a strong impact on whether employees would be willing to share knowledge; however, this impact varied according to whether the co-workers were considered close friends as well as the personality of the employee. The quasi-experiment found that recognition of knowledge sharing in an appraisal system had strong effects on employees' willingness to share knowledge with co-workers and friends. However, these effects were moderated by dispositional factors. Machiavellians responded instrumentally, whereas impression managers' responses were consistent with a desire to maintain a public image.

References

Alavi, M. and D.E. Leidner (2001). Review: Knowledge Management and KM Systems: Conceptual Foundations and Research Issues. *MIS Quarterly*, 25(1), 107–136.

Beck, U. (1992). *Risk Society: Towards a New Modernity*. London: Sage.

Chan Kim, W. and R. Mauborgne (1997). Value Innovation: The Strategic Logic of High Growth. *Harvard Business Review*, January–February, 103–112, Reprint Number: 97108.

Chay, Y.W., T., Menkhoff, B. Loh and H.-D. Evers (2005). Theorizing, Measuring, and Predicting Knowledge Sharing Behavior in Organizations — A Social Capital Approach. Paper presented at the 38th Annual Hawaii International Conference on System Sciences (HICSS-38), 3–6 January 2005, Hawaii. (Published in the HICSS-38 2005 Conference Proceedings, edited by Ralph H. Sprague).

Evers, H.-D. (1974). The Role of Professionals in Social and Political Change. In *Sociology and Social Development in Asia*, T. Fukutake and K. Morioka (eds.), pp. 241–250. Tokyo: University of Tokyo Press.

Evers, H.-D. and T. Schiel (1988). Strategische Gruppen. Vergleichende Studien zu Staat, Bürokratie und Klassenbildung in der Dritten Welt. Berlin: Dietrich Reimer Verlag.

Evers, H.-D. (1988). Strategische Gruppen. Über den Umgang mit Machteliten und ihren Plänen. *Entwicklung und Zusammenarbeit*, 30(3), 8–9.

Evers, H.-D. (2003a). Transition Towards a Knowledge Society: Malaysia and Indonesia in Comparative Perspective. *Comparative Sociology*, 2(2), 355–373.

Evers, H.-D. (2003b). Malaysian Knowledge Society and the Knowledge Gap. *Asian Journal of Social Science*, 31(3), 383–397.

Evers, H.-D. (2004). Local Knowledge and the Digital Divide. Background Paper to the UNESCO World Report 2004.

Evers, H.-D. and S. Gerke (2003). Local and Global Knowledge: Social Science Research on Southeast Asia. Southeast Asian Studies Working Paper No. 18, Department of Southeast Asian Studies, University of Bonn, Germany.

Evers, H.-D. *et al.* (2003). Entwicklung durch Wissen: Eine neue globale Wissensarchitektur. *Soziale Welt*, 54(1), 49–70.

Evers, Hans-Dieter and T. Menkhoff (2004). Creating an Effective Culture of Knowledge Production in Science and Technology Parks. Paper presented at the 2nd International Knowledge Management Symposium "Knowledge Governance in Science and Technology Parks" organized by T. Menkhoff and Y.W. Chay, Singapore Management University (SMU), School of Business, 17 March 2004.

Grant, R.M. (1996). Towards a Knowledge-based Theory of the Firm. *Strategic Management Journal*, 17, 109–122.

Hansen, M.T. (1999). The Search-Transfer Problem: The Role of Weak Ties in Sharing Knowledge Across Organizational Subunits. *Administrative Science Quarterly*, 44, 82–111.

Kaufmann, D. *et al.* (1999). *Governance Matters*. Washington, DC: The World Bank Development Research Group and the World Bank Institute.

Li-Hua, Richard (2004). *Technology and Knowledge Transfer in China*. Aldershot: Ashgate.

Liebowitz, J. (2000). *Building Organizational Intelligence*. Boca Raton, FL: CRC Press.

Menkhoff, T. and S. Gerke (2002). *Chinese Entrepreneurship and Asian Business Networks*. London: RoutledgeCurzon (paperback version was published in 2004).

Misra, D.C., R. Hariharan and M. Khaneja (2003). E-Knowledge Management Frameworks for Government Organizations. *Information Systems Management*, Spring, 38–48.

Nahapiet, J. and S. Ghoshal (1998). Social Capital, Intellectual Capital, and the Organizational Advantage. *Academy of Management Review*, 23(2), 242–266.

Pereira, A. (2003). *State Collaboration and Development Strategies in China: The Case of the China-Singapore Suzhou Industrial Park (1992–2002)*. New York: RoutledgeCurzon.

Stehr, N. (2004). *The Governance of Knowledge*. New Brunswick and London: Transaction Books.

Stewart, Thomas A. (1997). *Intellectual Capital: The Wealth of Organizations*. New York: Doubleday.

Szulanski, G. (2000). The Process of Knowledge Transfer. A Diachronic Analysis of Stickiness. *Organizational Behavior and Human Decision Processes*, 82(1), 9–27.

Sveiby, Karl Erik (1997). *The New Organizational Wealth, Managing & Measuring Knowledge-Based Assets*. Berrett-Koehler Publishers Inc.
Truch, Edward (ed.) (2004). *Leveraging Corporate Knowledge*. Aldershot: Gover.
World Bank (1999). *World Development Report 1998/99: Knowledge for Development*. New York: Oxford University Press.

Part I

What is Knowledge?

Chapter 1

Knowledge of Enterprise: Knowledge Management or Knowledge Technology?[1]

Milan Zeleny

1.1. Introduction

It was Albert Einstein who cautioned our world that "Information is not knowledge". Einstein also asserted that "Knowledge is experience. Everything else is information". This was some time before the Information theory, MIS, IT and KM, before many world cultures started treating knowledge as information. As "Knowledge Management (KM)" got carelessly reduced to information and data manipulation and processing and the oxymoron of "explicit knowledge" started making broad rounds, Einstein's wisdom (but not knowledge) became all but forgotten.

In the rapidly unfolding "Post 9/11" times of the 21st century, it has again become clearly insufficient to rely on our vast depositories of data and information. It has become quite unsatisfactory to rely on our information technologies. In this new world of new action we need to focus on continually produced, improved and shared knowledge and on new Knowledge Technology (KT) designed to support and expand the processes of knowledge formation, enhancement and transfer.

To serve the new realities well, it has become doubly important to define and establish essential differences between information and

[1]This is a reprint of an article published in the *International Journal of Information Technology and Decision Making*, Vol. 1, No. 2 (2002), 181–207. The authors are grateful to World Scientific Publishing Co. and the author for allowing us to include this pioneering piece in our monograph.

23

knowledge, information and data and also knowledge and wisdom. Simply dividing knowledge into tacit and explicit, without defining "knowledge" itself and without distinguishing it from information and data, is a curious phenomenon. It is bound to bring forth even more disasters, stemming from insufficient, incomplete decisions and less than coherent judgments.

In this paper, we argue that while information is a *symbolic description* of action, knowledge refers to the *action itself*, more precisely to its *purposeful coordination*. No amount of data or information will replace our coordination abilities, our knowing. In our view, information and data are mere inputs into the activity of coordinating production and generation processes towards achieving objectives or goals. We know because we do — and we do because we know. Being informed or having the information is necessary but not sufficient for a successful action in the knowledge era.

1.2. Knowledge Era

"It is the greatest truth of our age: Information is not knowledge"[2]

The change from Information Society to the Knowledge era is rapid, powerful and real. It is accompanied and supported by an equally swift change from information processing to knowledge production and management. At the core of the change is the fundamental shift from information to knowledge as a strategic foundation of business management, decision making and judgment.

That *information is not knowledge* is intuitively understood and evidenced by the shift in labels and vocabulary: "Knowledge" has quickly become a new keyword and yet "Knowledge management" has first emerged quite recently (Zeleny, 1987). The so-called "Information age" is all but over. We are starting to have quite a lot of information available worldwide and worry about information overload or information irrelevance. Yet, we all seem to be increasingly aware of being short of knowledge and no "knowledge overload" has entered our vocabulary.

L. Prusak (1999) recently reflected on the status of KM as being "...much more focused on explicit, articulated knowledge (or data),

---

[2]Caleb Carr, *Killing Time*, Random House.

which is really another way to say information. Now, there is nothing wrong with managing information". Indeed, nothing. What is wrong (and rather hopeless for the future of KM) is calling *that* managing knowledge.

1.2.1. *Knowledge as Capital*

Most importantly, *knowledge is the primary form of capital*. All other forms are dependent and derived, only secondary to knowledge. Without knowledge, money is just a pile of paper, machine of concoction of metals, building a heap of bricks and concrete and raw material remains just that: raw material. Knowledge gives life to it all.

Capital is characterized by the three requisite properties (Dewey, 1965):

(1) Is capable of being bought, sold, transferred, and held.
(2) Is capable of being used, deployed, and consumed.
(3) Must remain available for the next production cycle.

Many *capital assets* possess these properties and are therefore differentiated forms or components of capital. Capital is that part of the proceeds of production that has to be maintained, reproduced or produced in order to realize the next production cycle. Capital asset is that part of the proceeds that is set aside for the next cycle. Knowledge however, can be stored and consumed and still remain available for future use.

Capital is therefore a self-renewing *knowledge matrix* that is to be continually regenerated so that the individual capital assets are properly embedded and coordinated in it. Even if individual components (capital assets) are replaced, knowledge matrix remains and retains its character. Knowledge is the "glue" that holds all other forms of capital together.

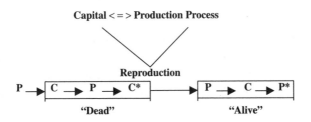

Fig. 1.1. Capital as the catalyst of production.

Capital is the catalyst of production (see Fig. 1.1), yet, for some, production is the catalyst of capital. If the only purpose of capital is more capital, then such capital is "dead". Capital becomes catalyst only if the purpose of production is more or better production: such capital is "alive". The purpose of knowledge is never just more knowledge: such knowledge would be "dead". The purpose of knowledge is better or more action (production): knowledge *is* a catalyst of production.

1.2.2. *Knowledge versus Information*

It can be demonstrated that the richest nations are those well equipped in knowledge and human capital, while the poorest countries have and rely on their natural resources and labor only (see Chapters 2–5 of this book). Man-made, built capital is quite useless without knowledge. Money bags cannot become productive capital without knowledge. Countries and cultures can be resources rich, even information rich, and yet remain knowledge poor. Having plenty of cows and libraries of cookbooks does not yet make great chefs.

Although it is quite common to declare that there is *too much information*, it would be rather difficult to even imply that there could be *too much knowledge*. Just trying to say aloud: "I know too much" or "There should be less knowledge" or "Too much knowledge is bad" is quite illuminating. Knowledge is good. It is too little or no knowledge that is bad. Not the same can be said about information.

There is a clear difference between a bread-making cookbook and baking bread. Baking bread and milking cows is not information but knowledge itself. Knowing the cookbook by heart is not knowledge, but only "knowledge" of information. The difference is fundamental.

"Knowledge" of information (having or possessing information) can be demonstrated through a statement, recall or display. Knowledge itself can only be demonstrated through action.

There is no other way of demonstrating knowledge of baking bread than by baking it. I know how to write books because I write them. I cannot claim knowing how to milk cows through a mere statement or even by writing a book about it. I do not know how to manage a company but I can provide you with plenty of information on that subject.

1.2.3. *Definition and Taxonomy of Knowledge*

What is knowledge?

Knowledge is *purposeful coordination of action*. Achieving intended purpose is the sole proof or demonstration of knowledge. Its quality can be judged from the quality of the outcome (product) or even from the quality of the coordination (process).

In Table 1.1, a taxonomy of knowledge is outlined. Its logical progression is from top to bottom, increasingly enfolding more and more context of a purpose or purposes. For example, data are very simple elements, their purpose still unclear and ambiguous, with many degrees of freedom. (Many different things can be "baked" from the elements, not only bread.)

Information is more purpose-specific, involving data aggregates plus their formulas and procedures. Ingredients plus recipe do not lend themselves to baking many other things than bread. Once we turn data into information, it becomes hard to deconstruct back into its elements. (It is impossible to reconstruct individual observations from their average or to reconstitute eggs from an omelette.)

Table 1.1. Taxonomy of knowledge.

	Technology	Analogy (Baking Bread)	Effect	Purpose
Data	EDP	Elements: H_2O, yeast bacteria, starch molecules	Muddling through	Know-nothing
Information	MIS	Ingredients: flour, water, sugar, spices + recipe	Efficiency	Know-how
Knowledge	DSS, ES AI	Coordination of the baking process → result, product	Effectiveness	Know-what
Wisdom	WS, MSS	Why bread? Why this way?	Explicability	Know-why
Enlightenment	?	Bread, clearly	Truth	Know-for-sure

Knowledge refers to the actual processing of inputs (data, information, recipes), involving coordination of action to achieve results, products or purposes. The rules, sequences and patterns of action coordination determine further *types of knowledge* with respect to internal or external validation of rules, procedures and outcomes.

We speak of *skills* when the rules are *internally* established and controlled by the subject. We speak of *knowledge* when the rules of coordination are established *externally*, by a social context and also expected outcomes are validated socially.

Skills are validated by the action itself. When we chop wood or type on a typewriter, the actor can evaluate, assess and judge the action itself, whether the action has been successful or not. A fallen tree or a typed page are the proofs.

Knowledge can only be validated as an act in social context of peer or professional institutions which, not the actors, establish the rules. One cannot claim knowledge without a social validation; one can only claim internally validated skills.

Expertise is socially sanctioned knowledge (coordination of action) combined with the attained ability to reflect upon a relationship between actor and the requisite *social system of rules*. One can master the rules of the profession, peer group or culture so well that they no longer need to be obeyed. Expert thus gains power over the rules and criteria that decide quality standards. Expertise just amounts to be able to (and be allowed to) change the rules. *The system (of rules) is learning from the individual.*

Observed or postulated modalities of knowledge (like implicit, explicit, tacit, objective, subjective, etc.) are exercises that are only secondary to the success of achieved goals. If I can consistently bake good bread then I *know* how to bake bread — regardless if it has been acquired or "learned" from cookbooks, training or experience.

Wisdom refers to explicability: if I also know why — not just what and how — then I am also wise, not just knowledgeable. Many can use information and follow the recipes efficiently: they possess dexterity and are specialists. They do not choose their goals, let alone knowing why they follow them. Only the master-chef knows how to coordinate action towards chosen goals. But only the wise man knows why such goals should be chosen and others rejected.

1.2.4. *DIKW Chain*

The progression from data and information through knowledge and to wisdom forms a *DIKW chain* of which all our searches for a competitive advantage are an integral part. Progressing from information to knowledge is as unstoppable and irreversible as the future transition from knowledge to wisdom and the past shift from data to information. The DIKW chain provides a framework for evaluating and forecasting our efforts. We are entering (reluctantly) its "K" stage.

Current "K" stage is characterized by coordination of action. *What is coordination of action?*

Coordination of action involves identification of objectives and goals, selection of inputs (both quantities and qualities), establishing the sequences, stages and progressions, assigning responsibilities, delegating the tasks, carrying out the processes, and submitting the outcomes for evaluation.

Coordination of action involves not just Know-how but a whole range of other knowledge components which must be woven into a coherent whole.

For example, *Know-what* refers to the knowledge of objects, facts, components and goals. This involves either information (what to have or to possess) or wisdom (what to do, act or carry out).

Know-why refers to the explicability of action, relationship or causality. This can either be information (why is) or wisdom (why do). Wisdom always involves the explicability of choice and presumes selection.

Know-how refers to skills and capabilities to act or to do something. This is knowledge.

Know-who becomes increasingly important. Who knows what and who knows how to do what is a critical resource. It involves the formation of special social relationships to gain access to external knowledge.

Know-when is also a part of coordination. In fact, timing of efforts is crucial to achieving stated purposes.

Know-what and know-why can be obtained through reading books, attending lectures and accessing databases, the other components of knowledge are rooted primarily in practical experience. Know-how will typically be learned in situations where an apprentice follows a master and relies upon him as the authority. Know-who is learned in social practice and sometimes in a specialized educational environment.

Know-when generally follows from one's own experience and the acquired sense of timing.

1.2.5. *Tacit and Explicit Knowledge?*

There is an academic fashion to classify knowledge into categories, like tacit and explicit, without attempting to define knowledge. Expanding such classifications is a safest way for entering the KM field for novices. It is fast, cheap and pointless: it has no practical import. The only practical or operational contribution is drawing a strong and useful distinction between information and knowledge and knowledge and wisdom.

All knowledge is tacit, in the sense of not being symbolically captured or described. As soon as it becomes recorded, made explicit through symbols or otherwise "captured" — it has become information. *Knowledge is action, not a description of action.* However, action is not really tacit in the sense of being implied, abstract or esoteric. Knowledge is fundamentally real and explicit. Although reading a book (information) on milking cows can be quite esoteric and intangible, there is nothing intangible or esoteric about actually milking cows and getting some milk from them.

So called *codified (explicit) knowledge* is therefore a symbolic description of action, that is *information.* So called tacit knowledge is action itself, i.e., process of *knowing* rather than knowledge as subject or object. Knowledge (knowing) is purposeful coordination of action. Symbolic description of action is information. In other words, "All doing is knowing and all knowing is doing" as Maturana and Varela assert.

K. E. Sveiby (1999:18–27) supports this understanding quite clearly: "All knowledge is either tacit or rooted in tacit knowledge. All our knowledge therefore rests in the tacit dimension". Yet, the KM filed itself is all about the explicit (capturable and transferable) knowledge, i.e., about information. This view comes from M. Polanyi's *Tacit Dimension* (1983), asserting that "Knowledge is an activity which would be better described as a process of knowing". *To know is to do,* according to Sveiby.

It remains difficult to explain why so much KM effort has been expended on manipulating simple information under the oxymoronic banner of "explicit knowledge".

The very roots of label "information" (symbolic description or codification of action) come from the original meaning of "in-formation": i.e., a physical deformation of the object or environment caused by action itself.

Can information alone be used to coordinate action? Yes, but the knower still must impose or inform the purpose. Automated (symbolically captured) instructions, rules and recipes are information. They can coordinate action but cannot impute purposes. Purposeful coordination of action is *human* knowledge. When knowledge becomes automated (turned into information), wisdom and explicability of objectives becomes the new frontier. It is already happening: as companies are becoming more informed and more knowledgeable, they are searching — the best ones — to become wise.

1.2.6. *Measuring Knowledge*

It is an often perpetuated myth that knowledge is somehow intangible or abstract, not really "real", and therefore difficult to measure. Nothing can be further from the truth.

Knowledge is very *real* and very *tangible*. What can be more tangible than automobiles we have produced, bread I have baked or milk I brought from the stable? Knowledge *produces* very tangible things and very tangible things are the measuring rods of human knowledge. The value of money is intangible, especially during the periods of hyperinflation. The value of information is intangible, unless it is translated into knowledge and thus into measurable action.

Because knowledge is so intimately related to action and the products of action, it is also eminently and simply *measurable*. My knowledge of skiing is well and precisely measured by how well I negotiate a slope (speed, style, grace), as is my knowledge of bread making measured by the bread itself (taste, price, quality, appearance).

Knowledge is measured by the value our coordination of effort, action and process adds to material, technology, energy, services, information, time and other inputs used or consumed in the process. *Knowledge is measured by added value.*

What is added value?

It is the value of shipped products or services, corrected by subtracting all internal and external purchases (or market value of) of inputs, operating cost (like 10% of production to sales department), and general administrative cost (supplies, light, heating, transportation, traveling expenses, rent, depreciation, etc.). Such total deduction of shipments is divided by the hours worked:

$$\text{Total Deduction/Total Hours} = \text{Added Value/Hour}$$

Observe that all salaries and wages can only be covered from the added value. If no value is added, no useful competitive knowledge has been applied, and no payment for successful coordination of action (knowledge) is possible for long.

Current knowledge indicators are primarily measures of knowledge *inputs* or codified knowledge — i.e., of information. Stocks and flows of *tacit knowledge*, such as learning that depends on conversation, demonstration and observation, cannot be measured by currently prevalent indicators. New indicators are needed to evaluate the *process of coordination* itself.

In the end, however, it is not the measurement that is the most important part of knowledge management. *It is the process.* If the process of knowledge production, use and enhancement is well designed and organizationally embedded, then its measurement will be safely provided by the market.

1.3. Knowledge Management

The "field" of Knowledge Management (KM) is suffering from the lack of distinction between data, information and knowledge (and also wisdom, of course), lack of definition and lack of action or process orientation.

KM should be less about managing "something" (like an object of knowledge) and more about the process of management *infused* with production, improvement and sharing of knowledge through action and interaction. KM is therefore more about *knowledgement* (processes of knowing and doing) than about knowledge management. Knowledge is not a thing.

Traditionally, KM is roughly concerned about the following:

(1) Producing (creating) new knowledge internally, within a corporation.
(2) Improving formal and informal flows of knowledge among individuals and teams.
(3) Codifying knowledge to facilitate its transfer, learning and sharing.
(4) Tapping into external sources of new knowledge.

One can readily see that all such efforts are about generating data and information transfers or about turning knowledge into information (codifying). All these efforts could very well be carried under the banner of *data and information management.*

Why is traditional KM failing so often?

There are many "local" reasons, but among the more general culprits we can list at least the following:

(1) Operational knowledge definition is not well established, distinctions from information and data are weak, implying simple *information management* (processing and use of symbolic descriptions), no perceptible competitive advantage and a sense of disappointment.
(2) Firms are already managing knowledge: they act, produce, coordinate, make decisions. KM is an ongoing and all-involving process, albeit unrecognized and out of focus. It cannot be tucked under convenient labels of KM department or CKO.
(3) Information Technology (IT) cannot be a substitute for social interaction. Description of action cannot replace action itself. ("It does not matter what they say they would do; what matters is what they actually do".) Knowledge Technology (KT), even where nonexistent, cannot be substituted by IT.
(4) Traditional KM concentrates on sharing, storing and recycling existing knowledge while the real game is in producing new knowledge, continuously.

(5) Most KM techniques are just traditional IT techniques, explicitly avoiding action and its coordination, manipulating symbolic descriptions.
(6) Mediocre or worst practice is the easiest to codify, share and "flow", while the best coordination of action remains necessarily tacit and explicitly unrecognized.

All knowledge that can be codified and so reduced to information can be transmitted over long distances at small costs. It is the increasing codification of certain elements of knowledge that has led the current era to be characterized as *"The Information Society"*. However, our society in the 21st century is "The Knowledge Society" (see Chapter 5 of this book) and it is the knowledge, not information, which is going to dominate it. It is the Knowledge Technology (KT), rather than the Information Technology (IT), which is going to enable it.

Thus, the *tacit knowledge*, in the form of skills and capabilities needed to handle codified knowledge (information), is more important than ever. Codified knowledge (information) might be considered as inputs to be transformed, while tacit knowledge, particularly the know-how, is the demonstrated capability for coordinating information with all other inputs.

The real purpose of knowledge management is *not* transforming knowledge into information — there is plenty of it. The real purpose is the very opposite: *transforming information into effective action, i.e., knowledge* — there is so little of that.

The process of *codifying knowledge* transforms:

KNOWLEDGE (action) $\Rightarrow$ INFORMATION (description of action)
Tacit knowledge thus becomes explicit "knowledge" (i.e., information).

The process of *activizing information* transforms:

INFORMATION (descriptions) $\Rightarrow$ KNOWLEDGE (coordination of action)
Codified information thus becomes explicit action (i.e., knowledge).

Information is but an input into a successful coordination of action. Codifying *knowledge (action) into information (description)* is one of the goals of KM (storage, transfer, sharing, etc. of necessary inputs).

Translating *information (description) into knowledge (action)* is the ultimate purpose of KM.

1.4. Theory of Knowledge

A useful theory of knowledge comes from C. I. Lewis's system of conceptualistic pragmatism (1956), rooted in the thought of Peirce, James and Dewey. Both knowledge and "truth" are necessarily social phenomena. We are able to bring our world forth only through the operations of separation and integration of sensory data. Knowledge, in order to be shared and validated through a social intercourse, must be expressed in words, which are further interrelated in language. We use language to coordinate our action in social domain.

Because knowledge coordinates human action, then socially divided or distributed knowledge can fulfill its coordinating function only through some form of language.

Especially John Dewey (Dewey and Bentley, 1949), through a thoroughly American philosophy of *pragmatism*, understood that action is internal and integral to knowledge. Action is not some tool for knowledge "acquisition" or belief "beholding": action is integral to whatever we claim to know. The process of knowing helps to constitute what is known: *inquiry is action*. Reciprocally, what is known by the knower is not stored as data or information, independently of the process of knowing: *action is inquiry*.

This simple, effective and powerful American philosophy of knowledge has been but abandoned by American proponents of knowledge management: they proceed without definition, on the basis of a vague concept of "justified belief" (totally devoid of action), and with the mechanistic but void differentiation between explicit and tacit "knowledge". Why would Americans abandon pragmatism and action and substitute a simple, computer-powered manipulation of symbolic data and information, even renaming it knowledge management, remains a perplexing mystery.

Lewis captured the social dimension of knowledge through his term *community of action*. Congruity of behavior and consensual human cooperation are the ultimate tests of shared knowledge.

We as humans not only think (interpret) but also act (behave) and so we are part of a temporal *process*: prediction or forecast of action shapes our present as much as our past experience. There is no knowledge of external reality without the anticipation of future action (experience).

It is proper to emphasize that thought or reflection can do only two things: (1) to *separate* (by analysis) entities which in their temporal or spatial existence are not separated; (2) to *integrate* (by synthesis) entities which in their existence are disjoined and distinct. Humans can either *divide* or *integrate* (more precisely *reintegrate*) *their* world. The nature of human knowledge must be correspondingly twofold: either analytic or synthetic. One can argue that we cannot integrate what has not been previously divided: any reintegration necessarily follows its preceding division. So, the early division and specialization of knowledge must be later followed by *knowledge reintegration*.

1.4.1. *Language*

Knowledge, in order to be shared and validated through social intercourse, must be expressed in words which are further interrelated in language. We use language to coordinate our actions in a social domain. Because knowledge coordinates human action, then socially *divided* or *distributed* knowledge can fulfill its coordinating function only through some form of language.

In addition, any coordinative language must display a sufficient degree of ambiguity, i.e., the same "word" conveys more or less restricted meaning (or even different concepts) on different occasions; words must exhibit *degrees* of clearness about their meaning; and identity of meaning derives from implied modes of behavior (action).

Fuzzy labels divide the field of experience into classes with overlapping qualitative ranges of denotation. Without such exquisite device, human mind could not succeed in imparting order onto a given experience.

For the purposes of bringing forth relationships among concepts and thus fostering consensual communication among coordinators of action, meanings and their linguistic labels have to be "fuzzified" so that they become "common to different minds". To reduce such powerful knowledge-building strategy to simple notions of imprecision, lack of information or vagueness would be self-limiting.

C. I. Lewis (1956:230) offers the following useful summary:

> *In experience, mind is confronted with the chaos of the given. In the interest of adaptation and control, it seeks to discover within or impose upon this chaos some kind of stable order, through which distinguishable items may become the signs of future possibilities. Those patterns of distinction and relationship which we thus seek to establish are our concepts. These must be determined in advance of the particular experience to which they apply in order that what is given may have meaning.*

A large part of science is therefore a search (or re-search) for things worth naming within a given consensual model of experience. All empirical knowledge of objects is only probable and all human judgments remain forever at the mercy of future experience.

1.4.2. *Community of Action*

Lewis also captured the social dimension of knowledge through his term *community of action*. Congruity of behavior and *consensual* human cooperation are the ultimate tests of shared knowledge.

Consensual cooperation of human beings does not stem from some vague identity of their psychological perception, experience or compatible worldviews. It stems from their inherent tendency to action, basic similarity of needs, and shared organismic structure. The wonder of consensual cooperation is that it can take place within the realm of vast diversity of sensual and social experiences.

Human beings possess a strong natural tendency to explicit and implicit cooperation. Socially engineered destruction of their consensually shared concepts and common action — like the social isolation stemming from the extreme specialization and division of task, labor and knowledge — reduces human consensual communication to a minimum and replaces it with man-designed non-consensual communication "bypass": an externally imposed and enforced form of coordination of action. The purpose of communication is coordination of behavior: it is therefore essential that all of its aspects remain consensual.

1.4.3. *Summary of Conceptualistic Pragmatism*

Lewis's system can be summarized in three principles:

(A) It must be false, that every identifiable entity is *equally* associated with every other.
(B) In any situation where identifiable entities fail to satisfy A ("random" associations), there will be other entities, connected with the former, which do satisfy A.
(C) The statistical prediction of the future from the past cannot be generally invalid, because future to any given past is in turn past for some future.

Agents who *continually revise* their judgment of the probability of a statistical generalization by its successively observed verifications and failures, cannot fail to make more successful predictions than if they would simply disregard the past. This "Principle of Statistical Accumulation" explains why statistical analyses of observations must be explicit (or implicit) part of *any* successful system of management.

1.5. Knowledge as a Process

Human knowledge thus cannot refer to simple static descriptions or "captures" of facts, things or objects, that is data, information and knowledge, "out there" that is outside us, in the "objective world". Such "captures" and "codifications" could only be labeled as data or information but they do not constitute knowledge because they describe separate objects and not their *relationships*. Knowledge is about *coordinating* and *relating* descriptions of objects into coherent complexes. The relationships among objects are not simply "out there", to be captured, but are being continually produced, constructed, deconstructed and re-established by the knower, the agent of action.

Knowledge thus cannot be separated from the process of knowing (establishing and coordinating relationships). Knowledge and knowing are identical: *knowledge is a process.*

What is meant when we say that somebody knows or possesses knowledge? We imply that we expect one to be capable of *coordinated action* towards some goals and objectives. Coordinated action is the test of possessing knowledge. Knowledge without action reduces to simple information or data. All doing is knowing, and all knowing is doing.

Vast repositories of data and information (data banks, warehouses, infomarts, encyclopaedias) are only passive recordings of the "raw material" of knowledge. Only coordinated human action, i.e., the process of relating such components into coherent patterns, which turn out to be successful in achieving goals and purposes, qualifies as knowledge.

Among the myriads of possible postulated relationships among objects, only some result in a successful coordinated action. Every such act of knowing brings forth a world of action.

Bringing forth a world of coordinated action is human knowledge.

Bringing forth such a world manifests itself in all our action and all our being. *Knowing is effective* [i.e., coordinated and "successful"] *action.*

Knowledge as an effective action enables a living (human) being to persist in its coordinated existence in a specific environment from which it continually brings forth its own world of action. All knowing is coordinated action by the knower and therefore depends on the "structure" of the knower. The way knowledge can be brought forth in doing depends on the nature of "doing" as it is implied by the organization of the knower and his circumstances (working environment).

1.6. Uses and Users of Knowledge

Knowledge is an effective coordination of action. For example, a baker coordinates his actions so effectively that the result is not only edible but also "good" and generally desirable. He *knows* how to make bread.

A successful baker can also share his knowledge: he can teach others how to make bread that is "good". He can also share his knowledge *by parts*, instructing others how to perform smaller parts of the entire task and retaining only the overall coordinative function. Ultimately, he might lose the detailed knowledge of all the subtasks and thus of the integrated knowledge of making bread. At such point, no single individual would know the entire task. Such is the situation present after the millennia of progressive division of task, labor and knowledge.

According to F. A. Hayek (1937), the central question of all social sciences is precisely that: how combining the *fragments of knowledge*, residing in different minds, can bring about results which, if they were to be brought about deliberately, would require a knowledge on the part of the directing mind which no single person can possess. No single individual or even group of individuals know how to build a space shuttle and yet space shuttles do get built.

Most of human knowledge has been dispersed into the bits and pieces of specialization, into all the incomplete and contradictory information possessed by separate individuals.

There are at least two essential modes of approaching this dilemma:

(1) All local knowledge is conveyed to the central authority, integrated and used to form plans which are then communicated down to the local agents for the purposes of coordinating their action by command and order.

(2) Central or strategic knowledge is supplied to the individuals and their localities as an *additional* knowledge, needed by them in order to coordinate *their own* plans and action with those of other similar localities (self-coordination).

The first mode (centralized planning) prevails in traditional corporations and separates coordination from action, limits the value of local knowledge and ultimately transforms local agents into executors of substantially limited responsibility and freedom to act. The second mode (decentralized planning) enriches local knowledge and enhances agents' responsibility for the purposes and execution of their own autonomous action of coordination.

Local agents (workers and employees) possess crucial and irreplaceable knowledge of the particular context and circumstance of time and place. Each individual agent thus possesses knowledge that is *unique*. We can treat this unique knowledge of people, local conditions and special circumstances as an asset to be enhanced and enriched, or we treat this unique knowledge (and its possessors) with contempt and replace it with context-free and locally useless directives of specialist expert coordinators.

What is the strategic frame to be communicated to the possessors of local knowledge? Do they need to know all the reasons why have quantities or qualities of particular items changed? Certainly not. They need a simple information index which would reliably indicate how scarce or abundant a particular item or its attribute is at any given moment. Such numerical index should not be derived from any intrinsic properties of things, because it has to be continually adjustable and changeable in order to reflect *immediate relationships* of the relative scarcity of things. In other words, a *system of free prices* is what is needed for the *effective* coordination of action *within a corporation*.

Prices are the necessary informational "glue" which allows free agents to coordinate action even under the conditions of significant division of knowledge. Free market prices are the most effective telecommunication system of broadcasting and circulating relevant information among economic agents and thus assuring their explicit (and implicit) cooperation.

1.7. Division of Knowledge

There is a wealth of economically and socially valuable concepts hidden in now overused and overrated notion of the "division of labor". Today, it is the *division of knowledge*, rather than the division of labor, that determines the limits and the potential of competitiveness and productivity of an enterprise. As usual, it is still Friedrich Hayek (1945:520) who was "there already":

> *Clearly there is here a problem of the division of knowledge, which is quite analogous to, and at least as important as, the problem of the division of labor. But, while the latter has been one of the main subjects of investigation ever since the beginning of our science, the former has been as completely neglected, although it seems to me to be the really central problem of economics as a social science.*

Division of knowledge *is* the central problem of economics as a social science. Especially today, when neither traditional economics or

knowledge management address the issues of the division of knowledge, important insights and opportunities continue being lost to the
business and management community.

One important exception is the current thought of Joseph Stiglitz
(1999:19) who appears to understand von Hayek's insights and
restates them in a modern language of knowledge economy:

> *The information transmitted upwards in a hierarchy to inform decisions is
> explicit codified information, so decisions are made in a hierarchical structure
> without lower level uncodified tacit knowledge. Better decisions might be made
> lower in the hierarchy closer to the source of the knowledge. Decentralized author-
> ity also partly unifies principal and agent to mitigate agency problems. When
> these local decisions require informational inputs from various different job cate-
> gories, it is best for the decision-makers to have rotated through those job categories
> to have acquired their tacit components. These arguments for fuzzy job bound-
> aries and job rotation cut against the traditional arguments for specialization
> and division of labor.*

The fuzzy job boundaries are represented in Fig. 1.2. Many arguments against the specialization, division of labor and division of knowledge have accumulated. Division of knowledge needs a hierarchy of
coordination, layers upon layers of bureaucracy. Division of knowledge does not promote cooperation but separates the agents through

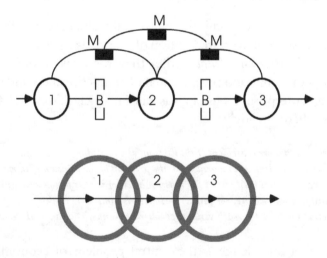

Fig. 1.2. Fuzzy job boundaries as an enabler of knowledge.

barriers and buffers interlaced throughout the process. Reintegration of knowledge enables the agents in cooperation, innovation, and coordination of their efforts.

How has the fragmentation of knowledge, task and labor surpassed its natural and economic limits?

First, any task can be broken into a large number of subtasks and operations. Such task disaggregation then allows parallel processing and could translate directly into increased productivity. This kind of division is directly related to the *number of parts* constituting the product. As long as such tasks are performed either by a single worker or by a number of automated machines, there is no reason to talk about a division of labor, but only about the *division of task*. Some products consist of thousands of parts, including all sorts of accessible or less accessible screws, nuts, washers, bolts, caps and pins. This type of "medieval" product design is bound to be of a low quality and reliability.

Second, in order to realize the *parallel processing* of thousands of specialized tasks, different tasks have to be performed and controlled by *different workers*: labor itself has to be appropriately divided. Only in this sense can we talk about the *division of labor* proper. Division of task may or may not be followed by the division of labor. If hundred workers, coordinated by a supervisor, were replaced by a hundred machines controlled by a supervisor, the division of labor would be reduced in a 100:1 ratio, although the number of subtasks remained the same.

Third, together with the division of labor we are also disaggregating, dividing and dispersing the knowledge necessary for coordination of the entire task. When one person makes a chair, from cutting the proper wood to selling it at the market, such person commands a full contingent of the chair-making knowledge. As the task and labor become divided, each person can claim only a part of that overall knowledge: "Nobody knows how to make a chair anymore". The knowledge itself becomes divided and the phenomenon of *division of knowledge* must be considered.

The concept of "division of labor" thus includes at least three separate, separable and relatively independent and differentially manageable phenomena: *division of task, division of labor, and division of knowledge*.

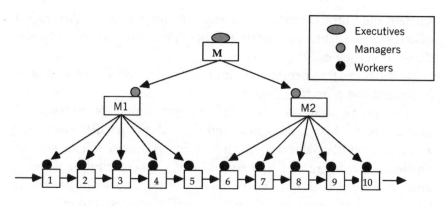

Fig. 1.3. Division of labor.

Originally, one person would perform the entire task: he would make his own clothes, starting from hunting for the animal and ending with the sewing and decorating. As the process of division of labor advances, more and more people become involved and their subtasks become more specialized. Coordinative agents and leaders (precursors of today's management) soon emerged. As markets grew, the division of labor and specialization expanded correspondingly.

In Fig. 1.3, we show how the division of labor leads to the emergence of coordinating agents (*M1, M2* and *M*) organized properly in a coordinative hierarchy, because of the individually limited *span of control* (Urwick's old dictum that no human brain should attempt to supervise more than five or six other individuals). Although the productivity increases, the complexity and the cost of coordination are increasing even faster. Division of labor is limited by its own requisite cost and complexity of coordination, *not* solely by the Smithian extent of the market.

Every subsequent doubling of the number of specialized subtasks (and laborers) leads to more than doubling of the requisite number of coordinators (managers). Coordinative hierarchy is bound to grow in size, complexity and costs.

Ultimately the cost and complexity of requisite coordination, accompanied by frequent breaks in communication and increase in misinformation, make further division of labor less and less attractive.

Coordinative hierarchies and bureaucracies can be viewed as representing a form of *social memory*. Since nobody knows how to make a space shuttle and yet space shuttles get built, coordinative hierarchies are a way of *preserving and storing societal knowledge*. The more splintered is the task, labor and knowledge, the larger and more complex must the coordinative hierarchies be.

Only a purposeful reintegration of task, labor and knowledge reduces bureaucratic hierarchies permanently.

Also, the distinction between labor and work becomes sharper. *Labor* is a direct consequence of the division of labor: it is measured by chronological time or by the output quantity per unit of time. It is separated from the final product (related to subtask or to subfunction) and it requires only the simplest, mindless mechanical moves. Drilling holes for 8 hours or shoveling earth for 8 hours is not work, but labor.

Work is a form of social relationship, a cultural concept: *"It is the way human beings make sense of the relations with their outside world and with each other"*.

Work is by definition related to a real, socially favored product or outcome. As such, work acts as a social regulator, a cohesive force linking individuals together. Making a chair, building a rocket engine, digging a drainage is work, not labor. Increased degradation from work to labor has therefore been characterized by the weakening of social cohesiveness.

After the period of rapidly rising costs, declining quality and rising prices, more globally aware and competitive producers and managers are starting (knowingly or unknowingly) to counteract these unfavorable trends:

Task is being reintegrated by reducing the number of separate parts constituting the product. Progressive product designs now have ten to hundred times smaller number of parts than the conventional "screw-it-together-with-a-nut-and-washer" approach to manufacturing. Smaller number of parts implies lower product cost, simpler assembly, lower labor cost, higher quality and more consistent reliability — directly satisfying the customer.

Labor is being reintegrated by increasing the number of subtasks to be carried out or controlled by a single multifunctional worker or

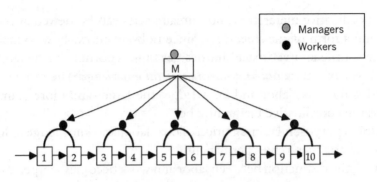

Fig. 1.4. Reintegration of labor.

group. Job rotation, multifunctionality, multipurpose machinery, etc. are all manifestations of the rapidly accelerating labor reintegration.

Knowledge is being reintegrated by increasing employees' responsibility, control and decision-making span over larger areas. Employee and department autonomy, self-coordination, self-management, participative decision making and co-ownership, are examples of the knowledge reintegration at local levels of operations.

As labor becomes work again, meaning is replacing alienation, professionality and craftsmanship are replacing expertism and specialization. Basic coordinative mechanisms of traditional administrative management of labor-performing operators are being replaced by self-coordinative systems of *mutual adjustment* and *consensual reciprocity* of modern "craftsmen".

In Fig. 1.4, we present the three reintegrations schematically. Compared to Fig. 1.3, if each worker now performs two instead of one task (with the aid of the requisite technology), task productivity would be maintained, number of workers cut in half, number of managers cut by two-thirds and the whole operation made simpler, more streamlined, cheaper, more flexible and of higher quality. Knowledge is being recovered from the splinters and knowledge management grows in importance.

1.8. Process of Reintegration

There are internal *systemic* limits to the old processes of task, labor and knowledge division. Coordination becomes more difficult, more costly and more complex. Although markets continue to grow and are in fact becoming global, processes of the division of labor do not keep the pace, slow down and ultimately reverse themselves towards the opposite direction of reintegration. One person performs the tasks previously carried out by two persons; one person controls two instead of one machine; group of workers manage themselves, without managers or supervisors; and so on. These reintegrative processes continue to gather their momentum.

These processes (division and reintegration) cannot be characterized as a "cycle" or "wave", nor as a "revolution" or "transformation", not even as a "metamorphosis" or "growth". The closest label seems to be Vico's concept of *corsi e ricorsi* in the evolution of social systems (Tagliacozzo, 1983).

Any real origin in human affairs — and the process of division of labor *certainly is* of a real origin — ultimately meets with a real end. After each *corso* there follows a different and yet organically related *ricorso*. There is a course and recourse, outswing and rebound, disaggregation and reaggregation. The processes of *corso* and *ricorso* cannot be divided or taken apart. Every *corso* in human affairs is internally self-binding and self-limiting, transforming itself into its inevitable *ricorso*.

Processes of the division of task, labor and knowledge, because of their own internal dynamics and self-organization, transform themselves spontaneously into their subsequent processes of the reintegration of task, labor and knowledge.

A good description of the self-limited corso-ricorso cycle in physical, social and human affairs can be borrowed from an M.I.T. metallurgist C. S. Smith (see Warsh, 1984:96):

A new thing of any kind whatsoever begins as a local anomaly, a region of misfit within the preexisting structure. The first nucleus is indistinguishable from the few fluctuations whose time has not yet come and the innumerable fluctuations which the future will merely erase. Once growth from an effective nucleus is well under way, however, it is then driven by the very type of interlock that at first opposed it: it has become the new orthodoxy. In crystals undergoing transformation, a region having an interaction pattern suggesting the new structure, once it is big enough, grows by demanding and rewarding conformity. With ideas or with technical or social inventions, people eventually come to accept the new as unthinkingly as they had first opposed it, and they modify their lives, interactions and investments accordingly. But the growth too has its limits. Eventually the new structure will have grown to its proper size in relation to the things with which it interacts, and a new balance must be established. The end of growth, like its beginning, is within a structure that is unpredictable in advance.

1.9. Knowledge and Technology

The nature of technology has changed: it is becoming more integrative and more *knowledge-oriented*. It tends to complement or extend the user, not to make him an appendage. The notion of technology has to be redefined: it should be viewed as a *form of social relationship*, with hardware and software enabling the brainware and technology support infrastructure. A quote from Stiglitz (1999:5) is appropriate as an introduction:

> *Take technology transfer as an example. The technical manuals, blueprints, and instruction books are the codified technical knowledge that could be seen as only the tip of the iceberg. The codified technical information assumes a whole background of contextual knowledge and practices that might be very incomplete in a developing country. Implementing a new technology in a rather different environment is itself a creative act, not just a copied behavior. Getting a complex technical system to function near its norms and repairing it when it malfunctions both draw upon a slowly accumulated reservoir of tacit knowledge that cannot be easily transferred or "downloaded" to a developing country.*

Stiglitz uses the labels of contextual and tacit knowledge in order to emphasize the insufficiency of information, codified "knowledge" and hardware-software mindset. Information can always be "downloaded", knowledge cannot. Knowledge has to be produced within the local circumstances and structural support.

At its most fundamental, technology is a *tool* used in transforming inputs into products or, more generally, towards achieving purposes or goals. For example, the inputs can be material, information or services. The product can be goods, services or information. Such a tool can be both physical (machine, computer) and logical (methodology, technique). Technology as tool does not have to be from steel, wood or silica, it could also be recipe, process or algorithm.

Many IT/S technologies are high technology. But what is high technology? Why is it labeled "high"? We often know it by listing: optical fibers, reprogrammable robots, ceramic engines, satellite communication devices and systems, optical scanners, etc. — all are high technology. But why?

1.9.1. *Structure of Technology*

Any technology can be divided into several clearly identifiable components:

(1) *Hardware*. The physical structure or logical layout, plant or equipment of machine or contrivance. This is *the means* to carry out required tasks of transformation to achieve purpose or goals. Hardware therefore refers not only to particular physical structure of components, but also to their logical layout.

(2) *Software*. The set of rules, guidelines, and algorithms necessary for using the hardware (program, covenants, standards, rules of usage) to carry out the tasks. This is the *know-how* to carry out tasks to achieve purpose or goals.

(3) *Brainware*. The purpose (objectives and goals), reason and justification for using or deploying the hardware/software in a particular way. This is the *know-what* and the *know-why* of technology. That is, determination of what to use or deploy, when, where and why?

These three components are interdependent and equally important. They form *technology core*: Components of technology core are co-determinant, their relations circular (non-linear and non-hierarchical) and mutually enhancing.

This concept of technology is clearly illustrated when we consider a car as technology: A car consists of its own physical structure and logical layout, its own hardware. Its software consists of operating rules of the push, turn, press, etc., described in manuals or acquired through learning. The brainware is supplied by the driver and includes decisions where to go, when, how fast, which way and why to use a car at all.

One could similarly define computers, satellites or Internet in terms of these three dimensions. Any information technology or system should be clearly identifiable through its hardware, software and brainware.

There exists a fourth and the most important aspect of technology:

(4) *Technology Support Net.* The requisite physical, organizational, administrative, and cultural structures: work rules, task rules, requisite skills, work content, standards and measures, styles, culture and organizational patterns.

1.9.2. *Technology Support Net*

Any technology core (hardware, software and brainware), in order to function as technology, must be embedded in a supportive network of physical, informational, and socioeconomic relationships which enable and support the proper use and functioning of a given technology. We refer to such a structure as *Technology Support Net* (TSN).

TSN is a network of flows: materials, information, energies, skills, laws, rules of conduct circulate to, through and from the network in order to enable proper functioning of the technology core and achieving given purpose or goals.

Ultimately, all the requisite network flows are initiated, maintained and consumed by people participating in the use and support of use of a given technology. They might similarly and simultaneously participate in supporting many different technologies through many different TSNs.

The entire structure of technology core and its support network of requisite flows are sketched in Fig. 1.5. It should now be clear that the shape and form of TSN is the main determinant of technology use.

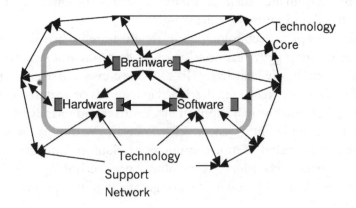

Fig. 1.5. Structure of technology.

Every unique technology core gives rise to a specific and requisite TSN and thus to a specific set of relationships among people. Ultimately, TSN can be traced to and translated into the relationships among human participants: initiators, providers and maintainers of the requisite flows in a cooperative social settings.

In this sense, every technology is a *form of social relationship* brought forth from the background environment. Only in this sense and only as such it can be properly understood, discussed and managed. Let us look at a car as technology again. Its TSN consists of a large number of people that has to be organized in a specific and requisite pattern in order to enable cars to function as technology.

All four dimensions are necessary in order to define technology: *technology is an interacting unity of hardware, software and brainware, embedded in its requisite support network of relationships.*

It is clear that technology and its four components can only be defined from the vantage point of the user or observer, not in context-free or absolute sense. In other words, roads, bridges and traffic signals can be technologies themselves, with their own hardware, software, brainware and support nets.

For example, traffic signal is a part of TSN of automobile, but its hardware can be driven by its own software (computer-controlled switching program or schedule) and brainware (purposes of safety, volume and flow control, interaction with pedestrians). It has its own support net of electricity, interpretations and car traffic (turned off at night?). Traffic light is a technology of its own.

Similarly, a piece of software from some technology can itself become viewed as technology (for achieving specific business purpose or goals) with its own hardware, software, brainware and TSN. The success of Microsoft is rooted in this realization.

Such observer-dependent definition of technology is also important for identifying important complementary, competing and collaborating technologies through the revealed intermeshing of individual TSNs into larger hypernetworks.

The relationship between technology core and its requisite TSN is that of mutual enhancement and codetermination. Specific technology core requires specific TSN, but the core itself is further shaped and defined by the intensity and depth of its embedding in its requisite TSN.

Although the technology core of automobile gives rise to a new and proper TSN, the evolution and properties of automobile TSN determine specific adaptations of the evolving technology core of automobile. Through this coevolution, technologies mature and are characterized by closer and more efficient fit between their core and TSN environment.

1.9.3. *High Technology*

The concept of technology support net allows us to *separate* the technology core of hard-soft-brainware from its requisite embedding. Different cores can fit the same net, different nets can be tried for the same core, and so on. In this sense, any technology can characterized as being "misplaced" or "unfit" as well as "right", "fitting" or "appropriate". In the cases of mismatch, both aspects of technology (core and TSN) have to be adapted in order to assure appropriate functioning.

Different changes in the core, both in hardware or software and brainware, will have differentiated effects on the requisite TSN. According to the nature and extent of such changes, we can offer the following definitions:

(1) *High technology* is any technology core that affects the very architecture (structure and organization) of the components of the technology support net. High technology changes the qualitative nature of tasks, their performance, interconnections and physical, energy and information flows, or also the skills required, the roles played, the styles of management and coordination, even the organizational culture. It allows (and often requires) not only to *do things differently* but often to *do different things.*

Clearly, high technology has to be differentiated from [just regular] technology.

(2) *Technology* is a core that affects only the efficiency of flows over TSN, i.e., it activates only quantitative changes over the qualitatively the same architecture of TSN. It allows users to perform the same tasks in the same way, but faster, more reliably, in larger quantities, or more efficiently, while preserving the qualitative nature

of flows, structure of the support, skills, styles and culture. Technology allows us to do the same thing, in the same way, more efficiently.

(3) *Appropriate technology* core essentially preserves everything: the support net as well as the flows through it; its effects are neutral with respect to TSN. It allows users to do the same thing in the same way at comparable levels of efficiency. Improving efficiency is not the purpose here, preserving and protecting the TSN is. Appropriate technology is very important in situations where the stability of the support net is primary for social, political, cultural or environmental reasons.

High technology cannot be compared and evaluated with the existing technology purely on the basis of cost, net present value or return on investment: it would be like comparing apples and oranges. Only within an unchanging and relatively stable TSN would such direct financial comparability be meaningful. In other words, you can directly compare typewriter with a better (electric) typewriter, but not typewriter with word processor. Therein lies the management challenge of high technology.

Appropriate technology implies that rather than improving the measures of performance, it is the preservation of the TSN itself which is the driving purpose of technology implementation.

The notion of high technology is therefore relative to the vantage point of the technology being replaced. No technology is fixed and — being a form of social relationship — it evolves. Technology starts, develops, persists, mutates, stagnates and declines just like living organisms.

High technology core emerges and challenges existing TSNs which are thus forced to coevolve with it. New versions of the core are being designed and fitted into an increasingly suitable TSN, with smaller and smaller high-technology effects. High technology becomes just technology, with more efficient versions fitting the same support net. Finally, even the efficiency gains diminish, emphasis shifts to product tertiary attributes (appearance, style) and technology becomes TSN-preserving appropriate technology. This technological equilibrium state is at times interrupted by a technological mutation — new high technology appears and the cycle is repeated.

Automobile was high technology with respect to horse carriage, it evolved into technology and finally into appropriate technology with a stable, unchanging TSN. The only high-technology advance in the offings is the electric car, because of its need for wholesale restructuring and redistribution of the TSN.

Implementing high technology is often resisted. This resistance is well understood on the part of active participants in the requisite TSN. Electric car will be resisted by gas-station operators in the same way automated teller machines (ATMs) were resisted by bank tellers and automobiles by horsewhip makers. Technology that does not qualitatively restructure the TSN will not be resisted and never has been resisted.

Proverbial "Resistance to change" is not a universal human trait. In fact, humans like change, seek it out and thrive on it, as long as the change preserves the support network they are part of. Electric typewriter, electric tooth brush or more powerful tractor were never resisted. Technologies and appropriate technologies are not resisted, high technologies are.

Middle management resists business process reengineering because BPR represents a direct assault on the support net (coordinative hierarchy) they thrive on. Teamwork and multifunctionality is resisted by those whose TSN provides the comfort of narrow specialization and command-driven work.

1.9.4. *High-Technology Environment*

We can compile a short comparative listing (Table 1.2) of current impacts of the transition from Technology to High Technology.

Within the framework introduced here, one cannot fail to observe that modern information- and knowledge-based technologies (including techniques and methodologies) currently tend to be high technologies with high-technology effects. They integrate task, labor and knowledge, transcend classical separation of mental and manual work, enhance systems aspects, promote self-reliance, self-service, innovation and creativity. The "low" technologies, no matter how new, complex

Table 1.2. Technology versus high
technology impacts.

Technology	High Technology
Efficiency	Effectiveness & explicability
Economies of scale	Economies of scope
Know-how	Know-what & know-why
Data & information	Knowledge & wisdom
Specialization	Reintegration
Working harder	Working smarter
Centralization	Decentralization
Hierarchy	Network

or advanced, are those which still require dividing and splintering of task, labor and knowledge, increase specialization, promote division and dependency, sustain intermediaries and diminish initiative.

Not all modern or advanced technologies are high technologies: they have to be *used* as high technologies, function as such and be embedded in their requisite TSNs. They have to *empower* the individual because only through the individual they can empower knowledge. It would be hasty to claim that all "information" or "informating" technologies (IT/S) have integrative effects. Some information systems are still designed to "improve" the traditional hierarchy of command and thus preserve and entrench the existing TSN: administrative model of management. They further aggravate division of task and labor, further specialize knowledge, separate management from workers and concentrate information and knowledge in centers.

As knowledge surpasses capital, labor and raw materials as the dominant economic resource, technologies are also starting to reflect this shift. Because knowledge is not a "thing", residing in a supermind, superbook or superdatabase, but a complex relational pattern of networks brought forth to coordinate human action, technologies are rapidly shifting from centralized hierarchies to distributed networks.

The use of computers provides a good example. The original centralized concept (*one computer, many persons*) is a knowledge-defying idea of our computing prehistory and its inadequacies and failures are becoming clearly apparent. The era of personal computing brought powerful computers "on every desk" (*one person, one computer*). This short and transitional period was necessary for getting used to the new computing environment; but it was inadequate from the knowledge-producing vantage point. Adequate knowledge creation and management come mainly from networking and distributed computing: *one person, many computers.* Each person's computer must form an access to the *entire* computing landscape or ecology: the Internet of *other* computers, databases, mainframes, as well as production, distribution and retailing facilities, etc.

1.10. Knowledge Technology (KT)

While IT/S type of technology was dominated by hardware and software, knowledge technology (KT) is driven by the brainware and technology support infrastructure. While IT/S creates, organizes and supplies *informational inputs*, KT enables and supports effective *coordination of all* inputs, processes and people.

It is important that knowledge and Knowledge Management (KM) returns to its pragmatic roots and Western scientific and professional traditions. The work of Dewey, Lewis and Polanyi provides sufficiently strong and healthy roots. It is not what we say but what we do that matters. *That* tradition provides a foundation for sound business and management in the 21st century.

References

Dewey, D. (1965). *Modern Capital Theory.* New York: Columbia University Press.
Dewey, J. and A.F. Bentley (1949). *Knowing and the Known.* Boston: Beacon Press.
Hayek, F.A. (1937). Economics and Knowledge. *Economica*, February, 33–45.
Hayek, F.A. (1945). The Use of Knowledge in Society. *Am. Econ. Rev.*, 35, 519–530.
Lewis, C.I. (1956). *Mind and the World-Order*, 2nd Ed. New York: Dover Publications.
Maturana, H.R. and F.J. Varela (1987). *The Tree of Knowledge.* Boston: Shambhala Publications.
Polanyi, M. (1983). *Tacit Dimension.* Peter Smith Publ.
Prusak, L. (1999). What's Up with Knowledge Management: A Personal View. In *The Knowledge Management Yearbook 1999–2000*, J.W. Cortada and J.A. Woods (eds.), pp. 3–7. Woburn, MA: Butterworth-Heinemann.

Sowell, T. (1980). *Knowledge and Decisions.* New York: Basic Books.

Stiglitz, J.E. (1999). *Public Policy for a Knowledge Economy.* Center for Economic Policy Research Document. 27 January, London.

Stonier, T. (1983). *The Wealth of Information.* London: Methuen.

Sveiby, K.E. (1999). Tacit Knowledge. In *The Knowledge Management Yearbook 1999–2000,* J.W. Cortada and J.A. Woods, (eds.), pp. 18–27. Woburn, MA: Butterworth-Heinemann.

Tagliacazzo, G. (ed.) (1983). *Vico and Marx: Affinities and Contrasts.* Atlantic Highlands, NJ: Humanities Press.

Warsh, D. (1984). *The Idea of Economic Complexity.* New York: Viking Press.

Zeleny, M. (1982). *Multiple Criteria Decision Making.* New York: McGraw-Hill.

Zeleny, M. (1986). High Technology Management. *Human Syst. Management,* 6(2), 109–120.

Zeleny, M. (1987). Management Support Systems: Towards Integrated Knowledge Management. *Human Syst. Management,* 7(1), 59–70.

Zeleny, M. (1989). Knowledge as a New Form of Capital: Division and Reintegration of Labor, Part 1. *Human Syst. Management,* 8(1), 45–58; Knowledge as a New Form of Capital: Knowledge-based Management Systems, Part 2. *Human Syst. Management,* 8(2), 129–143.

Zeleny, M. (1989). The Role of Fuzziness in the Construction of Knowledge. In *The Interface Between Artificial Intelligence and Operations Research in Fuzzy Environment,* Interdisciplinary Systems Research Series No. 95, J.-L. Verdegay and M. Delgado (eds.), pp. 233–252. Rheinland: Verlag TÜV.

Zeleny, M. (1991). Cognitive Equilibrium: A Knowledge-based Theory of Fuzziness and Fuzzy Sets. *General Syst,* 19(4), 359–381.

Zeleny, M. (1991). Knowledge as Capital: Integrated Quality Management. *Prometheus,* 9(1), 93–101.

Zeleny, M. (2000). Knowledge versus Information. In *IEBM Handbook of Information Technology in Business,* M. Zeleny (ed.), pp. 162–168. London: Thomson.

Part II

The Rise of Asian Knowledge Society

Chapter 2

"Knowledge" and the Sociology of Science[1]

Hans-Dieter Evers

2.1. Introduction

Land labor and capital are, in classical economics, regarded as the three "factors of production". Economic policy has been very much oriented towards improving the total and relative allocation of resources to these factors. In Asian developing countries integrated agricultural development, income generating activities and rural credit schemes are just examples of a rich arsenal of development programmes that can be directly related to the conventual wisdom that inputs into factors of production produce development. More recently a new factor of production has been added to the development debate; a factor that supposedly has overtaken the other factors in importance: *Knowledge* is now regarded as the main driving force of innovation, economic progress, modernization and development. A by now famous example is cited in the World Development Report of 1998/99. Ghana and the Republic of Korea started of with almost the same GNP/cap in 1960. Thirty years later the Korean GNP/cap had risen more than six times, the Ghanaian was still hovering at the same level (in 1985 prices). Half the gap could be explained in terms of the "traditional" factor inputs, the other half, according to World Bank experts, was attributed to "knowledge" as a factor of production (see the introductory chapter of this book).

[1]I am grateful to Farid Alatas, Zaheer Babar and other members of the Working Group on Knowledge Society that was active in the Department of Sociology, National University of Singapore in 1999/2000 for useful comments and additions to this chapter.

Knowledge has since been identified as one of the major factors, if not THE crucial factor of development. The idea is, indeed, fascinating. If natural resources are scarce, if foreign direct investment (FDI) does not flow into the country as expected, if land is not fertile or scarce, knowledge can be introduced and put to effective use. In the almost poetic words of the World Bank, "knowledge is like light. Weightless and tangible it can easily travel the world, enlightening the lives of people everywhere" (World Bank, 1999:1).

Furthermore knowledge governance is about to become a major field of development planning, which has attracted the attention of researchers around the globe. Knowledge governance is closely related to "good governance" on one side and "governance of natural resources" on the other. An interdisciplinary approach to solve problems of governance is therefore mandatory. While "Governance" is basically about how to govern a country or an organization through laws, rules and regulations and through instilling values and beliefs in the procedure and legitimacy of governing, "Knowledge Governance" refers to: (i) enacting and creating the institutions necessary for the development of a knowledge society; (ii) facilitating the development of an epistemic culture of knowledge production; and (iii) regulating the flow of knowledge, as well as safeguarding intellectual property rights. Most industrialized countries have embarked on policies to help the growth of their knowledge-based economies.

In the developing world, the idea that knowledge is a major factor of production, has been gaining ground particularly in Asian countries, that have so far been titled "NICs" — newly industrializing countries. Several South-east and East Asian Countries have thus planned and carried out strategies to bridge the digital divide, to close the knowledge gap between them and the OECD countries. They invented a framework to produce and utilize knowledge for economic and social development and follow an active policy of knowledge governance. The mainstays of these strategies are:

- heavy investment in ICT (information and communication technology) infrastructure;
- training programmes to increase computer literacy;

- government support of R&D (research and development) and R&D personnel;
- creation of research institutes in selected fields, like bio-technology, ICT and informatics, but also in the social sciences; and
- gearing the education systems towards elite education and the creation of "centres of excellence".

The following chapters will provide a background to the debate on knowledge societies and knowledge governance. We shall discuss general issues, starting from the classical sociology of science, explain the social structures and features of knowledge societies and provide some case studies on knowledge governance and knowledge management in selected Asian countries.

2.2. Knowledge and Existence

In his influential work "Die Wissensformen und die Gesellschaft" (Types of Knowledge and Society) Max Scheler (1924/1960) sees knowledge as an existential phenomenon, a "Seinsverhaeltnis", which serves different purposes: the development of personality, salvation in a religious sense and political domination as well as economic achievement. Positive scientific knowledge is only *one* of several forms of knowledge, which is in itself dependent on the absolute reality of metaphysics (Maas, 1999:15). There are two "Seinsbereiche", namely ideal factors ("Geist" or spirit), i.e., ideas and values, and real factors (social or material conditions), that determine the selection of which knowledge is created, formulated and believed to be relevant. Platonian idealism and cultural relativism are combined into the core field of sociology of knowledge.

Scheler as well as contemporary German sociologists working in the phenomenological tradition of Husserl use the concept of "milieu" as a methodological tool to analyze the formulation of knowledge situated within the social environment and within networks of interaction (Grathoff, 1989:413). Milieus are able to attach meaning ("Sinn") to a person's social, cognitive and emotional experiences and over time form distinct styles of experiences and *Weltanschauung*.

Mannheim has already warned researchers to distance themselves from the *Weltanschauung*, which they wish to analyze and to which they are also subjugated (Mannheim, 1931). Only then can the social scientist discover the basic principles underlying the formation of knowledge in a specific period of history in a particular civilization. It is the task of the sociology of knowledge to analyze the styles of knowledge and their social class basis.[2] The three methodological steps he is advocating entail: (i) keeping a distance between researcher and prevalent *Weltanschauung* and cognitive styles;[3] (ii) contextualization, i.e., relating knowledge to social condition; and (iii) particularization, i.e., defining the realm of knowledge under discussion.

In formulating the basic principles and assumptions of the sociology of knowledge, Mannheim drew upon and creatively synthesized three dominant intellectual currents of his time: German classical philosophy, particularly Hegelian ideas; Marxism and *Geisteswissenschaften*, represented by Dilthey among others. Hegel provided the view that facts and event are to be conceptualized not as isolated phenomena but as related to other events and the dominant forces and trends. From Marx, Mannheim borrowed the idea, formulated most forcefully in *The German Ideology* but elsewhere too, that the ideologies of a society in a given period bore some determinate relationship to the existing classes and to the conflict of interests among them. From Dilthey and the *Geisteswissenschaften* School, Mannheim accepted the assumption that due to the fundamental difference between the physical and cultural sciences, the latter required a specific method. While for the physical sciences, explanation (*Eklärung*) or the correlation of external facts was sufficient, this could not be the main objective of the cultural sciences. The latter required both explanation and understanding (*Verstehen*) or the involvement with the purposes, motives, and values of the actors concerned. In addition to these three main intellectual currents, Durkheim in his *Elementary Forms of the Religious Life* had already argued that ideas of time and space, force and contradiction,

---

[2]It appears that Habermas (1978) has later followed up this line of argument in his brilliant book on Knowledge and Interest.

[3]This argument has become better known through Max Weber's writings on Wissenschaft als Beruf (science as a profession).

etc. vary from one group to another, and within the same group from one historical period to another. He argued that our basic categories, conceptions of the sacred, etc. are socially and culturally contingent. Building on these intellectual currents of his time, Mannheim argued that "the greater art of the sociologist consists in his attempt always to relate changes in mental attitudes to changes in social situations . . . the human mind does not operate in vacuo; the most delicate change in the human spirit corresponds to similarly delicate changes in the situation in which an individual or a group finds itself, and, conversely, the minutest change in situations indicate that men, too, have undergone some change" (Mannheim, 1953:219). This formulation remained central to Mannheim's conception of sociology of knowledge that was refined and developed further in *Essays on the Sociology of Knowledge* (1952) and *Ideology and Utopia* (1936; 1960).

2.3. Idealism and Relativism[4]

As mentioned earlier sociology of knowledge seeks to grapple with the two tension points of Platonic idealism and relativism. One of the problems that Mannheim had to grapple with was the problem of radical cultural relativism. Mannheim rejected the notion of an abstract, totally impartial knowing subject, uninfluenced by any conceptual framework but he was not comfortable with radical relativism. Rejecting both these extremes, Mannheim argued that knowledge is not relative but perspectivistic and relational. By considering how different social locations and contexts influence the production of knowledge, one's knowledge of reality becomes more adequate. This is because they provide different perspectives of a given reality that do not contradict each other but "encircle the same . . . historical content from different standpoints and at different depths of penetration" (Mannheim, 1952:105). The method of relating the production of knowledge to the position and location of individuals or groups that produce it did not lead to total relativism. On the contrary, Mannheim felt that his method led to a

---

[4]We are grateful to the Working Group on Knowledge Society for valuable additions to this section.

"widening of our concept of truth which alone can save us from being barred from the exploration of these fields in which both the nature of the object to be known and that of the knowing subject make only perspectivistic knowledge possible" (Mannheim, 1952:120).

These early formulations of a sociology of knowledge are developed further by Mannheim in his *Ideology and Utopia* (1936; 1960). Taking seriously Marx's contention that the conditions of social existence influence humans' social consciousness, he argued that sociology of knowledge itself could not have arisen in medieval Europe where different strata dwelt in their own isolated world-views or *Weltanschauungen*. Social mobility and communication made possible by the development of capitalism led to forms of thought and experience developed in relative isolation to enter a common consciousness, impelling "the mind to discover the irreconcilability of the conflicting conceptions of the world" (Mannheim, 1960:7). Here, Mannheim was reflexively analyzing the specific social context that made the development of sociology of knowledge possible. Connecting the development of ideas and knowledge to the specific location and world-view of the carriers of knowledge, Mannheim arrived at his distinctive concepts of "ideology" and "utopia". In formulating these concepts, Mannheim sought to elucidate the significance of the historical and social location of the carriers of knowledge to the ideas and knowledge they produced. For example, the Christian formulation "The last shall be first" can only be meaningfully understood by placing it in the sociohistorical context in which it was first uttered. The early Christians and their Roman oppressors were located differently and their world-views expressed respectively as "utopia" and "ideology" reflected this differential location. The phrase "the last shall be first" is "utopian" in the sense that it expresses the countervalues to the dominant values or "ideology" of their Roman oppressors. The "utopian" countervalues (utopia) expressed in the depreciation of power and the glorification of passivity expresses the exact opposite of Roman "ideology". Both ideological and utopian thought are situationally determined in the sense that they reflect the different conditions of existence of rulers and ruled, oppressors and oppressed and each reflects the interests of its carriers.

Mannheim's sociology of knowledge was intended to facilitate the evaluation of a diversity of contending view-points, and thereby enhancing the ability of arriving at "truth" (Zeitlin, 1994). Mannheim's conception of the relatively unattached intellectual (*sozial freischwebende Intelligenz*) was meant to resolve the thorny issue of relativism that accompanies any attempt to contextualize the production of knowledge. Hence, his formulation that in the modern era, intellectuals, being relatively independent of structural dependence on patronage, as was the case in the medieval era, are potentially in a position to deploy a variety of perspectives toward any given social issue or phenomenon. Thus while all social thought and knowledge is relative to particular social contexts, positions and perspectives, intellectuals have the potential ability to adopt a variety of perspectives in order to enhance understanding and explanation of any phenomenon.

2.4. The Sociology of Science

Although Max Scheler and Mannheim explicitly developed the framework for sociology of knowledge, they explicitly exclude natural scientific knowledge from their scope. For Mannheim, the content of scientific knowledge could not be subject to sociological analysis (Mulkay, 1979). He refers to the concepts appropriate to the study of the natural world as "timeless and static". Valid knowledge about such objective phenomena can be obtained only by detached, impartial observation, by reliance on sense data and by accurate measurement (Mannheim, 1952:4–16). He comes close to generating a sociology of scientific knowledge when he writes that "we must reject the notion that there is a sphere of truth itself as a disruptive and unjustified hypothesis. It is instructive to note, that natural sciences seem to be, in many respects, in a closely analogous situation" (Mulkay, 1979:15). But overall, he stops short of including natural scientific knowledge within the purview of sociological analysis. Despite some indications to the contrary, scientific knowledge for Mannheim develops in a relatively straight line, as errors are eliminated and a growing number of truths accumulate. Scientific knowledge progresses through a steady, linear accumulation of true facts, unaffected by the larger social and organizational context of their production (Mulkay, 1979:11). The development of sociology of science, initiated largely by Robert Merton (1972) and his colleagues such as Bernard Barber (1952) largely accepted this view of scientific knowledge. Their early work focused on analyzing the social and institutional factors that influenced the growth of science, but scientific knowledge itself was judged to be unproblematic. The content of scientific knowledge was assumed to be uninfluenced by the social context of its production. In the 1970s sociologists began to subject the content of scientific knowledge to sociological analysis. Influenced heavily by the new philosophy of science and particularly by Berger and Luckman's *The Social Construction of Reality* (1966), they argued that social factors influenced the very content of scientific knowledge (Latour and Woogar, 1979; Barnes, 1977; Collins, 1985; Mulkay, 1979; Mulkay and Knorr-Cetina, 1983; Knorr-Cetina, 1981). The key idea here was that scientific knowledge like any other knowledge is partly a social construction. Scientific facts are produced or "manufactured" by a network of scientists in specific social contexts and an element of social contingency is part and parcel of the development of scientific knowledge. The constructivist perspective has been enormously useful in problematizing the idea that scientific knowledge represents an objective, neutral accumulation of facts about the natural world. The basic idea that scientific knowledge is contingently influenced by the conditions of its production has been particularly fruitful for critically scrutinizing the claims of experts and expert knowledge systems to offer ahistorical and universal models that can in principle be applied in any context (Brown, 1993). The constructivist perspective has also led to a reflexive awareness of the mechanisms through which certain structural and power relations are implicated in expert knowledge systems and how these elements marginalize specific views and perspectives while simultaneously claiming contextless, apolitical universality (Harding, 1986; 1993; Martin, 1987; Fuller, 1993; Rabinow, 1996; Evers and Menkhoff, 2004).

While a radical version of social constructivism raises all the problems associated with relativism (scientific facts are made, but they are not made up!) and has been criticized (Hacking, 1983; 1999; Murphy, 1994; Baber, 1992; 2000), "moderate constructivism", that takes the element of social contingency in the production of scientific knowledge seriously, provides a useful framework for making sense of the social processes of social negotiation, power struggles etc. that are integral components of the production of scientific knowledge.

2.5. Conclusion

In this introductory chapter we have drawn attention to the fact that the discussion on knowledge management and knowledge governance has its roots in the classical literature of the sociology of knowledge. Two important thoughts stand out in this debate: (i) There are different forms of knowledge. Rational scientific knowledge, available in the writings of researchers and experts is only one form of knowledge; and (ii) The production and use of knowledge is embedded in social, cultural and political relations. The current distinctions between knowledge and experience, tacit and open knowledge, local or indigenous and global knowledge owe much to the earlier debates of which we have provided a short glimpse.

References

Baber, Z. (1992). Sociology of Scientific Knowledge: Lost in the Reflexive Funhouse? *Theory and Society*, 21, 105–119.

Baber, Z. (2000). An Ambiguous Legacy: The Social Construction of the Kuhnian Revolution and its Consequences for the Sociology of Science. *Bulletin of Science and Technology Studies*, 20(2), 139–155.

Barber, B. (1952). *Science and the Social Order*. New York: Free Press.

Barnes, B. (1977). *Interests and the Growth of Knowledge*. London: Routledge.

Berger, P.L. and T. Luckmann (1966). *The Social Construction of Reality: A Treatise in the Sociology of Knowledge*. New York: Anchor Books.

Brown, R.H. (1993). Modern Science: Institutionalization of Knowledge and Rationalization of Power. *The Sociological Quarterly*, 34(1), 153–168.

Collins, H.M. (1985). *Changing Order: Replication and Induction in Scientific Practice*. London: Sage.

Evers, H.-D. and T. Menkhoff (2004). Expert Knowledge and the Role of Consultants in an Emerging Knowledge-based Economy. *Human Systems Management*, 23(2), 137–149.

Fuller, S. (1993). *Philosophy, Rhetoric and the End of Knowledge*. Madison: University of Wisconsin Press.

Grathoff, R. (1989). *Milieu und Lebenswelt. Einführung in die phänomenologische Soziologie and die sozialphänomenologische Forschung.* Frankfurt am Main: Suhrkamp Verlag.

Habermas, J. (1978). *Knowledge and Human Interests.* London: Heinemann Educational.

Hacking, I. (1983). *Representing and Intervening.* Cambridge: Cambridge University Press.

Hacking, I. (1999). *The Social Construction of What?* Cambridge, MA: Harvard University Press.

Harding, S. (1986). *The Science Question in Feminism.* Ithaca: Cornell University Press.

Harding, S. (1993). *The "Racial" Economy of Science.* New York: Routledge.

Knorr-Cetina, K. (1981). *The Manufacture of Knowledge.* New York: Pergamon.

Latour, B. and S. Woolgar (1979). *Laboratory Life: The Social Construction of Scientific Facts.* London: Sage.

Maas, S. (1999). *Wissenssoziologie.* Bielefeld: Transcript Verlag.

Mannheim, K. (1930). Wissenssoziologie. *Handwoerterbuch der Soziologie,* pp. 659–687. Stuttgart: Enke.

Mannheim, K. (1952). *Essays on the Sociology of Knowledge.* London: Routledge and Kegan Paul.

Mannheim, K. (1953). *Essays on Sociology and Social Psychology.* London: Routledge and Kegan.

Mannheim, K. (1936/1960). *Ideology and Utopia.* London: Routledge and Kegan Paul.

Merton, R. (1972). *Sociology of Science.* Chicago: University of Chicago Press.

Mulkay, M. (1979). *Science and the Sociology of Knowledge.* London: Allen and Unwin.

Mulkay, M. and K. Knorr-Cetina (eds.) (1983). *Science Observed.* London: Sage.

Murphy, R. (1994). The Social Construction of Science without Nature. *Sociology,* 28, 957–974.

Rabinow, P. (1996). *Making PCR: A Story of Biotechnology.* Chicago: University of Chicago Press.

Scheler, M. (1960). *Die Wissensformen und die Gesellschaft.* Gesamtausgabe herausgegeben von Maria Scheler. Muenchen: A Francke.

World Bank (1999). *World Development Report 1998/99: Knowledge for Development.* New York: Oxford University Press.

Zeitlin, I.M. (1994). *Ideology and the Development of Sociological Theory.* New Jersey: Prentice Hall.

Chapter 3

The Knowledge Gap and the Digital Divide

Hans-Dieter Evers

3.1. Defining the Knowledge Gap and the Digital Divide

Since the World Bank published the 1998/99 World Development Report on Knowledge and Development (World Bank, 1999), narrowing the knowledge gap and the digital divide between and within countries has become a prime target of international development agencies as well as of some national governments.

The World Bank report distinguishes two types of knowledge: knowledge about attributes leading to information problems and knowledge about technology (i.e., know-how), including knowledge gaps: "Typically, developing countries have less of this know-how than industrial countries, and the poor have less than the non-poor. We call these unequal distributions across and within countries *knowledge gaps*" (World Bank, 1999, Chapter 1). The international knowledge gap is thus defined in terms of the knowledge achieved in the OECD countries, in particular the USA. The meaning of knowledge is never clearly defined, but from the discussion on the knowledge gap we can deduce that education, expenditure for research and development and ICT infrastructure are seen as the crucial variables.

The digital divide refers to the uneven distribution of information and communication technology (ICT) between and within nations. In each country there are people who have access to modern communication technology while others are not enabled to make use of telephone connections, the Internet and other ICT features. There is no doubt that such a digital divide exists but its severity and depth is evaluated differently according to the indicators used to measure it. The knowledge gap as mentioned above is a more complex phenomenon and refers to the uneven intensity of knowledge production, availability and dissemination world wide. There appears to be a connection between the two: the digital divide determines to a large extent the capacity of producing and using new knowledge.

Usually the concept of a "digital divide" is used to relate to the technological aspect of the knowledge gap. The term "digital divide" refers to the gap between individuals, households, businesses and geographic areas at different socio-economic levels with regard to their opportunities to access information and communication technologies (ICTs) and their use of the Internet. It reflects differences among and within countries (OECD, 2001). Access to telephones appears to be the basic factor, because Internet use per telephone subscriber does not differ very much between countries (Dasgupta *et al.*, 2001). In general the concept "digital divide" is biased towards high technology and needs to be reconceptualized to pay greater attention to social exclusion and inclusion (Warschauer, 2003).

As shared by C.A.P. Braga, "The debate about the welfare implications of the information revolution for developing countries has given rise to diametrically opposed views. Some believe that information and communication technologies (ICT) can be mechanisms enabling developing countries to 'leapfrog' stages of development. Others see the emerging global information infrastructure as contributing to even wider economic divergence between developing and industrialized countries" (1998).

In any case, closing the knowledge gap and the digital divide are regarded as necessary steps towards economic development. Knowledge is the most important factor of production and its growth is essential to propel a country into self-sustained growth. Development agencies have been the most outspoken proponents of the gap-closing strategy. World Bank President James Wolfensohn, commenting on a massive study "Voices of the Poor", has again emphasized this view with the following words: "Poor people know as well as anybody else that what keeps them poor is lack of competitiveness and lack of knowledge" (Far Eastern Economic Review, June 27, 2003). Whenever a point of view is authorized by the World Bank, it advances to the status of an ultimate truth. But exactly at this stage we should sit back, take a closer look and re-think and re-search the issue at hand. Can and should a knowledge gap and the digital divide be closed to achieve development?

3.2. The Widening Knowledge Gap

Optimistic commentators argue that the fast expansion of information and communication technology (ICT) has improved the access to knowledge. Especially the spread of personal computers and the Internet has connected millions of people to the knowledge resources of the world-wide-web. In Malaysia, e.g. the number of Internet users has risen from 40 thousand to 3.7 million from 1995 to the year 2000 and the number of computers has risen from 37.3 per thousand people to 103.1 during the same period. For comparison: in the whole region (East Asia and the Pacific) the ratio was 12.8 in 2000 and 26.3 in 2002, putting Malaysia far above the average. (World Bank, Development Data Group, 2004). But access to ICT resources is not equally distributed and the digital divide has increased.

More and more people gain access to global knowledge resources and a fair proportion is probably making use of them. Comparing countries critical commentators are, however, not convinced that "the knowledge revolution will let developing countries leapfrog to higher levels of development. In fact, the knowledge gap is likely to widen the disparities between rich and poor, imprisoning many developing countries in relative poverty" (Persaud, 2001). It is equally uncertain that the new knowledge technologies will bolster democracy just on the basis of better access to information and improved knowledge of political issues.

The digital divide as well as the knowledge gap is widening because some regions within countries develop faster than others and some countries are on a faster track towards a knowledge society than the less endowed. Statistical indicators show that the global knowledge gap has been widening. This holds true for comparisons within as well as between countries and within and between ASEAN countries as well.

The knowledge gap is arguably deliberately or inadvertently widened by the monopolization of the application of knowledge through patents and the insistence on securing intellectual property rights by powerful organizations, especially the WTO. The TRIPS (trade-related aspects of intellectual property rights) Agreement, concluded in 1995, determines rights over intellectual property and grants temporary monopolies for innovations and inventions. Poorer countries and people are excluded from access to vital "knowledge goods" such as medicines, seeds, and educational materials (Oxfam, 2001). Selling knowledge in the form of licenses, franchising and overseas education has developed into a multi billion dollar business for the OECD countries, which capitalize on the knowledge gap between them and the developing world.

The digital divide and the knowledge gap are constructs within the world of development cooperation, but they can also be seen as the result of a global marketing strategy of the industrialized countries, especially the United States. The knowledge gap is constructed in such a way that it cannot be closed. Developing nations are instructed to follow a strategy of improving their knowledge base by investing heavily in ICT and by following the model of the most highly developed knowledge-based economies in the North. As this model is changing fast, the developing countries (and a large part of the other industrialized economies) are engaged in a futile race of catching-up, instead of trying to improve their competitive advantage by stressing local knowledge resources, occupying niches, and forming strategic alliances among themselves and with selected others.

We shall now take a closer look at the knowledge gap and the digital divide and its creation.

3.3. The Digital Divide Between South-east Asian and European Countries

Singapore and Malaysia have been singled out for their success in promoting economic development through stringent development policies, including support for the growth of a knowledge-based economy and the formation of knowledge societies. Statistical indicators show, however, that the digital divide has deepened, both within ASEAN and between single ASEAN countries and the EU, the US and Japan.

The divide is measured by indicators, selected by development professionals and large organizations. By constructing these indicators, they also define the digital divide and the knowledge gap. Often small countries are compared with the US, which is used as bench mark for comparative indicators. It does not make much sense to compare the largest and industrially most advanced country with much smaller ones without taking the specific conditions for creating a knowledge society into account. We have, therefore, opted to compare ASEAN countries among themselves and Malaysia and Indonesia with countries of similar population and geographical size. We should, however, never forget that the gap is constructed by interested parties and depicts a virtual world of development.

There are many indicators that may be used to describe a knowledge society. We shall look at a few of them and then try to locate Malaysia's and Indonesia's position in comparison to selected industrialized and knowledge based economies. The Malaysian Economic Planning Unit has calculated a Knowledge Development Index to monitor Malaysia's position in relation to other countries. Malaysia and Indonesia took the 17th and the 21st place out of 22 countries in the year 2000. This does not seem to be a convincing result with respect to Malaysia's and Indonesia's path towards a knowledge-based economy. Malaysia is, however, doing well on some ICT indicators, like mobile phones per 1,000 people. According to the Malaysian Communications and Multimedia Commission, in March 2001 there were 254 mobile phone subscribers/1000 population in Malaysia, i.e., there are more mobile phones per inhabitant in Malaysia than in Germany. On two other indicators, namely R&D researchers per million inhabitants or patents filed, Malaysia still trails far behind Korea, Germany (see Fig. 3.1), the Netherlands and other OECD countries, but is ahead in comparison with other ASEAN countries, like Indonesia (Evers, 2003).

The more important question would be, however, whether the gap is narrowed. Looking at time series data, this does not seem to be the case at present. The knowledge gap, in fact, is widening.

The picture does not change very much, if we use other indicators. In 1980 there was almost no knowledge gap between Korea and Malaysia. By 1995 the gap had widened dramatically, if measured by expenditure on R&D. The declining rate of relative R&D expenditure and the

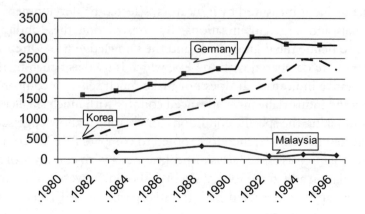

Fig. 3.1. Researchers per million inhabitants, 1980–1996 — Germany, Korea and Malaysia (moving averages).

Source: UNESCO (2001).

number of researchers have, among other factors, reduced Malaysia's competitiveness in relation to other countries.

3.4. The Cultural Construction of the Knowledge Gap and the Digital Divide

During the debate on the emergence of knowledge societies, knowledge-based economies and the widening knowledge gap, the "GAP" has become essentialized. In other words, the existence of a gap between those who possess knowledge and those who are less endowed is taken for granted, and is not deconstructed into its components or succumbed to critical evaluation. We shall therefore have a closer look at the concept itself and analyze its meaning.

First of all we have to recognize that knowledge gaps are not evil by themselves. In fact, knowledge gaps are a precondition for any development of knowledge, science, research and human development. It is obvious that adults are supposed to know more than children, a university student should know more than primary school pupils, a physicist can be expected to know more about nuclear fission than a sociologist, and an expert should know more than a laymen. These categories of people are all separated by knowledge gaps regarding their respective fields of specialization. Often new knowledge is created out of the cooperation between specialists without closing the knowledge gap between them. In fact all interdisciplinary research makes sense if a knowledge gap exists between the cooperating scientists. Without knowledge gaps there is no progress in research and development.

Similar arguments may be brought forward in regard to the digital divide. High-tech industries or computer software developers require different kinds of communication technologies than students or farmers. The needs of users have to be the guiding principle for an evaluation of the digital divide. Only if the requirements of industries and the digital needs of the population are not met, a digital divide exists.

But how do we deal with the gap in knowledge between industrialized knowledge economies and the developing countries? This, after all, is the crucial issue at hand. The concept of a "gap" indicates a hierarchy between haves and have-nots or haves and have-less. If this is the case we have to consider about which type of knowledge we are talking: knowledge about specific branches of science, knowledge about kinship terminology, knowledge about Islamic religious rituals, knowledge about survival under harsh ecological conditions? The value of knowledge is determined by experts (see Chapter 7 of this book), mainly from the industrialized knowledge economies and by processes in powerful organizations like the big transnational corporations, government departments, UNESCO, the World Bank and other large organizations. They determine what knowledge is essential and what is not. They construct the knowledge gap and the digital divide.

References

Braga, C.A.P. (1998). *Inclusion or Exclusion*. http://www.unesco.org/courier/1998_12/uk/dossier/txt21.htm.

Dasgupta, S. *et al.* (2001). Policy *Reform, Economic Growth, and the Digital Divide: An Econometric Analysis*. Washington, DC: World Bank Working Paper No. 2567.

Evers, H.-D. (2003). Transition Towards a Knowledge Society: Malaysia and Indonesia in Comparative Perspective. *Comparative Sociology*, 2(2), 355–373.

OECD (2001). *Understanding the Digital Divide*. Paris: OECD.

Oxfam (2001). *Intellectual Property and the Knowledge Gap.* Oxfam Discussion Paper 12/01.

Persaud, A. (2001). The Knowledge Gap. *Foreign Affairs,* 80(2), 107–117.

UNESCO (2001). Research and Development Personnel by Occupation. http:// www.uis.unesco.org. Paris: UNESCO Institute for Statistics.

Warschauer, M. (2003). *Technology and Social Inclusion. Rethinking the Digital Divide.* Cambridge, MA: MIT Press.

World Bank (1999). *World Development Report 1998/99: Knowledge for Development.* New York: Oxford University Press.

World Bank, Development Data Group (2004). http://devdata.worldbank.org/ external/CCProfile.asp December 2004.

Chapter 4

Local and Global Knowledge: Social Science Research on South-east Asia

Solvay Gerke and Hans-Dieter Evers

4.1. The Production of New Knowledge and the Growth of ICT

New knowledge is produced at an unprecedented pace (Stehr, 2004:xii) The growth of scientific knowledge production, supported by advances in information and computer technology, has been primarily responsible for the explosive rate of increase in knowledge. "There is a widespread consensus today that contemporary Western societies are in one sense or another ruled by knowledge and expertise" (Knorr-Cetina, 1999). This knowledge is governed, managed, monopolized or shared throughout the industrialized countries, but also increasingly in parts of Asia. In a recent survey of the Economic Intelligence Unit of the Economist (*The Economist*, 18 April 2004), the "E-readiness" of individual countries is measured in terms of their ICT infrastructure and the popular acceptance of digital equipment. Singapore is the "shooting star" of knowledge governance: It improved its position on the ranking order from rank 12 to rank 7 close to Sweden, Denmark and the UK between 2000 and 2003.

Knowledge is increasing with every patent granted and every paper, journal article or book written on a particular subject. If we consider only those articles that have been accepted in international journals and have been officially recognized or "authorized" by inclusion into a major databank, we see a steep rise not only in natural science and engineering knowledge but also of social science work on South-east Asian countries during the boom years of the 1980s and

1990s (Evers and Gerke, 2003). Of particular interest is the rising local social science production, as it indicates a rising concern for social and cultural processes under conditions of globalization and an increase in "reflexive modernization" (Beck *et al.*, 1994). We observe that the concern for the direction of social and cultural processes, particularly of the emerging education-conscious middle classes in Malaysia, Indonesia and elsewhere (Gerke, 2000) stimulates local knowledge production on society and culture.

Information and communication technology (ICT) is also growing fast, though at different rates. In 2001 in Northern Europe and North America, between 40% to 60% of all households had Internet access (OECD, 2002). In some countries, like the UK or Portugal the number of Internet subscribers more than doubled between 2000 and 2001. The use of hand phones has also increased substantially world wide, particularly in some of the Asian countries.

Access to knowledge used to depend on libraries and their resources. Today the Internet has fast advanced to become the prime source of knowledge and information. The number of Internet subscribers is therefore a good indicator of access to global knowledge. In terms of total numbers of subscribers, Malaysia has made great progress, though Singapore leads the field if we take population size into account (see Fig. 4.1).

Components of the information and communication technology (ICT) infrastructure and of institutions of knowledge production and dissemination are, however, unevenly distributed. In the year 2000 in the United States about a third of the work force was employed in ICT related sectors, in Korea only 4% or about half a million workers and much less in most of East and South-east Asia. About 30% of R&D expenditure worldwide is spent in the European Union, Asia and the United States respectively, a small proportion in the rest of the world (UNESCO, 2000). The result is a widening digital divide, which mirrors the income differences between developed and underdeveloped economies (World Bank, 1999). There are nodal points where digital equipment is concentrated, where knowledge is produced and from where it is globally distributed. Research on Indonesia, for example, may be extensively done by foreign scholars, affiliated to universities or research institutions around the globe, rather then Indonesian

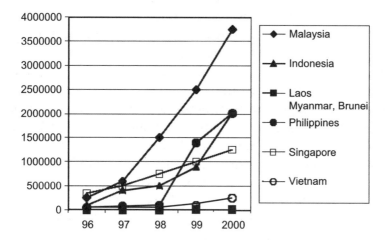

Fig. 4.1. Use of the Internet, ASEAN 1996–2000 (total number of Internet subscribers).
Source: World Bank (2004).

nationals or scholars attached to its local institutions (Evers, 2003). This raises the issue of how far knowledge is produced to meet local needs rather than the interests of a global community of scholars or the R&D interests of multi-national corporations.

The unequal production and distribution of knowledge is widening the knowledge gap between highly productive and less productive countries. The distribution of ICT and the production of knowledge are interrelated, but the exact nature of this connection is far from clear. An ICT infrastructure can only be developed if the necessary scientific knowledge and expertise is locally available. The production of new knowledge is, however, not primarily dependent on the availability of ICT, though being on the wrong side of a digital divide reduces the chances for innovative knowledge production.

4.2. From Global to Local Knowledge

Most knowledge about the developing world and the transition societies is still produced outside the region to which it pertains. The capacity to benefit from knowledge is governed by two basic elements: the ability to acquire and to apply knowledge that already exists, and the ability to produce new knowledge. It is not enough to transfer knowledge, e.g. knowledge embedded in a particular technology, from one country to another. Instead, in order to achieve a sustained development, it is necessary for the knowledge importing society to be able to acquire, to absorb the knowledge, to understand, to interpret it and to adapt it to local needs, and subsequently to produce knowledge endogenously along the same line (Cohen and Levinthal, 1990). Knowledge, therefore, has to be imported and adapted to local requirements, i.e., global knowledge has to be "localized". For any society and any nation state it will be crucial for further development whether or not this will be achieved (Evers, 2003).

The debate so far has focused on indigenous knowledge. Our emphasis will be on local knowledge rather than indigenous knowledge. Any knowledge production or use is local at the outset before it is, under certain circumstances to be discussed below, globalized. Indigenous knowledge is bound by language, tradition and values to a particular community (Antweiler, 1998; Sillitoe, 1998). Local knowledge is shared by a community of practice or is locally available or shared. The respective locality can be a nation state, a society, a university or a meeting. Local knowledge is globalized, e.g. when it is posted on the Internet, published in a widely available book or international journal. Only a fraction of indigenous or local knowledge is globalized and only a minor part of global knowledge enters local knowledge (Tomforde, 2003). Both forms of knowledge are mixed up in the post-modern world (Baruch, 2001) and the keen researcher can separate the two only by analytical arm-twisting and preposterous modeling.

4.3. South-east Asian Vision of Localizing Global Knowledge

Most ASEAN leaders and governments have developed visions of developing a knowledge-based economy and a knowledge society as a way to achieve parity with Western nations. These visions are invariably directed at using global knowledge to achieve economic progress.

In 1991 Malaysia's Prime Minister proposed in a much-publicized speech that Malaysia should become a fully industrialized country by the year 2020 (Evers and Gerke, 1997; Evers, 2003). Meanwhile the transition from a newly industrializing to a fully industrialized country has been superseded by a new development goal. Dr. Mahathir's "Wawasan 2020 (Vision 2020)" had to be up-dated and Malaysia has adopted a new strategy to move towards a knowledge-based society and economy.

Indonesia has followed suit and has pronounced "visions and missions" as a first step in the national and local planning process. "Terwujudnya Masyarakat Telematika Nusantara Berbasis Pengetahuan di Tahun 2020" ("Creating a Nusantara Telematic Society by the Year 2020") is the vision statement of the KTIN (Kerangka Teknologi Informasi Nasional), the National Framework for Information Technology. The document is broad-based, extending from support for e-business to good governance and e-democracy. This vision and the appended action plan are directed, however, at information technology (TI) and not at knowledge per se, on which information technology has to be based. Little has been done so far to put this plan into action.

Singapore launched its start into a knowledge society in 1992. By now Singapore has a very well developed knowledge infrastructure in terms of ICT, research institutes and knowledge workforce (Toh *et al.*, 2002). Considerable research is being conducted by scientists and researchers in Singaporean institutions of higher learning and research centres especially in the areas of biotechnology and the life sciences which the Singapore government is promoting in its bid to stay economically competitive in the knowledge-based economy (Singapore Economic Development Board, 1999). Universities, like the National University of Singapore, Nanyang Technological University and Singapore Management University strive for recognition as world class research centres, and institutions like A*Star are set up to carry out cutting edge applied research. If we look at local knowledge production in terms of the level of patenting activities, we will see a 34% increase in the number of patents applied in Singapore between 1999 and 2000 alone (A*Star, 2002) and also, as discussed below, a steep increase of papers published by Singaporeans in international journals.

The emphasis on impression management, like changing the names of statutory boards to make them more appealing to an international audience, the invention of visions and missions, the use of culture-bound place names like Cyberjaya indicate that an attempt is made to create an epistemic culture (Knorr-Cetina, 1999; Evers, 2000), a culture of knowledge production. The creation of a knowledge-based economy is therefore not just ICT driven, but has developed into a social and cultural process as well. Social science research is part of this process. It is significant as it creates knowledge on a particular society and its processes of change and development.

4.4. Regional Differences in Knowledge Production

South-east Asian countries can be divided into two groups, those about which a large global knowledge base exists and those with only limited knowledge resources.

The Global Knowledge Stock Indicator (GKSI) measures the volume of social science documents on a particular country in relation to

Table 4.1. Indicators of local knowledge production and the global social science knowledge stock on South-east Asian countries, 1970–2000.

Rank		Local K-Stock Indicator	Rank		Global K-Stock Indicator
1	Singapore	53.5	1	Philippines	0.32
2	Brunei	35.7	2	Vietnam	0.26
3	Malaysia	25.1	3	Indonesia	0.24
4	Philippines	24.1	4	Thailand	0.23
5	Thailand	18.8	5	Singapore	0.20
6	Indonesia	7.1	6	Malaysia	0.20
7	Cambodia	2.9	7	Cambodia	0.03
8	Vietnam	2.4	8	Myanmar	0.03
9	Myanmar	1.9	9	Laos	0.02
10	Laos	0.8	10	Brunei	0.01

Source: Own data analysis, based on the Sociological Abstracts, 1970–2000.

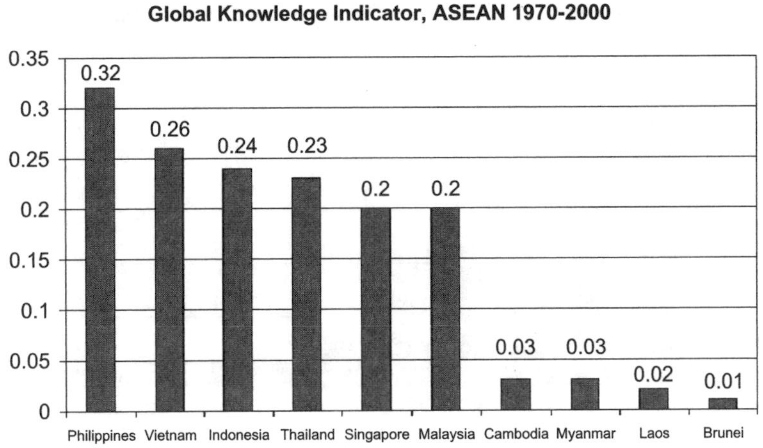

Global Knowledge Indicator, ASEAN 1970-2000

Fig. 4.2. Indicator of global knowledge production on
all ASEAN countries, 1970–2000.

Source: Sociological Abstracts.

all documents in the data base. It shows the strength of the research
interest in different countries. Personal preferences of authors and gate-
keepers, like peer reviewers and editors of journals, officials of funding organizations, international organizations and government agencies
have probably had a decisive impact on what social science knowledge
is produced and added to the global fund of accessible knowledge.
Figure 4.2 shows that globally the Philippines are the most researched
country in South-east Asia.

The Local Knowledge Stock Indicator (LKSI) — defined as locally
produced documents as a percentage of all documents available on a
particular ASEAN country — measures the strength of local social science (see Fig. 4.3). There is a knowledge gap between two groups
of countries, namely Singapore, Brunei, Malaysia, the Philippines and
Thailand in the upper group and Indonesia, Cambodia, Vietnam,
Myanmar and Laos in the lower group. It can, therefore, be said that
ASEAN countries are stratified into an upper and a lower knowledge
class.[1]

---

[1]There seems to be a high correlation between GNP/pc and the local knowledge
indicator, yet data cannot be presented here.

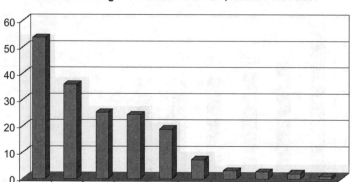

Fig. 4.3. Indicator of local knowledge production, all ASEAN countries, 1970–2000.
Source: Sociological Abstracts 1970–2000.

4.5. The Development of Social Science Knowledge

The production of local and global knowledge has varied over time. This may be due to a number of factors which will have to be analyzed. South-east Asian countries have different political systems, have followed different development strategies and have experienced different impact of the financial crisis of the 1990s. A look at the time series of knowledge production between 1970 and 2000 shows different long-term trends.

We hypothesize that the higher the percentage of globally produced documents the greater is the dependence on outside sources for the interpretation and construction of one's own society. If social science production is mainly carried out elsewhere, the process of "reflexive modernization" is impeded (Beck *et al.*, 1994). Our data do not contain most of the locally published research results and are therefore deliberately biased.[2] But still we may be allowed to argue that a knowledge gap or "knowledge dependence" is either widened or closed. Figure 4.4 shows four different paths of local knowledge development. Indonesia has a low but stable output of local knowledge, Malaysia

---

[2]A look through the reading lists of social science courses in South-east Asian universities shows that mainly international books and journal articles, i.e., "global knowledge", are used as teaching materials.

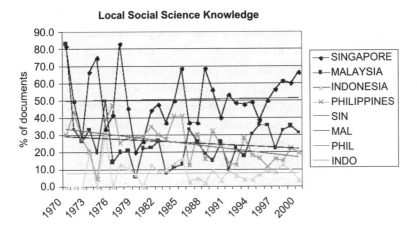

Fig. 4.4. Trends of local social science knowledge production on selected South-east Asian countries, 1970–2000.

Source: Sociological Abstracts 1970–2000. Trends are shown by bold linear regression lines.

and the Philippines have relatively high but declining local output and Singapore has a high and increasing local knowledge production. Argued from a global point of view the social science knowledge stock on Indonesia is stable on a high level of dependence on outside knowledge, Malaysia and the Philippines have increased their dependence on foreign sources, whereas Singapore has successfully globalized their social science output. It is, of course, possible that the countries of the lower knowledge class produce reasonable amounts of local knowledge which is simply not published in internationally recognized journals and therefore not globalized, but the interpretation and construction of their own societies is nevertheless based on this globally not recognized local knowledge. Therefore, the process of reflexive modernization as stated above would not be impeded and the hypothesis "the higher the percentage of globally produced documents the greater is the dependence on outside sources for the interpretation and construction of ones own society" would be invalid. The fact that only little local knowledge of those countries is globalized does not yet prove that they depend on global knowledge instead in the process of interpreting and constructing their own societies, which essentially is a search of their own identity.

The large differences between ASEAN countries can be exemplified by contrasting Singapore and Vietnam. The global output on Vietnam is much higher than on Singapore, which attracts only limited interest among social scientists, but the local contribution of Vietnamese scholars to global knowledge is still minimal (see Fig. 4.5 below).

Another contrasting case would be Brunei, about which very little is published each year in international journals, out of which scholars located in Brunei itself have a fair share. Publications on Laos are also rare, out of which hardly any are produced locally in Laos itself. The data used in this paper yield rough indicators to diagnose the development of social science production in the form of internationally recognized journal articles. The indicators are rough in the sense that they do not give any clue as to the form and contents of the knowledge contained in the documents, except that they refer in one way or another to a particular South-east Asian country.[3] To end on an optimistic note: South-east Asian researchers have at least kept up their internationally recognized production of knowledge at the same pace and at the same yearly rates of increase as outsiders (see Fig. 4.6). The trouble with growth rates is, as the developing world has experienced, that those

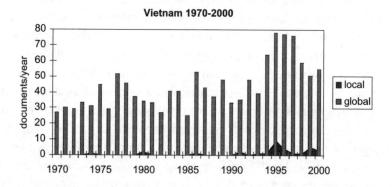

Fig. 4.5. Local and global social science production on Vietnam, 1970–2000. Source: Sociological Abstracts 1970–2000.

---

[3]The scope and contents of South-east Asian studies has been analysed in Evers (1999), *Crisis and Beyond: Theorising Southeast Asia*. 4th ASEAN Inter-University Seminar on Social Development, 15–18 June 1999, Prince of Songkla University, Pattani.

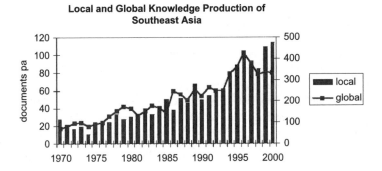

Fig. 4.6. Local and global knowledge production on South-east Asia, 1970–2000. Source: Sociological Abstracts 1970–2000. Left scale: locally produced documents, right scale: globally produced documents.

starting from a high plateau gain more: a gap develops. Closing the k-gap will not be easy, but looking at the past five years the future looks promising.

4.6. Conclusion

Local knowledge production of South-east Asian scholars has kept pace with global knowledge production. Percentage increases from year to year have been similar. In the past decade local knowledge production has increased even more than global production. If the trend remains in tact we can assume that South-east Asia will move forward in the world of social science.

References

Antweiler, C. (1998). Local Knowledge and Local Knowing. *Anthropos*, 93, 469–494.

A*Star (2002). *National Survey of R&D in Singapore 2001*. Singapore: Agency for Science, Technology and Research (A*Star).

Baruch, Y. (2001). Global or North American? A Geographical Based Comparative Analysis of Publications in Top Management Journals. *International Journal of Cross Cultural Management*, 1(1), 109–126.

Beck, U. *et al.* (1994). *Reflexive Modernization. Politics, Tradition and Aesthetics in the Modern Social Order*. Cambridge: Polity Press.

Cohen, W.M. and D.A. Levinthal (1990). Innovation and Learning: The Two Faces of R&D. *The Economic Journal*, 99, 569–596.

Evers, H.-D. (2003a). Transition Towards a Knowledge Society: Malaysia and Indonesia in Comparative Perspective. *Comparative Sociology*, 2(S), 355–373.

Evers, H.-D. (2003b). *Malaysian Knowledge Society and the Global Knowledge Gap.* Department of Southeast Asian Studies, University of Bonn, Germany.

Evers, H.-D. (2000a). Die Globalisierung der epistemischen Kultur: Entwicklungstheorie und Wissensgesellschaft. In *Vom Ewigen Frieden und vom Wohlstand der Nationen*, U. Menzel (ed.), pp. 396–417. Frankfurt am Main: Suhrkamp Verlag.

Evers, H.-D. (2000b). *Epistemic Cultures: Towards a New Sociology of Knowledge.* Working Paper No. 151, Department of Sociology, National University of Singapore.

Evers, H.-D. and S. Gerke (1997). *Global Market Cultures and the Construction of Modernity in Southeast Asia.* Thesis Eleven 50, pp. 1–14. London, Thousand Oaks/CA and New Delhi: SAGE Publications.

Evers, H.-D. and S. Gerke (2003). *Local and Global Knowledge: Social Science Research on Southeast Asia.* Southeast Asian Studies Working Paper No. 18, Department of Southeast Asian Studies, University of Bonn, Germany.

Gerke, S. (2000). Global Lifestyles under Local Conditions: The New Indonesian Middle Class. In *Consumption in Asia. Lifestyles and Identities*, B.-H. Chua. pp. 135–158. London and New York: Routledge.

Knorr-Cetina, K. (1999). *Epistemic Cultures: How the Sciences Make Knowledge.* Cambridge: Harvard University Press.

Mahathir, M. (1991). *Wawasan 2020.* Kuala Lumpur: Government Printing Office.

OECD (2002). *Measuring the Information Economy.* Paris: OECD. www.oecd.org/sti/measuring-infoeconomy.

Sillitoe, P. (1998). What Know Natives? Local Knowledge in Development. *Social Anthropology*, 6(2), 203–220.

Singapore Economic Development Board (1999). http://www.sedb.com/edbcorp/sg/en_uk/index.html?loc=home.

Stehr, N. (ed.) (2004). *The Governance of Knowledge.* London and New Brunswick: Transaction Publishers.

Toh, M.H. *et al.* (2002). *Mapping Singapore's Knowledge-Based Economy. Economic Survey of Singapore*, Singapore, 56–75.

Tomforde, M. (2003). The Global in the Local: Contested Resource-use Systems of the Karen and Hmong in Northern Thailand. *Journal of Southeast Asian Studies*, 34(2), 347–360.

UNESCO (2000). *Facts and Figures.* Paris: UNESCO Institute for Statistics.

World Bank (1999). *World Development Report 1998–99: Knowledge for Development.* New York: Oxford University Press.

World Bank (2004). Development Data Group. http://devdata.worldbank.org/external/CCProfile.asp, December 2004.

Chapter 5

Transition Towards a Knowledge Society: Malaysia and Indonesia in Global Perspective[1]

Hans-Dieter Evers

5.1. Visions of a Knowledge Society

Malaysia and Indonesia see themselves as being on the way to develop into knowledge societies. The characteristics of this new stage of development are only vaguely circumscribed by Indonesia's political leadership. Malaysia's political elite has, however, developed a vision when and how to reach the stage of a fully developed industrialized nation with a knowledge-based economy. This chapter will outline the basic features of a knowledge society and it will analyze some of the social and cultural preconditions as well as consequences in reaching the stage of a knowledge society. It will finally attempt to answer the question how far Malaysia and Indonesia have advanced towards the stage of a knowledge society.

In our fast moving world concepts and policies spring to life at an amazing speed. The epistemology of development reflects the diversity of a world that only a few years ago was seen as moving towards an integrated world society, but is now understood as increasingly differentiated and complex. Some mega-trends have, however, been diagnosed. Globalization as an expansion of a world market is thought to be such a mega-trend, the move towards a knowledge society another.

---

[1]This chapter is a revised version of Evers, Hans-Dieter (2003), "Transition Towards a Knowledge Society: Indonesia and Malaysia in Comparative Perspective", *Comparative Sociology*, 2(2), 355–373. The authors are grateful to Brill Academic Publishers for allowing us to include the essay in this monograph.

In this chapter we attempt to provide an overview over the current discussion on the role of knowledge in creating a knowledge society and highlight some characteristics knowledge societies are thought to have. We shall also provide some evidence on how far Malaysia and Indonesia have moved on its way towards a knowledge-based society.

Malaysia's Prime Minister, in 1991, proposed in a much publicized speech that Malaysia should become a fully industrialized country by the year 2020 (Mahathir, 1991; Evers and Gerke, 1997). The Malaysian Government has made the move towards a knowledge-based society and economy its primary target.[2] As knowledge is of critical importance in a fully developed K-economy, "... the challenge for Malaysia is to develop this knowledge amongst our citizens so that our success will be due to the contributions of Malaysian talents and knowledge workers" (Dr. Mahathir bin Mohamad, Putrajaya 8 March 2001 — advertisement in the New Straits Times 13-04-2001). A knowledge economy is defined as one in which information and communication technology (IT or ICT), other high-tech activities and e-commerce play a leading role.

Indonesia has followed suit as indicated by the development of "Terwujudnya Masyarakat Telematika Nusantara Berbasis Pengetahuan di Tahun 2020" ("Creating a Nusantara Telematic Society by the Year 2020") which is the vision statement of the KTIN (Kerangka Teknologi Informasi Nasional), the National Framework for Information Technology. The document is broad-based, extending from support for e-business to good governance and e-democracy.[3] This vision and the appended action plan is, however, directed at information technology (IT) and not at knowledge per se, on which information technology has to be based.

---

[2]"The chief architect of this vision is Malaysia's former Prime Minister, Dato' Seri Dr Mahathir Mohamad. Malaysians have responded robustly to his challenge to become a fully-developed, matured and knowledge-rich society by the year 2020" (http://www.mdc.com.my/msc/index.html).

[3]"Teknologi Informasi (TI) merupakan faktor pendukung bagi pembangunan di Indonesia yang mencakup aspek politik, aspek ekonomi, aspek sosial budaya dan aspek hukum".

5.1.1. *A Hypothesis on Transition and Productivity*

The current situation and trends in Malaysian and Indonesian social and economic development should not be seen in isolation. We have to pinpoint Indonesia's and Malaysia's present position in both a historical and a comparative perspective. For this purpose I should like to introduce a hypothesis, taken from transition theory. It says: The transition from one period of history or type of economy and society to another takes place, whenever a new innovative productivity factor is introduced.[4] Those entrepreneurs or those countries that make use of this new productivity factor can collect an innovation rent that allows them to prosper and progress at a rapid speed, outpacing their competitors.[5]

Table 5.1 gives a very rough overview over mega-trends in the region. It intends to illustrate the hypothesis put forward above rather than provide an accurate picture of the rather complicated flow of history.

The establishment and intensification of long-distance trading networks enabled the glory of Melaka, Malaysia's golden past, followed by the profitable entrepôt trade of the Straits Settlements. The introduction of modern technology into the tin mining sector and the new and economically efficient organization of rubber plantations led to the boom years of the early 20th century in Peninsular Malaya. Finally, specialized industrial manufacturing with low R&D but high value added production led to the "Asian Miracle" of independent Malaysia. In Indonesia the emerging historical trends are more diverse and differ from region to region. The independent trading empires of Pasai, Banten, Demak and Makassar declined with the ascent of Dutch power and where displaced by the Dutch controlled trade centres of Batavia, Surabaya and a number of smaller ports. Indonesia also participated

---

[4]This hypothesis is to be seen in the context of general theories dealing with the transition from one type of society to another, from Karl Marx to Max Weber, Karl Polanyi and Schumpeter.

[5]Without going into details here, it is obvious that this hypothesis is derived from a combination of Schumpeter's definition of entrepreneurs and the more contemporary comparative advantage paradigm.

Table 5.1. Transition hypothesis of social and economic development.

Productivity Factor		Transition		Malaysia/Indonesia
		From	To	
I	Early long-distance trading networks	Subsistence agriculture	Trading empire	Melakka/Makassar
II	Labor intensive estate agriculture and industrial mining	Peasant society	Colonial raw material producing economy and society	Federated Malay states/Netherlands Indies (19th century)
III	Industrial production and organization	Colonial raw material producing economy and society	Light industrial and commercial agricultural society	Malaysia after independence/ Indonesia after 1980
IV	Knowledge	Light industrial and commercial agricultural society	Knowledge economy and society	Malaysia/Indonesia after 2020?

in the boom of estate agriculture, first sugar and coffee, then rubber in Sumatra. Industrialization started much later in Indonesia, but industrial output and employment rose fast during the late 1980s and throughout the 1990s, at least on Java.

But as we know all too well the boom years induced by the introduction of new factors of productivity are invariably followed by years of crisis and boom. Without going too much into detail we should like to propose the hypothesis that these boom periods were phases of social and economic development, during which a "transition rent" was collected in a phase of socio-economic and at times also political restructuring. Once this "rent" was spent and a new platform had been reached, the "normal" mechanisms of supply and demand, of efficiency and waste, of the ups and downs of business cycles, of political imperfections and market failure came into being again. Some countries could manage this transition well and maintain self-sustainable growth, others with less luck (i.e., under less fortunate global conditions) and less political foresight (i.e., authoritarian rather than democratic systems) retarded into economic coma.

If we follow this line of argument, a big issue comes up. If "knowledge" is the new factor of social and economic productivity, the long-lasting boom of the US American economy may be explained in terms of our productivity-rent hypothesis. In fact, many economic gurus (Drucker and others) follow this line of argument. This, however, raises further questions: If the application of knowledge was the driving factor of the economic development of the OECD countries, has the innovative power of this productivity factor been spent? Have these countries concluded their transitions and reached a new platform of high productivity of a knowledge economy, with little hope for further extraordinary productivity gains?[6] Will Malaysia in particular enter a new phase of transition towards a knowledge society or will access to this status be barred by those countries that have already achieved the august stage of a knowledge economy? Will Indonesia's initial attempts to introduce knowledge into its industrialization process be stopped at an early stage? Probably nobody is able to answer these questions in full, but we can, at least, try to clarify some features and stumbling blocks on the path towards a knowledge-based society.

If knowledge is a primary factor of production, if information and communication technology is a platform upon which a knowledge economy is built and if the existence of a knowledgeable workforce is both a precondition and an indicator for the existence of a knowledge society, then we may well ask the question, how far Malaysia and Indonesia have advanced on the path towards becoming a knowledge society.

5.2. What is a Knowledge Society?

5.2.1. *The Productivity of Old and New Knowledge*

Some experts, the shamans, *dukuns* or *bomos* of modern society, allege that knowledge has replaced industrial organization and production as

---

[6]The losses of ICT and dot.com companies and the rapid decline of the NASDAQ point to this direction.

the major source of productivity. In fact the largest share of value added in modern intelligent production does not rest on the value of the material used or the input of labor and capital, but on the knowledge embedded in the final product. In the current phase of the economic transformation, knowledge has taken its place as the most important factor of production passing capital and labor. "The central wealth-creating activities will be neither the allocation of capital to productive uses, nor 'labor' ... Value is now created by 'productivity' and 'innovation', both applications of knowledge to work" (Drucker, 1994). Malaysia's former Prime Minister has taken up this theme as well in his well known statement "Vision 2020": "There was a time when land was the most fundamental basis of prosperity and wealth. Then came the second wave, the age of industrialization. Smokestacks rose where the fields were once cultivated. Now, increasingly, knowledge will not only be the basis of power but also prosperity.... No effort must be spared in the creation of an information rich Malaysian society."[7]

During the transformation from industrial to knowledge societies, knowledge has assumed the prime position as a factor of production. There are, however, considerable differences between knowledge and the other factors of production like labor and capital. To mention just three aspects:

1. Knowledge is more difficult to measure than the other factors. "Knowledge is like light. Weightless and tangible, it can easily travel the world, enlightening the lives of people everywhere" (World Bank, 1999). Once it has been produced it can easily be reproduced or copied and transaction costs are low. This explains why leading industrial nations have put great emphasis on the enforcement of intellectual property rights and patents, safeguarding the Internet and controlling access to data banks and other sources of knowledge. "Hackers" breaking the monopoly of knowledge and distributing secret information for free have become the Robin Hoods of modern knowledge society. Software pirating,

---

[7]"Malaysia: The Way Forward" presented by His Excellency YAB Dato' Seri Dr Mahathir Mohamad at the Malaysian Business Council, 28 February 1991.

knowledge poaching and industrial espionage are as much part of the emerging knowledge society as Internet conferences and electronic publishing.

2. Whereas other goods are succumbed to the law of diminishing returns, knowledge actually experiences rising marginal utility. The more an expert, a group of consultants or an organization know, the more valuable become individual pieces of knowledge; or to put it differently: Knowledge is needed to utilize knowledge effectively. A critical mass of knowledge workers is therefore necessary in any one locality to achieve a productive knowledge economy. The Silicon Valley in California, the Munich electronic belt in Germany, the Hsinchu region of Taiwan or possibly, in the near future, the MSC in Malaysia are examples to illustrate this point.

3. The concepts of "knowledge society" or "knowledge-based economy" have a tendency to be divorced from reality. A knowledge society becomes a vision (a *wawasan*), which is constructed as a virtual world. But also a vision, if believed in by many, is a social fact which may impact on societal and economic reality.

Though it appears to be an established fact by now, that knowledge is a major factor of production, it is extremely difficult to estimate the contribution of knowledge to economic growth. Most estimates consist of residuals, i.e., what is left after all other known contributions to economic growth have been factored in. One historical study estimates that between 1929 and 1948 knowledge contributed only 26% to the economic growth of the US, but about 54% between 1948 and 1973 (Stehr, 2001). The World Bank estimated that a large proportion of the economic growth of Korea was due to an increasing input of knowledge throughout the 1970s and 1980s (World-Bank, 1999). Often the investment in formal education or in R&D (research and development) is used as an indicator of the input of knowledge into the society. Scientists, technicians and engineers rather than priests, *ulama* or artists are counted as productive knowledge workers. Informal education and training, experience, wisdom and accumulated local knowledge is widely neglected. The pursuit of knowledge as such is increasingly subjugated to the demands of the global capitalist market economy, both in reality and in the virtual reality of economic modeling and rational choice theory.

5.2.2. Characteristics of a Knowledge Society

A knowledge society is believed to have the following characteristics:

- Its members have attained a higher average standard of education in comparison to other societies and a growing proportion of its labor force is employed as knowledge workers.
- Its industry produces products with integrated artificial intelligence.
- Its organizations (private, government and civil society) are transformed into intelligent organizations.
- There is increased organized knowledge in the form of digitalized expertise, stored in data banks, expert systems, organizational plans and other media.
- There are multiple centres of expertise and a poly-centric production of knowledge.
- There is a distinct epistemic culture of knowledge production and knowledge utilization. (Evers, 2000a; 2000b)

Some of the above mentioned points and concepts warrant further explanation.

Often the concept of a knowledge society is confused with the concept of an information society, and the importance and prevalence of ICT (information and communication technology) is emphasized. This is definitely misleading and represents a way of thinking still colored by the epistemic culture of an industrial society. It is not the hardware, but the software, that is the keystone of a knowledge society. In a knowledge society, systems are not technology driven but determined by contents, meaning and knowledge.[8]

A distinction has to be made between knowledge-based work and knowledge work proper. An industrial society has to rely on the knowledge-based work of skilled workers and professionals, like

---

[8]This point is also stressed in the contemporary knowledge management literature. Kusunoki (2004:310) draws attention to the reluctance of Japanese firms to use IT and argues that "IT does not promise a competitive edge by itself".

doctors, lawyers, engineers or social scientists. Knowledge work, however, characteristic of a knowledge society, goes beyond the work done traditionally by skilled workers and university or college educated professionals. The new type of knowledge is not seen as definite, it is not regarded as the final truth but it has to be constantly revised. New knowledge is complex; it produces ignorance and therefore entails risk when it is applied.[9] It needs to be systematically organized and institutionalized to be productive and it requires information technology to be developed further.

Universities seem to have lost their near monopoly of basic knowledge production (see Chapter 9 in this book). The so-called triple helix of science-industry-university indicates that knowledge production has become poly-centric and the knowledge networks connect the respective organizations. The imbalance of enumeration of knowledge workers in the three components of the "triple helix" can be partly at least explained by the shift of relevant research from the university to the corporate sector. Strangely enough universities are no longer seen as "intelligent" or "learning organizations" in contrast to business or industrial companies in the corporate sector. Critics (in Germany for instance) have called universities "stupid organizations with many intelligent people". Of course as academics we might retort that many business corporations are "intelligent organizations" and can therefore afford to employ many dumb managers at horrendously high wages.

The sociology of the emerging knowledge society has been explored for some time and a fair number of publications have appeared on the subject (among others Long and Long, 1992; Gibbons *et al.*, 1994; Nonaka, 1994; Stehr, 1994; Willke, 1998; Evers, 2000a; 2000b). Enthusiasts have even founded a Global Knowledge Society, "devoted to the creation, diffusion, and usage of knowledge in relationship to knowledge economies at the Macro, Meso, and Micro levels".[10] But next to the euphoria of the advocates of knowledge-based economies there appears to have crept up some doubt whether neo-classical economic theory can provide the right questions let alone the answers

---

[9]The growth of ignorance in knowledge society is further explored in Evers (2000a; 2000b). For an interesting early discussion, see Hobart (1993).
[10]Advertised on its homepage *http://www.gksociety.org*.

to explain a knowledge driven economy.[11] The social structure, the institutional arrangements and the cultures of globalized knowledge societies appear to be even less well researched, if one assumes that radically new forms of a social organization of knowledge are emerging. Let me therefore concentrate on different aspects of the sociology of emerging knowledge societies: Malaysia and Indonesia in comparative perspective, strategic group formation and on the culture of knowledge.

5.3. On the Way Towards a Knowledge Society?

5.3.1. *Malaysia and Indonesia in Comparative Perspective*

Some societies are well on their way to become knowledge-based. A new "great transformation" (to use Polanyi's term) is taking place. How far have Malaysia and Indonesia approached the status of a Knowledge Society? Though we are not sure at all whether all societies will follow the *same* path towards a knowledge-based economy, we shall nevertheless compare Malaysia and Indonesia with other nations on some relevant indicators. We have selected Korea, a country that was often mentioned together with Malaysia as one of the Asian tiger economies and the Netherlands and Germany for comparison. The Netherlands is comparable to Malaysia in terms of its population and shares a common history with Indonesia, Germany can be compared to Malaysia in terms of its land size and is the largest economy in the European Union, as is Indonesia in ASEAN. Both Germany and the Netherlands are part of the world's largest economy, the European Union.

5.3.2. *Knowledge Society Indicators*

There are many indicators that may be used to describe a knowledge society. We shall look at a few of them and then try to locate Malaysia's and Indonesia's position.

The Malaysian Economic Planning Unit has calculated a Knowledge Development Index to monitor Malaysia's position in relation to other

---

[11]The new institutional economy may, at least, provide some answers. The literature on knowledge management is also providing interesting, empirically based insights.

Table 5.2. Knowledge society indicators, 1995/1998.

Indicators	Malaysia	Indonesia	Korea	Netherlands	Germany
Population	21	220	46	16	82
Land area, ths sq km	329	1919	99	34	349
GNP billion US$	98.2	221.9	485.2	402.7	2319.5
GNP at PPP per capita	10920	3450	13500	21340	21300
Mobile phones per 1000 people	74	3	70	52	71
PCs per 1000 people	42.8	4.8	131.7	232.0	233.2
Internet hosts per 10,000 people	19.3	0.54	28.77	219.01	106.68
Scientists and engineers in R&D per million people	87	181[12]	2636	2656	3016
High technology exports, % of manufacturing exports	67	18	39	42	25
No. of patents filed, residents	141	n.i.	59249	4460	51948
No. of patents filed, non-residents	3911	n.i.	37308	59279	84667

Source: Statistical Appendix, *World Development Report 1998/99*, Tables 1 and 19, World Bank (1999).

countries. The ranking list is topped by the USA and Japan. Looking at the five countries under consideration in this paper, Malaysia and Indonesia take the 17th and the 21st place out of 22 countries in the year 2000.

As our disaggregated data in Table 5.2 shows, Malaysia is, however, doing well on some ICT indicators, like mobile phones per 1,000 people.[13] According to the Malaysian Communications and Multimedia Commission, in March 2001 there were 254 mobile phone

---

[12]Estimate for 1988 (UNESCO, 2001). The figure is probably inflated.
[13]See also Ng and Jin (2000) on the importance of teleworking in Malaysia.

Table 5.3. Knowledge development index, 2000 — Indonesia, Malaysia, South
Korea, Germany and the Netherlands compared.

Country	Knowledge Index Score	Knowledge Index	Computer Infra-structure	Info-structure	Education and Training	R&D and Technology
Indonesia	1,518	21	21	20	21	21
Malaysia	2,645	17	17	17	17	16
South Korea	4,053	15	16	11	16	13
Germany	4,615	12	12	13	12	7
Netherlands	4,777	10	10	9	13	8

Source: Third Outline Perspective Plan, Chapter 5, pp. 131–130 Malaysia (2001). For
a calculation of the index see p. 129 of the plan and Chapter 3 of this volume.

subscribers/1000 population in Malaysia,[14] i.e., more mobile phones
per inhabitant in Malaysia than in some of the highly industrialized
countries. The Malaysian telecommunication system is comparatively
well developed, but the development of knowledge production is still
low, both in terms of investment and the manpower alloted to R&D
(see Fig. 5.1). In terms of knowledge output, measured by the number of patents filed, Malaysia still trails far behind the OECD countries,
but is ahead in comparison with other ASEAN countries, like Indonesia
(Evers, 2003).

The picture does not change, when we use other indicators, like the
expenditures for R&D. Korea is still increasing its investment in applied
knowledge production, the Netherlands remain stable, Germany has
settled on an even keel at a high level, but Malaysia is on a downward
trend during the 1990s, long before the Asian financial crisis broke.
For Indonesia we have not been able to obtain later data, but it is very
unlikely that the number of research personnel has increased in recent
years (Gerke and Evers, 2001).

The declining rate of relative R&D expenditure and the number
of researchers have, among other factors, reduced Malaysia's competitiveness in relation to other countries. If we follow the rather complex (and admittedly somewhat biased) World Competitive Indicator,

---

[14]In March 2001 there were 254 mobile phone subscribers/1000 population in
Malaysia (Malaysian Communications and Multimedia Commission).

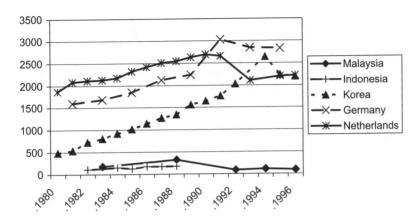

Fig. 5.1. Researchers per million inhabitants, 1980–1996 — Malaysia, Indonesia, Korea, Germany and the Netherlands.

Source: UNESCO (2001).

Malaysia is sliding back from a knowledge economy, rather than catching up (see Fig. 5.4). Malaysia has, despite its efforts to develop ICT especially in the Multimedia Super Corridor (MSC), receded from place 25 (in 1997) on a relative competitiveness scale of infrastructure development to place 38 (out of 49 countries in 2001). It has thus lost its competitive advantage over Korea and the gap to the two European countries in our chart (Netherlands and Germany) has in fact increased. The same holds true for Indonesia, that now occupies the last place on the World Competitiveness Index.

If other aspects, like business and government effectiveness are factored in, the situation looks somewhat brighter for Malaysia (see Figs. 5.2 and 5.3). Sadly enough the slow development of the technology infrastructure, i.e., the knowledge base of the Malaysian economy, accounts for the fact that Malaysia has fallen back in the very competitive race towards a knowledge society.

What may be the reasons for this pace of knowledge development in Malaysia? Government policy has been very supportive. The building of the MSC, the founding of new research institutes and universities and various programmes assisting innovation in industries have been important steps towards building a knowledge economy (NITC, 1999).

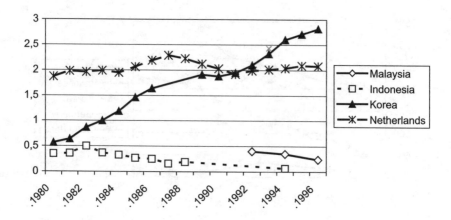

Fig. 5.2. Expenditure on R&D as a percentage of GDP, 1990–1997.
Source: UNESCO (2001).

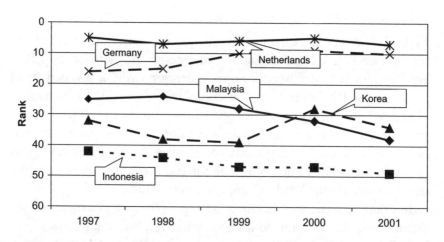

Fig. 5.3. World competitiveness index — infrastructure (including ICT), 1997–2001.
Source: *http://www.imd.ch/documents/wcy* and *http://www.weforum.org/site/ homepublic.nsf/Content/Global+Competitiveness+Programme%5CGlobal+ Competitiveness+Report* (2004).

Malaysia has a large highly skilled workforce and a good system of public and private higher education. There are, however, many other problems encountered on the path towards a knowledge-based society that have to be taken into account.

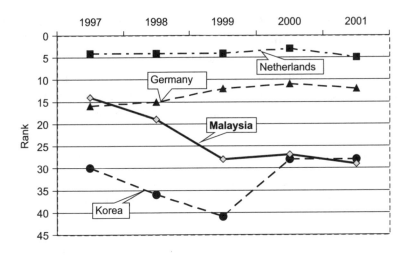

Fig. 5.4. World competitiveness index — global score.
Source: *http://www.weforum.org/site/homepublic.nsf/Content/Global+
Competitiveness+Programme%5CGlobal+Competitiveness+Report* (2004).

5.4. Strategic Groups in a Knowledge Society

5.4.1. *Changing Occupational Cultures*

The introduction of ICT into industrial production and even into the service sector is changing the occupational structure and culture of the emerging knowledge society. Let us consider the supermarkets that have been built in the wake of industrialization. They have replaced many of the small stores, shop-houses and wet markets where people used to shop in Malaysia and Indonesia. A few employees work the check-out points, but even these are on the verge of being replaced by automated stations into which the customer inserts his or her chip card, if he/she has not ordered his/her items beforehand through the Internet. Turning a shopping centre into an intelligent organization has many consequences. The unskilled workers are replaced by skilled technicians servicing the computer driven equipment, new industries have sprung up to supply the machinery for the high-tech mega-stores, and software houses apply knowledge to produce the software to drive the organizations. There are also other, less tangible effects. Social contacts in markets vanish; the senses are no longer stimulated by the foul smell of markets, the feel of freshly slaughtered chicken, the movements and colors of the hustle and bustle of the early morning market. All this richness of feeling, sound and smell is replaced by the virtual world of the Internet, the coldness of the plastic packaging, the computer generated voice and the "animation" of dead images. Up to now we are only at the beginning of a cultural process with an uncertain outcome.

5.4.2. *Who Gains and Who Loses in a Knowledge Society?*

Gold has been considered one of the great and shining resources of the pre-industrial and early industrial resources. When gold was discovered in California, the great gold rush of the 19th century took place. When rubber became an essential item for the production of motor cars, the plantation boom in Malaya and elsewhere enticed the imagination of investors, claiming as much land as they could lay their hands on. As knowledge is the major resource for the New Economy, a new gold rush is taking place. The man hunt for intellectual talents is on, ICT specialists and bio-informatics scholars are recruited and induced to cross national borders to accept new and better paid positions. Recruitment companies for highly skilled labor have sprung up in Kuala Lumpur, Jakarta and Singapore wherever knowledge is produced. Local companies and national governments have to compete for knowledge workers in a transnational labor market beyond the borders of ASEAN.

Though it is extremely difficult to come up with any predictions on who is going to gain and who is going to loose in an emerging knowledge society, at least a likely scenario can be developed.

5.4.3. *Strategic Groups of Knowledge Workers*

In a knowledge society new occupational groups emerge, that are essential for the production, dissemination and application of knowledge. It can be expected that they eventually realize their common interest in gaining a share of the new wealth, prestige and power, created by the utilization of knowledge as a productive force. In other words a new strategic group will merge and either join hands with other strategic groups like the state bureaucracy and big business or will compete with them in structuring society in such a way as to maximize their

Table 5.4. Strategic groups of knowledge workers.

Institutions	Production	Dissemination and Utilization
Higher Learning and research	researchers research staff	teachers lecturers
Business and industry	R&D scientists technicians	experts, consultants managers
Media	journalists artists	publishers editors

chance for appropriating wealth and power during the implementation of a knowledge society.

There are overlaps and omissions in Table 5.4, which is designed to reduce the complexity of a knowledge society to manageable proportion and aid the design of research projects or the construction of indicators. The most obvious strategic group are, of course, researchers and their supporting staff. They partly overlap with lecturers and other university staff who are also doing research, and also publish their results. But also creative artists are important knowledge producers. They set artistic standards, they may interpret history and everyday life in their novels and create values that influence the flow of social change.

The strategic groups of a knowledge society are bound together by networks of communication. They form "communities of practice" with vague boundaries. Their networks extend beyond national boundaries of Malaysia and Indonesia, even if they are firmly embedded in the local political and social processes of their own society. In a way they are pirates on the sea of knowledge, acquiring (or at times pirating) knowledge wherever they can. Because of their critical minds they are sometimes looked upon with suspicion or admiration, as the case may be, by politicians or other strategic groups.

5.5. Conclusion: The Knowledge Gap and the Digital Divide

The World Development Report 1998/99 proclaims that knowledge: "...can easily travel the world". Can it really? According to an OECD report "the relationship between technological progress, innovation

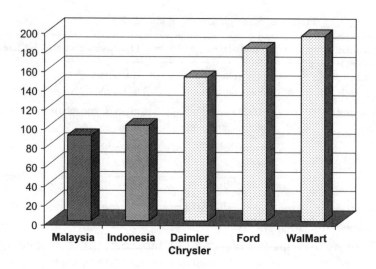

Fig. 5.5. GDP Malaysia, Indonesia and revenue of major companies, 2000 (in US$ billion).

Source: ASEAN Statistics (http://www.aseansec.org/macroeconomic/), *Der Spiegel* (2001).

and growth appears to have changed in the 1990s" (OECD, 2000:9). Networking, co-operation between firms and the fluid flow of knowledge have activated the knowledge market and innovations are spread more rapidly through the economy of the industrialized countries. On the other hand the knowledge gap between the major knowledge producing nations and the rest of the world is widening (Persaud, 2001) and the treasure throve of knowledge is jealously safeguarded by the powerful industrial nations. Our comparative data show divergent paths towards a knowledge society, with no guarantee, whether those catching up will look in 2020 like the more advanced knowledge societies do as of now. Today mega-companies are created by mergers and alliances that are made possible only by the advancement of information technology, the reduction of transaction costs and the infusion of new knowledge into the production process. These companies control budgets, exceeding those of many governments. Among the biggest one hundred economic units (in the year 2000) are 49 countries and 51 corporations (*Der Spiegel*, 23 July 2001). They increasingly determine what knowledge is created and who will have access to it.

Government ministries, let alone universities and research institutes, are dwarfed by the R&D divisions of these large conglomerates (see Fig. 5.5).

So far the benefits of globalization and the "knowledge revolution" have remained in the hands of the managers and shareholders of large corporations and the OECD states, mainly the US. The gap between rich and poor nations has widened and one has to be rather sceptical whether the knowledge gap will be closed and the digital divide bridged. The glamor of dot.com companies has waned, the computerization of the poorer sections of any society has been minimal and patents and Nobel prizes are concentrated on a few countries and regions. Nevertheless knowledge in many fields is expanding, most of it is translated into information and applied to production, services and to the every-day life of most people around the globe, being either beneficial or destructive as it may be. The global knowledge society *is* emerging, at all cost. But the global knowledge society is fragmented, divided and differentiated. The epistemic landscape still has hills and valleys, fast running streams and backwaters. Research is needed, how to channel the stream of knowledge into ones own backyard, how to utilize local knowledge and local cultural traditions, how to gain a competitive advantage by maintaining ones cultural identity. Knowledge does not consist of ICT alone, without a social, political and cultural context ICT and a knowledge economy will not flourish.

References

Der Spiegel, 23 July 2001.

Drucker, P.F. (1994). *Postcapitalist Society.* New York: Harper Business.

Evers, H.-D. (2000a). Die Globalisierung der epistemischen Kultur: Entwicklungstheorie und Wissensgesellschaft. In *Vom Ewigen Frieden und vom Wohlstand der Nationen,* U. Menzel (ed.), pp. 396–417. Frankfurt am Main: Suhrkamp Verlag.

Evers, H.-D. (2000b). *Epistemic Cultures: Towards a New Sociology of Knowledge.* Working Paper No. 151, Department of Sociology, National University of Singapore.

Evers, H.-D. (2003). Transition Towards a Knowledge Society: Malaysia and Indonesia in Comparative Perspective. *Comparative Sociology,* 2(2), 355–373.

Evers, H.-D. and S. Gerke (1997). *Global Market Cultures and the Construction of Modernity in Southeast Asia.* Thesis Eleven, 50, 1–14.

Evers, H.-D. and S. Gerke (2001). *Hochschulen in Indonesien*. Bonn, Department of Southeast Asian Studies, University of Bonn.

Evers, H.-D. and T. Menkhoff (2004). Expert Knowledge and the Role of Consultants in an Emerging Knowledge-based Economy. *Human Systems Management*, 23(2), 137–149. (See Chapter 6 in this volume for a revised version of this paper.)

Gibbons, M. *et al.* (1994). *The New Production of Knowledge: The Dynamics of Science and Research in Contemporary Societies*. London: Sage.

Kusunoki, K. (2004). Synthesizing Modular and Integral Knowledge. In *Hitotsubashi on Knowledge Management*, H. Takeuchi and I. Nonaka (eds.), pp. 309–338. Singapore: John Wiley & Sons (Asia).

Long, A. and N. Long (Hg.) (1992). *Battlefields of Knowledge: The Interlocking of Theory and Practice in Social Research and Development*. London, New York: Sage.

Mahathir, M (1991). *Wawasan 2020*. Kuala Lumpur: Government Printing Office.

National Information Technology Council (1999). www.nitc.org.my.

Nonaka, I. (1994). A Dynamic Theory of Organizational Knowledge Creation. *Organization Science* 5, 14–37.

OECD (2002). *Measuring the Information Economy*. Paris: OECD. www.oecd.org/sti/measuring-infoeconomy.

Persaud, A. (2001). The Knowledge Gap. *Foreign Affairs*, 80, 107–117.

Stehr, N. (1994). *Knowledge Societies*. London: Sage.

Stehr, N. (2001). *Wissen und Wirtschaften: Die gesellschaftlichen Grundlagen der modernen Ökonomie*. Frankfurt am Main: Suhrkamp Verlag.

UNESCO (2001). Research and Development Personnel by Occupation. http://www.uis.unesco.org. Paris: UNESCO Institute for Statistics.

Willke, H. (1998). Organisierte Wissensarbeit. *Zeitschrift für Soziologie*, 27(3), 161–175.

World Bank (1999). *World Development Report 1998/99: Knowledge for Development*. New York: Oxford University Press.

Part III

Strategic Groups as K-economy Drivers

Chapter 6

Knowledge Management: An Essential Tool for the Public Sector

Thomas B. Riley

Prologue

There is a shift of focus from "state action" to a broader field identified by policies, programs, strategies, projects, and tactics; the "practices" thus generated extend well beyond the traditional boundaries of the state apparatuses. Increasingly the production of knowledge comes to form a crucial focus of attention ... Social action increasingly revolves around and is directed toward the collection, classification, collation, compilation, calculation, and circulation of information (Hunt, 1993:310).

The above contains within it the notion of change that has occurred in our society and the ways in which governments have increasingly become reliant on the gathering, formulating, organizing, disseminating and usage of information. In the emerging Information Society of the last thirty years "information" has become a commodity and an indispensable tool for government in its role of governance. With the rise of information technologies and the Internet, the concept of information management and the means by which information is a strategic tool for both government and citizen alike, have become of paramount importance. This changing climate of societal norms has, as a by-product, created an evolving discipline known as "knowledge management" or, a more recent term, "knowledge sharing".

Recent changes within governments, who have increasingly reorganized themselves to become more like the private sector, have altered the ways in which governments now govern. Also, new technologies are creating vast arrays of information holdings which citizens want to access. But that is just a small part of the wider discipline of "knowledge management". Knowledge management is a discipline that can be used as an essential tool by all governments, no matter their size. This paper shall look at knowledge management in relation to Public Sector organizations.

6.1. Introduction

> *By sensing and understanding its environment, the knowing organization is able to engage in continuous learning and innovation. By applying learned decision rules and routines, the knowing organization is primed to take timely, purposive action. At the heart of the knowing organization is its management of the information processes that underpin sense making, knowledge building, and decision making* (Chun, 1998:xi).

This paper explores the subject of knowledge management (KM), or as it is now commonly known, knowledge sharing, particularly as it relates to knowledge-intensive organizations in the public sector. Research and interviews on this subject area were conducted in Canada, the United States and the United Kingdom, as well as through the World Wide Web.[1] The subject matter is crucial to understand when assessing and developing tools to transform governments into an effective public sector organization in the new global information technology infrastructure. However, the principles of knowledge management are not just about information technology. More important this evolving discipline is all about capturing knowledge to better improve public administration principles. These principles can be of intrinsic value to both developed and developing countries.

Knowledge management is considered by many as an emerging, new discipline to assist organizations to change and adapt in our new, knowledge-driven world. The importance of intellectual capital (IC) management (a component of knowledge management) first became widely recognized as a result of a FORTUNE magazine cover story in 1991. This article led to an explosion of interest in IC concepts and the

---

[1] Much of the knowledge in this paper has been drawn from a larger study conducted by the author for the National Research Council of Canada (CISTI). Any citations are reprinted here with their permission.

underlying processes of how to manage and liberate knowledge as a key intangible organizational resource. KM is now becoming an important discipline for many public sector organizations internationally.

This paper will explore the meanings and applications of KM with specific attention to how the concepts apply to government. The focus here is to look at KM applications in both public and private sector organizations with the purpose of illustrating and developing particular applications relevant for organizations seeking to use knowledge sharing as a strategic application in the evolution of a national knowledge-based economy.

This paper will look at:

- some definitions of knowledge management;
- the relevance of knowledge management to both the public and private sectors;
- case studies where KM has been applied in the public sector;
- the relationship of the knowledge worker and the knowledge economy; and
- knowledge management strategies in the knowledge economy and recommendations for possible implementation.

6.2. Knowledge Management Definitions

Intellectual capital is intellectual material — knowledge, information, intellectual property, experience — that can be put to use to create wealth. It is the collective brainpower (Stewart, 1997:12).

Professionals specializing in KM are constantly striving to determine what constitutes "knowledge". The term knowledge is subjective, with different social and organizational contexts shaping the definition. Knowledge includes experience, judgment, intuition, and values.

This broad scope of knowledge translates into an equally broad definition of KM as an articulated philosophy that cuts across many disciplines. The Public Service Commission of Canada defines it as "the process of creating, capturing, and using knowledge to enhance organizational performance" (McDowall, 1998:1).

Sveiby (1997:35), a founding father of knowledge management, defines it as "the art of creating value by leveraging the intangible assets". According to Sveiby, an individual's competence, consists of the following factors:

- Explicit knowledge *involves knowing facts acquired mainly through information, often through formal education.*
- Skill *involves practical proficiency acquired mainly through training and practice. Experience learnt from mistakes and successes.*
- Value judgments, *what the individual believes to be right, that act as filters for the process-of-knowing.*
- Social networks *made up of the individual's relationships with other human beings in an environment and a culture that is transferred through tradition.*

Knowledge management includes both the active creation, transfer, application and re-use of individual (tacit) knowledge and of codified (explicit) collective knowledge, supported by new approaches, relationships and technologies, to increase the speed of innovation, decision-making and responsiveness to organizational objectives and priorities.

Another aspect of extracting individual knowledge is through the use of storytelling. This involves engaging the individual in relating in anecdotal form, particular details of incidents regarding the subject at hand.

As a tool KM is an enabler of change that transforms behaviors, shared mental models, deeply held assumptions and metaphors through which we interpret the world and take action.

6.3. Tacit, Explicit and Cultural Knowledge, and Storytelling

Understanding the differences between "explicit" and "tacit" knowledge and "storytelling" is crucial to the application of KM. In fact, one of the most valuable assets in an organization, next to its corporate memory, is the tacit knowledge of individuals. According to Nonaka and Takeuchi (1998:2), "explicit knowledge can be articulated in formal language and transmitted through, for example, manuals, written specifications, etc. Tacit knowledge is seen as personal knowledge, based on individual experience and values and therefore not as easily transmitted". Extracting tacit knowledge has also been identified by some as storytelling, a unique way to gain knowledge from an individual, on any given subject of expertise or experience, based on the individual's unique perspective.

Nonaka and Takeuchi make the point that once an organization incorporates this tacit knowledge into its organizational memory banks, then this knowledge will not be lost once the individual moves on. Tapping into the tacit knowledge of individual employees in public sector organizations can have long-term benefits.

Chun (1998:xvi) adds another dimension to the types of knowledge inherent in organizations. He articulates that, in addition to "tacit" and "explicit" knowledge, there is "cultural" knowledge which is "expressed in the assumptions, beliefs and norms used by members (of the organization) to assign value and significance to new information or knowledge".

He expands on this crucial point by explaining how new knowledge is created by knowledge conversion and knowledge linkage: "In knowledge conversion the organization continuously creates new knowledge by converting between the personal, tacit knowledge of individuals who produce creative insight, and the shared, explicit knowledge which the organization needs to develop new products and innovations" (Chun, 1998:xvii).

In the burgeoning knowledge economy, knowledge management is central to the functions of private sector organizations. To compete in the knowledge economy, companies must utilize effectively all types of knowledge held within their organizations. KM can add or create value by more actively leveraging know-how, experience and judgment resident within and, in many cases, outside of an organization.

This ability to harness knowledge within an organization can be a key determinant in future growth, contributing to the realization of new opportunities, the more rapid and successful development of new products and services, more efficient manufacturing and distribution processes and, most importantly perhaps, better problem prevention and resolution.

The ability to innovate faster is one of the key results of more effective knowledge. Whether KM occurs internally or externally, organizations now have ready access to powerful software resources to manage and utilize vast information holdings and human knowledge. However, it must be remembered that however much technology is used in the deployment of knowledge management, technology itself is only an enabler.

6.4. Storytelling

Nothing serves a leader better than a knack for narrative. Stories anoint role models, impart values, and show how to execute indescribably complex tasks (Stewart, 1998).

Storytelling plays a large role in extracting informational history of organizations from an individual, which includes tacit and explicit knowledge of the individual. This can range from the experiences of engineers to clerks who have been with the organization for a long time, to heads of departments who have a broad, deep overview of the organization. The point of storytelling is that it doesn't just extract some basic factual information about a particular situation. Rather, it gives a broad overview of an individual's subjective experience of any given situation. The individual can relate, in often informative and lively ways, particular pieces of information not recorded. For example, oral traditions have always handed down, through storytelling, incidents in history never recorded. We have witnessed this in the form of ancient sagas, such as Beowulf, which was originally an oral tale and then put to writing. But the most important part of storytelling is encouraging the individual to relate how he or she solved a particular problem or what worked in approaching the problem.

As KM expert Snowden (2000) has said: "Storytelling can engage the individual in imaginative discourse and serve to bring out knowledge that would hitherto be unknown. An example, in public sector organizations, is that long-term employees in a department have a history of the department and approach their work based on their knowledge of what has happened in the department over the decades. Often individuals can understand that approaches to policies and programs may not work having been through a particular experience many years previously. An individual might know details about the development of legislation, and some of the intricate issues that arose during the process. Getting that individual to relate events that occurred from the past, when matters regarding the legislation, policy or program arise, could prove invaluable. A person might recall details unknown in the present but could have an important bearing in interpretation of the policy to hand or decision-making. Knowing the history of the organization, which is often as not, unwritten, can add value at some point. Often individuals are reluctant to write down their experiences, mostly because many people have difficulty expressing their thoughts in writing. However, storytelling can serve as a means to overcome this barrier".

Storytelling can be used to gain explicit knowledge from an individual, of any given circumstances, of a decision-making process. A number of people, for example, could be asked to give their views of what occurred when a decision was made. This exercise could help the organization to make changes for future decision-making by extracting the errors made or lessons learned from the individuals involved.

According to Stewart (1998:2), stories carry values and memory: ". . . many companies share the story of the day an underling stops the boss from breaking a rule. In the IBM version, Tom Watson praises the security guard who forces him to go back for his identification. But when a Revlon receptionist won't let Charles Revson walk off with a sign-in sheet, he fires her. In one company the moral is, 'We obey rules'; in the other, 'We obey rulers' ". Thus, the rules vary from organization to organization based on the culture of any one particular organization. The primary thing to do, when extracting data, information and knowledge from an individual, is to develop a system of how to be able to sort out the relevant data and important lessons from the story being told. This is a major challenge but can be invaluable in helping an organization to be more efficient and productive. Storytelling can also be invaluable, in and of itself, as it creates a sense of involvement in all the people in the organization and gives credence to individuals and assigns importance to what the individual has to say. This can contribute to good morale in the group.

As Stewart concludes from his research, there must be involvement from all levels of the organization. "The moral of the story?" he asks. "A very simple one: If stories are powerful and if stories are going to be told — true and false, official and underground, flattering and humiliating — then leaders and managers need to be part of the process. First, suss out how story-rich the place is. A lack of storytelling betokens an environment where management is too controlling. Ask yourself whether the stories — about the founder, about the guy who got canned, about why the boss got her job — are ones that tell people to shut up or step up, that include or exclude. Is there room for mistakes in the company story?" Stewart says that he believes that the oft-told tale of how Xerox fumbled the future — inventing the fax and the personal computer only to see others turn them into successful commercial projects — has been a good thing for the company. It offers a warning about cockiness but at the same time the assurance that one can make mistakes and recover from them. The argument is made that storytelling is about getting members of an organization to be in communication with each other. It is also about creating a sense of harmony in the workplace and recognizing the worth of each and every individual in the organization.

Tacit knowledge is information, knowledge and experience unique to the individual. Tacit and explicit knowledge can be obtained from an employee in the organization in many ways, such as a written report or notes, and storytelling. It would appear from the evidence now accruing that storytelling, an ancient art in all cultures, is a means to effectively draw out the tacit knowledge of an individual. A by-product of this process is that it helps to build camaraderie and closeness in a group, making the workplace a better place to be.

6.5. The Relevance of Knowledge Sharing to the Public Sector

> One of the curious things about living through a time of whirlwind change is that it is often difficult to understand exactly what is changing. In recent years, new technology has given us the ability to transform basic aspects of our lives: the way we converse and learn; the way we work, play, and shop; even the way we participate in political and social life (Shapiro, 2000:11).

Knowledge is an overriding, important commodity well understood by business and government alike. While knowledge has always been central to the work of many employees, there exists a rich resource of knowledge that often lies dormant. The challenge for the organization is to re-awaken this knowledge within the working environment and put it to good use. This fortifies the importance of extracting tacit, explicit, and cultural knowledge from individuals in the organization.

Many experts also state that such knowledge management has been with us for a long time but has been articulated in different ways and other forms. They contend that, although the term "knowledge management" may not have been used, knowledge initiatives reflecting KM concepts "have become the next phase in the continuous process of improving business performances" (TFPL, 1999:2).

A background paper on KM in the Public Sector (prepared for the Federal Government of Canada's Interdepartmental Knowledge Management Forum in 1999) articulated the importance of knowledge to the Canadian Government. The paper laid out the importance of knowledge management to Canadian society and to public sector organizations in particular: "A number of federal public sector institutions play a key role in providing leadership and support for leveraging knowledge for the Canadian society. Indeed, the move toward a knowledge-based society has underscored the importance of a number of knowledge-intensive public sector responsibility areas such as: education; historical and cultural heritage preservation and promulgation; health and the well-being of Canadians; law and order; the economy; and other areas" (National Research Council, 1999:5).

The paper goes on to state, "it is important to acknowledge the linkages between the government's responsibilities which relate to the 'knowledge-based society' and the role of knowledge in conducting the business of government" (National Research Council, 1999:5). This is an important concept to grasp when public sector institutions turn to the application of knowledge management principles.

The paper further states that: "Knowledge is not a distinct objective in itself, it contributes to the achievement of governmental objectives and plans, but it is often not explicitly considered in terms of the business planning and operational management processes. It is usually assumed that the knowledge will be present when needed, rather than thinking of it as a resource which needs to be managed, as one would consider managing structural capital, financial capital, etc." (National Research Council, 1999:8).

The 1999 study also notes that public sector organizations have faced many changes over the past few years. The growing importance, and use, of information technologies, downsizing in government departments, priorities for new programs to deal with the cultural shifts in society, all lead to wide challenges for public sector organizations. Knowledge management is a tool that can assist leaders and workers alike in government to adapt to the changes. Public sector organizations, in order to adapt to the changing needs of the future, need to implement new strategies, projects and priorities. This partially involves "the public sector's ability to anticipate the future, to prepare itself adequately, and to achieve the kinds of innovation necessary. It includes such things as scenario planning, forecasting, trend analysis and prediction, etc. With the pace of change, it is a significant challenge" (National Research Council, 1999:10).

There are, says the Report, distinct advantages of knowledge management for the public sector. Potential benefits from managing knowledge more effectively include: (National Research Council, 1999:12)

- improved productivity and service delivery efficiencies;
- increased innovation capability;
- core competency development;
- improved decision-making;
- greater responsiveness to changes;
- more unified strategy;
- improved service to customers through greater customer knowledge;
- improved employee morale;
- strengthened relationships; and
- cost efficiency.

However, in order to achieve the goals of effective KM it is important that there be a number of factors at play to make this work. There should be strong *leadership* within any public sector organization, which endorses and champions the importance of knowledge management. This leadership should not be just from the very top of an agency or department within the government but from heads of sectors and divisions within the organization. There also needs to be a *coordinated strategy* for what knowledge management principles should be applied that is developed in tandem with the overall operating goals and aims of the particular organization. Knowledge is a strategic tool that is resident in numerous places in an organization. This ranges from the tacit, explicit and cultural knowledge and experience of individuals to the vast reservoir of information that is resident within public sector organizations. This is why good information management practices can bolster attempts at implementing knowledge sharing practices. The two disciplines, knowledge management and information management, are quite distinct from each other. However, one complements the other.

As Hession (2000:20), Chief Information Officer of Fisheries and Oceans Canada, has observed, information management has an important part to play in developing professional knowledge workers: "In equipping professionals and knowledge workers to handle the challenges of information management, we have many problems to solve: lack of formal training in working with a digital workspace; lack of education in formal information classification and indexing; and lack of a framework for even filing their own e-mail. Without an architectural foundation on sound information management principles, it becomes very difficult to build, enhance, and co-ordinate the knowledge that is needed to deliver the services". It is clear that training is a key element in both information management and knowledge management.

Partnerships, within public sector organizations, are needed to extract and share knowledge for the overall common good of a government program. This is quite an important principle as, if properly applied and implemented, it can lead to increased efficiency, productivity and overall improvement of program delivery since it involves the citizenry.

6.6. The Knowledge Worker in Organizations

The emergence of knowledge management as a workable philosophy for public sector institutions is also the result of the increasingly sophisticated information and communication technologies now at the disposal of the organization. This has led, in turn, to the identification of specific roles and responsibilities to various categories of KM managers within an organization. TFPL Ltd., a UK consulting firm, has identified a range of full and part time roles supporting working units or communities:

- knowledge leaders, responsible for championing the KM approach in their business unit, quality of knowledge activities, decisions over confidentiality, etc;
- knowledge managers, responsible for the acquisition and management of internal and external knowledge;
- knowledge navigators, responsible for knowing where knowledge can be located;
- knowledge synthesizers, responsible for facilitating the recording of significant project/unit knowledge;
- content editors, responsible for codifying and structuring;
- publishing, responsible for internal publishing functions, principally on an intranet basis;
- coaching and mentoring roles, responsible for assisting individuals throughout their business unit or practice to develop and learn KM activities and disciplines;
- help desk activities, including the delivery of KM and information related;
- "knowledge workers" in that they are using, manipulating, interpreting and acting on information, and require a knowledge level that empowers them to make decisions and act on their own initiative; and
- information intensive roles such as Strategic Planning and Competitive Intelligence (TFPL, 1999:4).

Many organizations, including the public sector, recognize that they need to harness the knowledge of all of their workers, not just the highly skilled, innovative and creative worker, to compete effectively and to respond to the changing culture due to the impacts of new technologies. Since a person with talent and drive can easily move around within the marketplace, we have seen aggressive programs within business and government both to attract new, skilled workers and to keep current employees. It is the function of the knowledge management worker to ensure that the knowledge assets of such highly valued employees is also put to the most effective use in pursuit of corporate objectives while the worker is with the organization.

Speaking at a knowledge management seminar in Ottawa, Saint-Onge (1999) identified the emerging contract between the knowledge worker and the organization. The old contract had the worker claim loyalty and exchange it for a promised future. The new contract is based on the worker being self-initiated, owning his/her own performance, learning and career. So the new contract is: "I will give you my commitment in exchange for the ability to constantly increase my capabilities. If that contract is met I will stay with you. If it is not met I will look elsewhere".

The importance of the knowledge-sharing worker is identified in the TFPL study in the UK. Concluding that no single department or function can deliver corporate objectives alone, the TFPL study isolates six characteristics that determine how the overall corporate knowledge management capability is created, shared and utilized. These are through:

- the skills and expertise of the staff;
- their ability to learn and to build knowledge;
- the processes which enable their skills and knowledge to be applied and shared;
- the culture and values which encourage knowledge building and sharing;
- the infrastructure (IT and physical), which supports knowledge building, flow and sharing; and
- the intellectual assets which the organization builds, maintains, organizes and exploits (TFPL, 1999:2).

Findings of the American Productivity and Quality Centre determine that knowledge flourishes where you have influential thought leaders, a sense of higher purpose and urgency surrounding change, peer pressure from communities of practice to share knowledge, and where contributions are recognized. Six factors have been recognized as fostering a knowledge-sharing culture:

- a demonstrable link to the business strategy;
- fit with the overall culture;
- open sharing of ideas by leaders and managers, even at a "half-baked stage";
- trust in the members of human networks;
- a shared sense of responsibility for results; and
- knowledge sharing is a visible highly sought-after activity, imbedded in daily work (Nicholson-O'Brien, 1999a:5).

6.7. Knowledge Management between Government and Citizenry

The Internet has brought about a decentralization of power. In the wired world, individuals can now make their own choices as to which authorities and information sources they will accept. This is leading to a greater democratization of knowledge, empowerment of the individual, and the potential for more informed interactions between the citizenry and organizations, including government. Moreover, since individuals now have ready access to a variety of information resources, organizations have to adopt new proactive measures to compile and disseminate information in a competitive information environment. Defining a clear role and responsibilities of a knowledge worker, and setting up small, effective teams to assess information demands and plan accordingly, can help in the transformation to information-intensive, citizen-centric web sites. Such approaches are going to be necessary as people more and more work and live online.

A citizenry that is able to seek and obtain information and knowledge from any place in the world through the Internet will, in all likelihood, also expect more from government. There is also the opportunity for a paradigm shift in which governments benefit even more from the intellectual capital of the citizenry. In a knowledge driven economy, the intellectual capital of the citizen could become government's and society's most important asset. Knowledge management principles can be the key to managing this transition and effectively creating this new, interactive knowledge-sharing environment.

Application of KM principles will also be necessary if government institutions are to maintain a role as an authoritative source of useful and relevant information. With public perceptions continuously changing due to the empowering nature of communication technologies, new creative and innovative environments will continually evolve on the Internet. Many authors, including this one, contend that the nature of government and governance will be transformed as a result, driven by the changes technology is creating in society (Riley, 2001).

6.8. Case Study where Knowledge Management has been Applied in the Public Sector[2]

Overall, whatever the term employed to describe it, knowledge management is increasingly seen not merely as the latest management fashion, but as signalling the development of a more organic and holistic way of understanding and exploiting the role of knowledge in the processes of managing and doing work, and an authentic guide for individuals and organizations in coping with the increasingly complex and shifting environment of the modern economy (Denning, 1998:6).

6.8.1. *Knowledge Management within the World Bank Group*[3]

The Washington DC-based World Bank Group provides loans and technical assistance to developing countries around the world, maintaining offices in 80 countries. Developments within the Bank suggest that the organisation is changing its vision from that of a financial bank to that of a knowledge bank with greater emphasis on supporting knowledge institutions in its borrowing member countries. Such

---

[2]Note: The case studies below and facts presented are based on interviews with employees of the World Bank in Washington, D.C. and the Department of Trade and Industry in the United Kingdom.
[3]The case study of the World Bank was originally published in a publication entitled "Knowledge Management: An Evolving Discipline". This was done for, and published by, the National Research Council of Canada (CISTI) in March 2000. The paper was prepared by the author.

support has a variety of dimensions, including knowledge codification (i.e., so useful knowledge is not embedded in individuals); enhancing the learning environment (e.g. less delivery of EDI courses in Washington, and more development of local knowledge institutions); connectivity and networking, to take advantage of the rapid development of telecommunications and related technologies; and a focus on pilot countries to see how these issues fit together in practice.

To achieve the objectives, the Bank has a six-person knowledge management secretariat whose sole responsibility has been to reorganize the Bank's international activities using KM principles and to apply them internally. Among 8000 staff members there are now 500 full time and 300 part time knowledge management workers. World Bank Group President, James D. Wolfensohn, has stated that the application of knowledge management within the organization and to all the countries the Bank deals with (especially developing countries) is more important than the lending of money.

The Bank describes KM as "collecting information, connecting people and applying experience and expertise to relevant situations". The strong focus on the importance of knowledge and its applications, which began in 1997, has also included renewing the skills of the organization's office workers, fine tuning strategic missions, and reorganizing the administrative structure of the Bank.

To prepare for the rapid rate of change in the 21st century, the Bank is embedding a philosophy that management and sharing of knowledge should be an integral part of the institution. While the Bank has always transferred and shared knowledge, it is now viewing this process as a distinct activity, backed with specifically identified human, administrative, financial and technological resources. The World Bank staff are also becoming facilitators, as they put workers in different countries together to share particular knowledge.

The Knowledge Management Secretariat is the strategic hub for the Bank's KM activities and, in turn, is directed by a Knowledge Management Board. The Board, which develops and ensures implementation of the overall KM strategy, includes operational vice-presidents, support vice-presidents and other senior officials within the Bank. The

Board has provided the KM Secretariat with a budget of U.S. $55 million over three years (1997–2000).

Bank knowledge workers themselves worked in communities that have been created throughout the institution, reflecting specific areas of expertise and responsibility, all of which report up through an administrative structure to the KM Board. Knowledge workers are expected to actively engage in knowledge sharing, including their area of research, the information libraries they have, and information concerning electronic transfer of funds and loans' activity.

While the KM structure has been articulated, application has been a challenge as the Bank attempts to achieve its objectives that, wherever a staff member may be in the world, there should be access to the Bank's knowledge resources.

Ensuring the relevance and value of knowledge also requires obtaining information, knowledge and insights from Bank clients in various countries around the world that is then transferred back to the Bank. Field employees are being taught to further this sharing concept. When a Bank employee gains some insight or knowledge in a country where he is working, he or she is encouraged to transmit this back to the appropriate person within the Bank. One of the main ways this is done is through email.

The Bank has other means of collecting and disseminating information. To bring people together electronically or physically to facilitate what individual staff members are trying to achieve, in addition to meetings in Washington, the Bank regularly convenes meetings through the Internet, video conferencing and other technology such as conference calls.

The Bank has a distance learning studio with satellite links and other communication technologies in Washington as well as a publishing arm through which papers and a variety of other information is available. Top experts are invited by the Bank to do presentations and seminars to employees. Brown bag lunches are organized within the Bank to encourage employees to discuss various projects they are working on. Inherent to all of these activities is implicit recognition of the importance of knowledge sharing and knowledge management.

Overlying this activity is the KM Secretariat's objective of a community of practices — based on thematic groups. These are the engines for their knowledge banks. For example, within the energy, mining and telecommunications sector, there are seven thematic groups, including one on information infrastructure, the mission of which is to promote effective implementation of telecommunications and information technology applications for poverty alleviation and social development. This thematic group is addressing such key sub-sectoral issues as telecommunications liberalization, rural telephony, networking, national information infrastructure policy development, strategic information, and systems portfolio development. The efforts of thematic groups will lead to more rapid cross pollination of ideas between countries and cultures.

The concept of community of practice — people who gather knowledge in their field and share a common area of expertise and/or an interest in common problems — also encompasses seven surrounding support activities described in Fig. 6.1:

- **Development Statistics** — On-line statistics and indicators, includes key sector statistics and other data needed to help clients
- **Help Desk/Advisory Services** — people who connect others with the right knowledge and/or people — serving internal and external clients
- **Directory of Expertise** — a tool to search for the people with the right skills

Fig. 6.1. KM within the World Bank.

- **Engagement Information** — transaction information related to bank activities such as preparation, appraisal, and supervision of operations past, present, and future
- **Dialogue Space** — an electronic world where people working together on projects can exchange knowledge, ask questions, and get answers, whether the participants are situated in or outside the Bank
- **External Access** — a mechanism to ensure the availability of relevant materials to external clients and partners, as well as incorporate external contributions into the Bank's knowledge base
- **KMS On-line** — the Bank's electronic knowledge system, where know-how is stored and made accessible, initially to Bank staff and ultimately to external clients and partners. [4]

This KM activity is positioning the World Bank as one of the leading creators, connectors, and facilitators of knowledge in the development community.

Despite this powerful vision backed by commitment, funding, people, and technology and administrative resources, the KM Secretariat has encountered some problems getting Bank staff to accept this new system. Problems encountered include:

- resistance to change;
- entrenched ideas on "how something works";
- unwillingness to share knowledge for fear of giving up some "power" one might have; and
- silo thinking — i.e., the information flows only within one division of an organization and does not cross to other parts of the organization.

To help overcome these problems, in the future Bank staff will be assessed, as part of their employee evaluation, on the degree to which they are able to share knowledge. This is a broad goal that is now only being applied in theory. The results will hinge on the degree to which knowledge can be shared, and people within organizations can

---

[4]Source: World Bank Brochure "Making development knowledge available and accessible for clients, partners and staff", p. 3.

develop the idea that sharing is essential, both for their own careers and to further the goals of the organization and their clients.

The World Bank has acknowledged that changing employee attitudes about information sharing is a huge task and will involve a major cultural shift. Individuals will have to learn that by sharing knowledge they are not losing anything from their power base (no matter how small or large). This will come through training and experience, say many experts.

The Bank's strategy has been to organize internally first. Now the next major step will be to organize in the field to improve services to clients and help them to solve their problems in more effective ways. Through application of KM, the Bank believes useful knowledge will be more rapidly shared to achieve the overall goal of alleviating poverty in client countries.

It is still too early to assess the effectiveness of the Bank's application of KM principles. Nevertheless, initial results show that many clients want to know about the principles and are looking for a template that can be applied in their own jurisdictions. It is considered that the internal marketing of KM principles, stressing the importance of internal knowledge sharing, will remain a critical attribute for long term success of the initiative.

6.8.2. *Examples of KM Implementation: Some Canadian Federal Government Initiatives*

> We need to develop resilient people who operate in nimble organizations where learning is considered a crucial asset. Most organizations, and the TBS and the federal government are no exception to this, are seeking to encourage knowledge-sharing at a faster rate than ever before, across organizational boundaries and disciplines (Nicholson-O-Brien, 1999b:1).

There has been an informal, Interdepartmental Knowledge Management Task Force in existence for the past five years (as of the year 2000). The 40 members on this Task Force represented most federal agencies, and have come from middle management and senior levels of government. In the past few years the Task Force has invited members of the private sector to join them. This is done in the spirit of the development and sharing of knowledge between people in their respective communities. With the emergence of the Office in the senior echelons of the Treasury Board, knowledge management is now working its way into the strategic thinking of the Federal government. Support from this level means that the knowledge management agenda should move significantly forward in the coming years. The Canadian government is considered a leader in knowledge management. The examples of leadership, from the senior echelons of government, for Knowledge Management activities in Canada, the United Kingdom and the United States, is important. Leadership is central to the development and implementation of knowledge management principles in public sector organizations.

At Human Resources and Development Canada (HRDC) a group of Assistant Deputy Ministers, together with the Deputy Minister, established a Knowledge Management Task Force that cuts across all business lines and regions to develop related strategies to meet future challenges. Four teams looked at:

- the design and production of knowledge;
- human capacity;
- delivery of information to clients and employees; as well as
- governance and accountability issues.

The Service and Innovation initiative in Treasury Board is being delivered, in conjunction with Human and Resources Development Canada, Industry Canada, and others, to ensure the integrated delivery of services to citizens, whether these services originate with the federal government, or with other governments and partners. Maximum use is being made of technologies that offer a user-friendly, timely and cost-effective interface.

Health Canada has launched a major knowledge management initiative in pursuit of a larger goal — the creation of a Canada Health Infoway, or pan Canadian health information highway. As described in the report, *Canada Health Infoway: Paths to Better Health*: "the Canada Health Infoway can help significantly to improve the quality, accessibility, portability and efficiency of health services across the entire spectrum of care. [This report] is also about how the Infoway can enable the creation, analysis and dissemination of the best possible evidence from across Canada and around the world as a basis for informed decisions by patients, citizens, informal caregivers, health professionals and providers, and health managers and policymakers"[5]

Health Canada has deployed several strategic initiatives to achieve its vision of effective knowledge management to expand the evidence base for health planning, improve policy planning and enhance services delivery. These include the following steps:

1. Develop a knowledge culture including the establishment of a Chief Knowledge Officer, the creation of a capacity to improve and implement knowledge strategy (frameworks, priorities, plans), and to lead knowledge culture initiatives (communities of practice, knowledge-maps, sharing). Knowledge business specialists would ensure that knowledge, information and data are developed, found or acquired and that technology tools (discussion databases, intranet) are identified and built, to meet business needs.
2. Conduct analysis and research by creating an internal capacity (staff, analytical frameworks, methodologies, publications, reports, briefing notes, seminars, conferences), influencing the national health research agenda, and developing skills (all staff), and "absorptive" capacity.
3. Create a health info-structure by identifying, nurturing, investing and partnering in projects, consulting stakeholders, and developing and influencing policy and standards (privacy, security, connectivity).
4. Provide enterprise IM and IT services by developing and maintaining architectures, infrastructure and tools.

6.9. Governing Knowledge in the Knowledge Economy

In a knowledge economy, it is evident that the key to success is "knowledge". In terms of governance, this implies the need to invest in, and develop, knowledge workers as well as allocation of funds for skills

---

[5]"Canada Health Infoway: Paths to Better Health". Final Report of the Advisory Council on Health Infostructure, March 1999 (executive summary).

development and education (Stiglitz, 1999:4). The Internet has tipped the scales in favour of both businesses and governments. For example, for scientists in business and government, the Internet is a major tool to assist in the sharing of research and the findings. Scientists can now do this in an increasingly global environment. Exchange of research and ideas has accelerated innovation, inventions, and creation of new goods and products, at a rate never before known in human history.

The rapid development of the Internet in the past ten years has resulted in an escalation of the global economy. This globalization has had a profound impact on both the economies of nations and the pressures on countries to compete effectively in this new global environment. Globalization of the economy has also raised new issues of nationalism and protection of local culture. Yet, the pressures for change, brought by this new phenomenon, have also meant that countries can compete on a global scale. In this new environment two of the most important commodities of a nation are becoming information and knowledge.

Globalization has been spurred on by the Internet, which operates 24 hours a day, 7 days a week (24/7, as it has become known). This has meant that ideas and innovation can be occurring around the clock. In this new environment, it will be important for government to development mechanisms to encourage the private sector, and public sector research organizations, to be innovative and able to deploy knowledge. More and more individuals and companies are engaged in businesses that are connected to the Internet. In 1999 it was estimated that Britain was the leader in e-Commerce in Europe, spending £2 billion online. It was predicted that by the year 2004, the United States might reach sales of $1 trillion online. But this is not just about the Internet. The Knowledge economy is about how the new technologies have transformed the way we think and act, and the ways in which we use the Internet and ICTs to improve the world economies.

Yet, despite these glowing accolades about the benefits of the transformed world economies, there are the deeper issues as to whether or not many of the developing nations can also benefit. The digital divide, economies of scale, trans-global organizations dominating the world markets, powerful economic engines of a few rich countries, and other concerns, can leave the impression that the gap in the world between the rich and the poor will widen over time.

It is the thesis of this paper that, in fact, the powerful new technological tools, and the Internet, are media that can be harnessed to benefit developing countries. Malaysia is one such country that appears to be on a fast track to becoming a developed country by 2020. The steps taken by the country to develop a technological infrastructure is a first good and important step. To succeed in the knowledge economy there are certain very basic policies that are needed. The first is to create a cultural change within the institutions of the country (see Chapter 5 in this book).

Joseph Stiglitz (1999:4), Senior Vice President and Chief Economist, the World Bank Group, in London, UK, maintains that "in industry, the shift towards a knowledge-based economy involves a shift in organization away from top-down hierarchical systems to horizontal structures such as networks of semi-autonomous teams". He maintains that it is essential for any country, in developing structures for their knowledge-based economies, to develop their own best practices based on their history and cultural development. Best practices from other jurisdictions cannot simply be imposed on a country. Stiglitz points out that any attempts by external agencies to impose their own set of "Best Practices" for a knowledge economy, "will not produce lasting change. It will undermine people's incentives to develop their own capacities and weaken their own confidence in using their own intelligence. The external development agency, instead of acting as a catalyst or midwife to empower change, will only short-circuit people's learning activities and reinforce their impotence. The external incentives may temporarily overpower the springs of action that are native to the institutional matrix of the country but that will probably not induce any lasting institutional reforms" (Stiglitz, 1999:4). This is an important principle to understand as, for any country to succeed, it must, by necessity, rely on its own internal understanding and the wisdom of its culture. Malaysians, for example, are the ones best suited to change their own culture. But the lesson for any country is the same: to transform a country into a viable, knowledge-based economy, institutional change will be crucial. Who better to develop its own strategy but the government of a particular country? A Knowledge Management strategy in place can determine what is needed for the country and put the necessary process in place to create the transformation.

One of the prime tools a government needs, in order to embrace as much of their citizenry as possible, is wide access to both the Internet and Information and Communication Technologies (ICTs). Thus, to achieve this, connectivity programs, funded by government, are necessary. Also, where there is access in the school, or in the workplace, or in the community, programs are needed to widen computer literacy. Of course, in many countries, raising the overall literacy of the population is a primary goal. Part of this should be built into programs to ensure that the current and next generations become computer literate.

This is essential for the development of knowledge workers at all levels of society. Importance is placed on computer literacy because in many countries, such as Canada, the United States, Great Britain, Singapore, and Australia, it is now estimated that 60% of production is created by knowledge workers. This does not mean that 60% of the workforce is creating knowledge that can be bartered and sold on the world markets. Though this is partly true, the fact is that information technologies are now driving the economic engines in most of the industrialised world. Chips embedded in the infrastructure now drive most technologies in the workplace and home. Technology pervades our lives, from the kitchen, to our means of transportation, to the workplace. Some form of information technology drives nearly all facets of life. This is not just isolated to developed countries, but is evident in most of the developing countries. In the case of the latter, the technology and the economic prospects they bring, are not as universal. But to thrive in the global knowledge economy it is going to be important to change the whole educational system to ensure a wide base of knowledge workers who understand and use these information technologies. Thus, education is a key, in order to ensure the skills for the knowledge economy exist in abundance. It is important that there be an army of skilled technical experts who understand and can apply technical knowledge. These workers are the underpinnings of the knowledge economy.

Part of the challenge in allowing wide access to the rich resources that exist through the Internet and other ICTs, is ensuring that there are sufficient opportunities for businesses to be online. This is a step beyond providing the education of citizens to create opportunities. There need to be programs to fund businesses to get them online. This is an important lesson many of the developed countries have had to learn. Getting businesses online is not just ensuring wide access to the Internet. It also requires extensive educational programs so business leaders understand the opportunities and benefits of having an online presence. This is important so that they can take advantage of the world as a potential customer.

Equally crucial is that business be able to thrive in a competitive environment, and can compete, not only within their own country but also in the wider global economy. Diversity is a key characteristic of the knowledge economy. It is important that there be intellectual property laws to protect businesses and innovators. However, the laws themselves must be flexible to ensure that monopolies do not develop (Stiglitz, 1999:6–9). It is important that there be innovation, creativity and diversity in the emerging knowledge economy and in the culture of government departments in order to adapt to the changes being brought by information and communication technologies.

The combined precepts of the developing knowledge economies are changing the way many national and international institutions operate. For example, the World Bank has changed its focus to the intangibles of knowledge, institutions and culture. The World Bank is now transforming itself "into more of a knowledge bank and is forging a more comprehensive development framework to put the new focus into effect. In more advanced, industrial economies, the challenge of creating and nurturing a culture of innovation ... is no less daunting" (Stiglitz, 1999:15).

Thus, it is evident that the world is rapidly moving towards information and knowledge intensive societies. Four key policy areas of the tools for the knowledge economy are:

- information policies;
- using the principles of knowledge sharing;
- data protection laws; and
- secure networks (known as public key infrastructure) to allow online transactions.

In summary, to succeed in the knowledge economy, governments need to:

- develop programs to create a climate to nurture knowledge workers; education is the key in this process, starting with front-end entrance institutions to higher education institutes;
- invest in online connectivity to embrace as much of the citizenry online;
- invest in technology to build infrastructures that support knowledge workers and strategies for growth of the national knowledge economy;
- build programs to stimulate innovation and creativity;
- enact legislation to create security and confidence for businesses to operate in the growing knowledge economy;
- create web sites within government with information that will assist businesses and entrepreneurs seeking to engage in knowledge-based economic activity; and
- work to bring about cultural change in institutions to adapt to the new economy emerging in the world.

6.10. Conclusions and Recommendations for the Public Sector

Communities of practice consist of people who are informally as well as contextually bound by a shared interest in learning and applying a common practice. Their focus on learning, competence, and performance bridges the gap between organizational learning and strategy topics and generates new insights for theory and practice.[6]

While the above examples are of embryonic KM initiatives within the federal government, it is clear that government recognizes the value of KM principles to adapt to the demands of this knowledge-based environment. Public sector organizations are beginning to capitalize

---

[6]Synder, William M., Communities of Practice, *http://www.km.gov* (as of 5 October 2001).

on the four identifiable elements of knowledge management:

- collective information resources;
- the intellectual capital of individuals;
- the multitude of external resources available to government; and
- the input of citizens who now have the capacity to play an interactive role in the process of government.

It is also clear that success of these initiatives will depend upon both leadership and commitment at senior levels of government organizations to break down barriers and "silo thinking". It will also require more refined use of one of the most important resources — the intellectual capital of people who work in the public service.

Building on in-house knowledge presents a strong challenge. It is not sufficient simply to tell employees in an organization that they need to share their knowledge. There has to be an understanding as to what particular pieces of knowledge held by the individual are important to the organization. The following are some basic principles that can be applied to this process:

- recognizing and building on in-house individual expertise;
- formalizing to varying degrees the harnessing of knowledge through the use of appropriate systems;
- passing on knowledge;
- developing knowledge from an individual asset into a corporate/organizational one; and
- encouraging the growth of an open corporate culture in which knowledge is viewed as being central to organizational development and to the efficiency of methods of business operation.

To be successful, the leadership within an organization must embrace knowledge sharing concepts and its precepts. More importantly, it must be a key component in the strategic vision of the organization. An additional, vital component is that there need to be designated officials and supporting staff to reorganize the organization and implement the principles of knowledge management to maximum benefit.

It is inherently clear that virtually every employee is a potential source of data, information and insights that constitute, in one form or another, a source of knowledge that is or could be invaluable to the goals and aims of the organization. The degree to which an organization manages knowledge to its advantage and forwarding of its strategic vision, is the degree to which the leaders of the organization can draw upon this source of potential wealth.

References

Chun, W.C. (1998). *The Knowing Organization: How Organizations Use Information to Construct Meaning, Create Knowledge and Make Decisions*. Oxford University Press.

Denning, S. (1998). *What is Knowledge Management?* Publication of the World Bank Knowledge Management Board, Washington, DC.

Hession, P. (2000). Information Management: Renewal and Reconstruction. *Canadian Government Executive*, Issue 3, June.

Hunt, Alan (1993). Law, State and Class Struggle. In *Exploration in Law and Society: Toward a Constitutive Theory of Law*, A. Hunt. New York: Routledge.

McDowall, P. (1998). Conference Report on International Knowledge Management Summit '98.

National Research Council (1999). *Leveraging Public Knowledge*. Background Paper for Knowledge Management in the Public Sector Seminar, National Research Council, CISTI, Ottawa, Canada, June (Paul McDowall and Brian Hamilton, Co-Chairs Interdepartmental Knowledge Management Forum, Federal Government of Canada).

Nicholson-O'Brien, D. (1999a). Knowledge Management in the Treasury Board (TB) and the Federal Knowledge Landscape. Paper presented at the TB of Canada, April 1999 (citing the American Productivity and Quality Centre, http://www.apcq.org).

Nicholson-O'Brien, D. (1999b). Building Organizational Capability Through Knowledge and Talent Development. Speech delivered at the Human Resources and Development Canada Leadership Conference, 16 June, Toronto.

Nonaka, I. and H. Takeuchi (1998). *The Knowledge-Creating Company*. Oxford University Press.

Riley, T. (2001). *Electronic Democracy and Electronic Governance: Living and Working in the Wired World, Lessons from Experience*. London, UK: Commonwealth Secretariat.

Saint-Onge, H. (1999). Knowledge Management: What This Means and How it Can be Applied. Contribution to KM Seminar, National Research Council, CISTI, 10 June.

Shapiro, A.L. (2000). *The Control Revolution: How the Internet is Putting Individuals in Charge and Changing the World We Know*. New York: Public Affairs (A Member of the Perseus Books Group).

Snowden, D. (2000). Comments at a Knowledge Management Seminar, October, Commonwealth Secretariat, Marlborough House, London, UK.

Stewart, Thomas A. (1997). *Intellectual Capital: The Wealth of Organizations*. New York: Doubleday.

Stewart, T. (1998). The Cunning Plots of Leadership. In *Fortune Magazine*, 7 September.

Stiglitz, J. (1999). *Public Policy for a Knowledge Economy*. Center for Economic Policy Research Document. 27 January, London.

Sveiby, K.E. (1997). *The New Organizational Wealth: Managing & Measuring Knowledge-based Assets*. Berrett-Koehler Publishers Inc.

TFLP (1999). Skills for Knowledge Management. A Briefing Paper by TFPL Ltd. based on research undertaken by TFPL on behalf of the UK Library and Information Commission, July, London, UK.

Chapter 7

Expert Knowledge and the Role of Consultants in an Emerging Knowledge-based Economy[1]

Hans-Dieter Evers and Thomas Menkhoff

7.1. Introduction

7.1.1. *Knowledge Society*

We are currently witnessing a major transition from the old type of industrial society with its traditional dominance of manufacturing work and old industrial classes to an information and knowledge-based society (Drucker, 1994) which shows the following characteristics:

- Its members have attained a higher average standard of education in comparison to other societies and a growing proportion of its labor force is employed as knowledge workers. In other words, there is a significant reduction in the number of people working in operational roles, while employment in professional, knowledge-based roles has risen (Evers, Kaiser and Mueller, 2003).
- Its industry produces products with integrated artificial intelligence (usually with the help of IT as in the case of JIT production) such as *voice-recognition software and technology* which is used increasingly in smart cars.

[1] This is a revised version of a paper presented at the 2003 Academy of Management (AOM) Conference in Seattle, USA (August). The essay was nominated by AOM for the "2003 Carolyn Dexter All-Academy Award for Internationalizing the Academy". Thanks are due to World Scientific Publishing Co. for granting as the privilege to reprint this piece which first appeared in *Human Systems Management*, Vol. 23, No. 2 (2004), 137–149.

- Service-based industries, retailing etc. are also undergoing dramatic changes as indicated by an increasing number of virtual stores such as Amazon.com or CD World.
- Its organizations — private, government and civil society — are transformed into intelligent organizations (Tuggle and Goldfinger, 2004).
- There is increased organized knowledge in the form of digitalized expertise, stored in data banks, expert systems, organizational plans and other media.
- There are multiple centres of expertise and a polycentric production of knowledge.
- There is a distinct epistemic culture of knowledge production and knowledge utilization (Knorr-Cetina, 1998; Evers, 2000).
- We see the growing importance of so-called communities of practice in and between organizations, i.e., self-organizing informal social structures which have the capacity to create and use organizational knowledge through informal learning and mutual engagement to leverage both internal and external stakeholders.

As outlined earlier, this process is very much evident in the case of Southeast Asian countries, Singapore and Malaysia in particular, who are following an intense strategy of knowledge governance (Evers and Gerke, 1994). In this chapter we shall focus on one group of knowledge workers, which we believe to be typical, and of strategic importance for a knowledge society: *experts and consultants* (Hitzler, Honer and Maeder, 1994). Experts and consultants sell knowledge. They are either working free-lance as self-employed professionals or as members of consultancy firms. They are distinct from producers as well as end-users of knowledge, very much like traders and trading companies buy and sell goods and services. Consultants do not own any physical means of production (at least not to a significant degree), but they have access to information and experience. As we are going to show, the number of experts and consultants is growing world-wide and the quality of their professionalism is a bench-mark for the stage which a knowledge-driven economy and a knowledge society has reached.

Why are experts strategically important and why is their importance — socially in terms of number of persons and economically in terms of output or turnover — growing?

Three reasons account for the strategic importance of experts and consultants:

- The growth of ignorance, which will increase the demand for expert knowledge;
- The increasing rather then diminishing marginal utility of the use of knowledge, which will add importance to, specialised expert knowledge; and
- The usefulness of expert knowledge as legitimization of political decisions.

Let us elaborate on these three points in greater depth.

7.1.2. *Expert Knowledge and its Functions*

7.1.2.1. The growth of ignorance

Globalization brings about a vast increase of what we know, but an even greater amount of ignorance, i.e., of what we know that we do not know (Evers, 2000a). While on one hand we are truly heading into the direction of becoming a knowledge society, we also become more ignorant at the same time. Each time a research project is successfully concluded, a number of new questions arise. While knowledge is increasing fast, the knowledge about what we do not know is increasing even faster (see Fig. 7.1). Reflexive modernization (Beck, 1992) is stimulating the growth of ignorance, because new knowledge is put into question as soon as it appears. Thus the growth of ignorance is a reflection of the

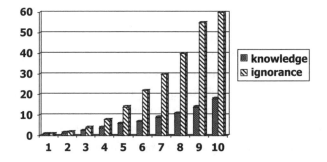

Fig. 7.1. The growth of knowledge and of ignorance (fictional).

growth of knowledge. The faster the wheel of knowledge production is turning, the greater uncertainty is likely to become.

This condition can be illustrated by the following examples. We do not know for certain whether or not an atomic energy plant will experience an accident with disastrous consequences and even experts are not able to tell us in advance, in which direction exchange rates will head. It is extremely "risky" to speculate in the futures market of commodities, stocks or currencies. It is only after the fact, after the crash that economists or social scientists come up with an explanation, which more often than not is based on conjecture rather than on hard facts or knowledge.

Risk consultancy, including political risk or environmental risk analysis has therefore become an important field of activity for consultants and their companies.

7.1.2.2. The increasing marginal utility of expert knowledge

Another important aspect of knowledge in a "new economy" is its specific characteristic as a factor of production that has grown in importance in relation to the other factors of labor and capital. Whereas other goods are succumbed to the law of diminishing returns, knowledge actually experiences *rising* marginal utility. The more an expert, a group of consultants or an organization know, the more valuable individual pieces of knowledge become; or to put it differently — knowledge is needed to utilize knowledge effectively.

7.1.2.3. The legitimizing function of expert knowledge

The third aspect explaining the increased demand for expert knowledge is its legitimizing function. Experts reduce the unscrutinable complexity of the globalized world and allow planners, politicians, business executives and other decision makers to base their actions on the executive summaries of the reports prepared by experts and management consultants, rather than on their own knowledge. Ignorance is thus transformed into expert knowledge. From the perspective of the firm, experts and consultants provide "instant knowledge" and "instant solutions".

The attitudes of clients towards knowledge work to the advantage of the large and well-known consultancy corporations. A government officer or a middle management executive will prefer to ask "world-class consultants" to advise his department or company, because he or she will not be blamed if the advice given by the consultants is not applicable, the proposed measures are not successful and the consultation proves to be an utter failure. If one has hired "the best", one is in a better position to legitimize one's decision as if one has hired a local and less glorified consulting firm that will have a hard time to convince its client that it has the right knowledge to successfully complete a consulting assignment.

As ignorance has grown under the conditions of globalization, "rational planning" in the narrow sense of the word has become almost impossible. In fact, ignorance is the prerogative of the expert. Only the expert can assess the risk involved in planning under conditions of minimal knowledge and maximal ignorance. When the balance between what we know and what we do not know is tilted towards the latter, experts are needed to fill the void of ignorance with authorized opinions.

The social function of experts and consultants is, among other things, to enable and to legitimate political action. Without experts the political decision-making machine would not be able to function. Politicians and bureaucrats can, so to speak, "off-load" their responsibilities to experts, and can get easier off the hook if they fail in their assessment, because they can pass on the blame to experts without loosing their political legitimacy. This poses a problem for the legitimacy of the political system as a whole, as the accountability of decision makers is by-passed through an excessive use of experts (Reddy, 1996). In this context it may be wise to remember a statement made by US President Woodrow Wilson in a campaign speech in 1912, in which he said: "What I fear ... is a government of experts, God forbid that in a democratic country we should resign the task and give the government over to experts" (Smith, 1991).

7.1.3. *Who is a Consultant?*

Consultants are a special kind of experts. Consultants acquire, package and sell specific knowledge that is to be applied or acted on by their clients. In contrast university lecturers and members of research institutes or R&D divisions are supposed to create new knowledge, but also pass on generalized knowledge to a general public, mainly students and colleagues. University-produced knowledge has to be published to be valued. Consultants, however, have specific clients to whom specific confidential knowledge is delivered. Consultants are usually bound by a contract that demands confidentiality.

Consultants may work free-lance, often part-time or as employees of consultancy companies mostly with a high degree of freedom and responsibility. The word "consultant" in itself is interpreted differently by those that see themselves as working in the consulting business. The term itself is not protected and any person may use the designation "consultant" as he or she may like. This makes it difficult to define the field of consultancy and to give exact figures on how many consultancy firms and how many free-lance consultants operate in a given country, like Singapore or Malaysia. The Singapore Yellow Pages list 740 companies alone under the heading "management consultants", the Malaysian Yellow Pages 526. But there are many other categories from acoustical consultants to vibration measurements consultants. There are also swimming pool consultants, recreation program consultants, and image consultants. In the medical profession, the term consultant is also used in the sense, that it designates a medical practitioner, one might like to consult. In addition there are companies which would fit our definition but do not call themselves consultancy firms, but go under different labels. We shall therefore attempt to give a formal definition first and then list a number of significant clusters of companies and consultants that fall into our categories.

The following is a very short and formal definition of experts and consultants:

- An expert has obtained knowledge. He is a professional knowledge broker, a middleman between knowledge producers and knowledge users.
- A consultant is an expert, who acquires, packages and sells specific and confidential knowledge for a fee with the expectation that his knowledge is applied and his advice is acted upon.

7.1.4. *The Knowledge Market: Experts, Consulting Firms and Think-tanks*

The marketing of knowledge has, indeed, become a multi-billion Dollar business (see Fig. 7.2). There are about 100,000 people worldwide working full-time in the management consulting industry that generate about US$25 billion in annual revenues (Collis, 1998). The by now defunct US based firm Anderson Consulting, at times worldwide the largest consulting firm, employed less than 10,000 consultants in 1987. Their number increased to over 21,000 in 1991 and over 27,000 in 1994 (UN, 1993). More than half of these consultants worked in foreign countries outside the USA. The number of consultants in the ten largest companies increased by 99.6% between 1987 and 1994, the revenues by 221.6%. The rapid growth of the consulting industry is shown in Fig. 7.3.

Management is only one of many other fields of the consultancy industry, though most probably the most important in terms of turnover, profits and professionals employed.

Total Annual Revenues (in billions)

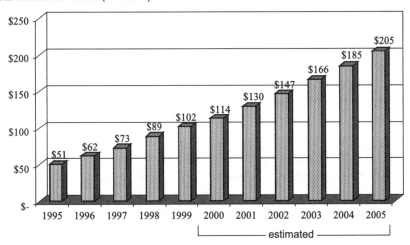

Fig. 7.2. Total annual revenues of the global consulting industry, 1995–2005.
Source: Kennedy Information Research Group (2001).

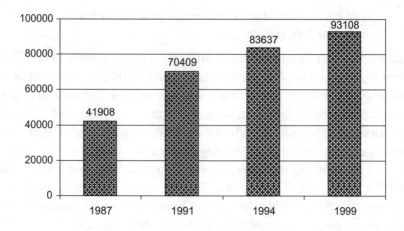

Fig. 7.3. Number of consultants, 1987–1999.
Source: Collis (1998); Lu (2002); United Nations (1993:13).

Experts and consulting firms sell what is considered to be superior knowledge. Consulting in engineering, business management, government development projects, construction of housing estates, setting up golf courses — and a host of other activities is carried out by local and foreign experts in many countries around the globe. To cite just one other example: In one field of consulting, namely development cooperation, we have estimated that there were approximately 42,000 professionals employed or self-employed in the Federal Republic of Germany in 2000/2001.[2]

The number of research institutes and think-tanks has proliferated, selling advice to private corporations and government departments. Though not all can turn in a profit from the marketing of expertise and knowledge, most of them can at least convince their governments, charitable foundations and other donor agencies that it is worthwhile to sink their money into institutions engaged in the production and sale of knowledge.

---

[2] Preliminary results of a survey within the research project on "Globalisation of Knowledge", carried out by Hans-Dieter Evers and Markus Kaiser.

Governments have become major consumers of knowledge, but so have large multinational corporations. It is very likely that the knowledge market is going to expand further as part of the expansion of the service sector. Experts, consultants and consultancy companies will be increasingly in demand with the spread of a knowledge society and the new economy.

Economic globalizations, the continuous influx of technological innovations, intense competition have made the world very complex for both small and large companies (McCune, 1997). Many large companies were forced to downsize and to become leaner. Hence they do not have sufficient internal staffs to get certain projects completed. As companies have cut back the number of middle managers, there are not enough executives for long term strategy planning and other corporate activities in an era of e-commerce and virtualization.

Due to the lack of qualified staff and size, even small and medium enterprise (SME) owners are increasingly forced to seek the services of external consultants (Cheok, 1991). Most SMEs are too small to justify specialized in-house staff to troubleshoot company problems, e.g. in terms of accounting or strategy or to employ HR specialists (Menkhoff and Kay, 2000; Nahavandi and Chesteen, 1988). Due to the structural peculiarities of SMEs, many small entrepreneurs do not systematically develop and upgrade their human resources or invest in information technology (Tung, 2002). As in other areas, management consultants have tried to fill this gap by providing virtual HR and other services.

External consultants are especially appreciated by management when there is an urgent need for outside help. The Asian crisis has been a major trigger in this respect, motivating managers of both small and large firms to approach external consultants for assisting them in restructuring operations and, more importantly, to prevent them from going into receivership and bankruptcy (Yoshihara, 1999). Due to Asia's economic downturn 1997–99, many local firms were forced to reposition their competitiveness, often with the help of external management consultants. Singaporean management consultants interviewed in the context of this study reported an increase in clients during the crisis as both small and large firms had not been spared from the rapidly changing environment and in view of their need for effective change consultants/OD specialists as facilitators of change processes.

We shall now discuss the case of the management consulting industry in Singapore, which appears to be well suited to illustrate some of the points made so far. Singapore is a small country of some 4 million inhabitants with no resources except its labor force and its location at the crossroads of shipping lanes from the Indian to the Pacific Ocean. The development of a knowledge economy is therefore the pronounced aim of the Singapore government. The infusion of knowledge through consulting services is the prime strategy employed by the government to overcome the Asian economic crisis of the late 1990s. The strategy is based on the assumption that knowledge rather than just capital is the source of increased productivity and economic growth.

7.2. Consulting Firms in Singapore

The field of consulting in Singapore is dominated by the big European and American Consulting giants on the one hand and the statutory bodies of the Singapore government on the other (see Fig. 7.4). According to a 1990 survey on the usage and provision of management consultancy services commissioned by the then National Productivity Board (NPB),[3] the total billings by management consultancy firms

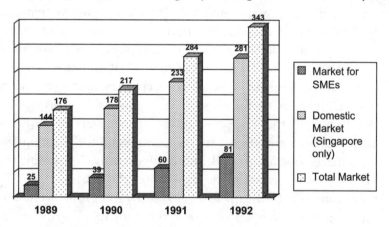

Fig. 7.4. Profile of the Singapore management consultancy market (in S$ million). Source: Cheak (1991:2).

---

[3]According to Singapore's Standards, Productivity and Innovation Board (SPRING Singapore) more recent figures/surveys are not available.

were expected to double from $175 million in 1989 to $342 million by 1992 (Cheok, 1991). The hiring of external experts allows both SMEs (small and medium enterprises) and larger firms to get important jobs done without adding employees or having an additional fixed cost. Such benefits were stressed by small Singaporean entrepreneurs who were interviewed in the context of a related study on change management practices (Menkhoff, 2001). As the owner of a small fish farm in Singapore who had enlisted external consultants to aid him in upgrading the firm's technology argued: "a good outsider can provide generic diversity to an inbred organization". Another local SME owner pointed out: "a consultant gives us an outside perspective and can act as a coach for change since we all have anxieties about the uncertainties of tomorrow" (Source: authors' interviews in 1999/2000).

The total number of staff in management consultancy firms in Singapore was estimated at about 2,800 in 1989, with an average of 14 staff per company (see Table 7.1). Some 50 management consultancy firms are organized in the Singapore Management Consultancy Association, which publishes a list of its members. Members are vetted by the Economic Development Board (EDB) and are allowed to

Table 7.1. Profile of the Singapore consulting industry, 1990.

- Over 200 firms employing 2,772 consultants
- Average strength:

Total Management	2
Managers	3
Senior Staff	5
Junior Staff	4
Total	14

- Breakdown of Most Common Consulting Products

	% of 1989 Billings
Computerization/IT usage	12
Productivity/Training	11
Financial Management	10

- 56% of consultancies have undertaken overseas assignments. 18% of total industry billings came from overseas assignments.

Source: Cheok (1991); De Guzman (1993).

receive subsidies set aside for consultations with emergent companies. EDB spends more than one billion S$ on loans to emerging companies, marketing support and consulting services. Very high sums are also allotted by the Standards, Productivity and Innovation Board (previously known as Productivity and Standards Board or PSB) and International Enterprise Singapore (previously known as Trade Development Board or TDB). The approved local companies get employed directly or indirectly by the big statutory boards, which also engage the services of the big multinational consultancy firms.

Big multinational corporations often contract the big consultancy corporations through their headquarters and local branches have to service the multinational corporations (MNCs) in Singapore and elsewhere in the region accordingly. Some key informants allege that despite all the rhetoric on globalization, the big companies engage increasingly only consultancy firms from their home-countries. Large corporations usually have their strategic planning departments in their headquarters rather than in Southeast Asia. They then order data from consultancy or market research firms, which they interpret themselves. They do not ask for knowledge but for information. There is tough competition but also some animosity between local and foreign consultancy firms.

In Singapore as elsewhere consulting firms depend on powerful clients such as governments or private sector firms who are willing to pay for the products and services being produced by them. How consulting firms are affected by the economic and political power of these primary stakeholders (power may be exercised through the refusal to pay, legislation, regulations, lawsuits, etc.) and how they initiate, structure, maintain and cultivate ties to them, however, is not easily analyzed. Academic studies on business networks and interlocking directorships in the US and elsewhere indicate that there might be a visible socio-economic network linking local consulting firms, government bodies and perhaps even some of their competitors characterized by active mutual networking activities and the exchange of resources such as knowledge. On the other hand there are tendencies to monopolize knowledge by creating management tools protected by copyrights. Thus the importance of *trade secrets* in the world of consulting suggests that the opposite is also possible, i.e., that networking is not that pronounced and confined, to a handful of knowledgeable individuals or knowledge brokers, propositions which should be further examined. In this context it would also be necessary to scrutinize the role of professional consulting associations such as Singapore's Institute of Management Consultants (ICM) as well as the consulting divisions of public sector clients. It appears that they function primarily to protect the interests of the industry rather than function as communities of practice or networks for the exchange of knowledge.

7.2.1. *Professional Associations*

Management consultants are often organized in a professional organization, like architects, accountants and similar professions. In Singapore, the Institute of Management Consultants (Singapore) was registered with the Registrar of Societies on 9 October 1992. It replaced the *Association of Management Consultants (AMC)* formed in 1986, the members of which comprised 44 consultancies including the consulting arms of all the big six accounting firms. On its formation IMC had 39 founder members, drawn from the existing membership of AMC. IMC's ordinary membership comprises individual members, not institutional members. IMC (Singapore) became a full member of the International Council of Management Consulting Institutes (ICMCI) on 1 January 1993. Through IMC's membership of ICMCI, Certified Management Consultants will have reciprocal recognition in the US, UK and other participating countries worldwide.

According to its prospectus, the prime object of the IMC is to promote the skills and knowledge of, and the adoption of the highest standards of conduct by, members of the management consulting profession. With the formation of IMC a process is now in place to certify management consultants in Singapore. Those who meet the criteria set could be admitted as Certified Members of the Institute and be entitled to use the designation CMC or Certified Management Consultant.

Certified members will be persons, age 30 or over, who are and have been engaged in management consultancy for 1200 hours per annum for three consecutive years immediately preceding the date of application and can demonstrate his/her competence and experience in management consultancy.

The situation in Singapore confirms a general trend in the consulting industry, namely an increasing professionalization of its practitioners. By adhering to standards of ethics and professionalism and by submitting themselves to the scrutiny of professional bodies consultants will be able to convince clients to trust their competence. The certification of its practitioners and generalization of quality standards can also be interpreted as a move to improve the knowledge management within the consulting firms and to turn them into intelligent organizations.

7.2.2. Educational Background and Life Histories of Consultants

So far we have only some tentative data on the education and job history of Singapore consultants. Work experience in a large MNC, a university education with an engineering or management degree, work with one of the large management consulting corporations seem to be a precondition for later free-lance work or for setting up of an own company. The guiding question appears to be which experience and knowledge is a precondition for making money. Academic knowledge as such is seen as totally irrelevant. In fact, most consultants hide their academic degree, as they do not wish to project an overly academic image. Clients may otherwise regard their analysis and advice as too for removed from reality, difficult to apply and in the long run irrelevant.[4]

Consultants take great care in "profiling" themselves. The word "consultant" in itself is constructed differently by those that see themselves as working in the consulting business. International consulting firms with branches in Singapore do not hesitate to advertise their "experience", "expertise", "their "professionals with extraordinary qualifications", "thought leaders", "innovators". They claim to possess "a tried and tested methodology", "high ethical standards", "rigorous quality standards". But despite all the boasting academic

---

[4]In the PSB survey mentioned earlier, "relevance of experience", "experience in consulting work for local companies" and "well trained staff" (rather than academic qualifications and cost of the consultancy project) were cited as the most important criteria for selecting a management consultant (see Cheok, 1991).

degrees are seldom mentioned. Local companies are more modest and also here academic degrees are seldom mentioned.

There seems to be an attempt to distance oneself from the producers of knowledge, though following a popular management guru is seen as a viable sales ploy. Interviews with consultants elsewhere in Southeast Asia confirm that many work in fields in which they have no formal training. In the process of their career they have gained "experience", which is held in great esteem. University education is seldom mentioned as a factor in professional attainment.

7.3. Constructing Virtual Problems and Offering Real Solutions

7.3.1. *Consultants as Change Agents, Catalysts, and Healers*

Consultants often play an important, catalytic role, e.g. in organizational change processes (French and Bell, 1978; Ginsberg and Abrahamson, 1991). They can assist key decision makers and others by contributing to the creation and evolution of new perspectives in business management, strategizing, organizational transition and so forth. Change is about taking people outside of their comfort zone. Management consultants and change agents in particular find themselves working simultaneously across the borders of conflicts and almost always outside their own comfort zones since they often challenge the existing cognitive order:

> "They state the obvious, ask foolish questions and doubt — all of which helps organizational members get outside of themselves" (Smircich and Stubbart, 1985:731).

External consultants have the advantage of being experienced observers and analysts which allows them to challenge previously established positions and/or ways of thinking. By ushering in new viewpoints, conceptualizations and jargon, they act like fashion setters, creating new frames of references that may force owners of both small and large firms to recognize the "antiquated" nature of previous strategic orientations and the criticality to embrace new business approaches and practices.

The role of external change advocates has been characterized as both holistic and healing. The change agent's concern is on alleviating problems in the organization's social system by focusing on past, present and future constructions of reality. By focusing on the past, a change agent acts as a guide for understanding the impact of past organizational events on the current context. By focusing on future realities in terms of probabilities, a change agent helps the client to trace the implications of alternative current time activities on effecting desired future realities.

One of the interviewed SME owners in our study on change management (Menkhoff and Kay, 2003) stated, "external change agents should act as doctors". He subscribed to the belief that change agents must be able to "heal the ailments" of his company:

> "... by transforming employees from behaving like stereotypical Chinese businessmen into actors who have adopted professional business practices".

As he pointed out, most of his staff members had been working for him for more than 15 years. But despite their loyalty, he found them unwilling to adapt to the changes he was trying to institute. He felt that "it is inevitable that they change". However, the external consultant he had hired was "not effective" because he had developed a "general strategy" for his company rather than catering to "individual needs". He would have preferred the consultant to work with individual employees and to "transform" them. The prescribed medicine apparently had no positive effect.

As with shamans, change agents are sometimes positioned as modern day medicine men (and women) that are expected to "cure" the organization even it is terminally ill. The concept of consultants as healers has been addressed by Barber and Nord (1977) who have argued that the true power of the external change agent as shaman lies in empowering and assisting others to determine their own process of change and offering a process for individual discovery and self healing. External change agents act as shamans in helping organizations to bridge the transition from former ways of acting, believing and being to new ones. In this way, external change agents act as spiritual guides in the transformational process (Beck and Beck, 1989). If the consultation is successful, the shamanic consultant's impact can indeed remain long after he or she has left the organization.

7.3.2. *Packaging Knowledge*

As we have argued above, the use of knowledge does not seem to suffer from the law of diminishing utility, but to the contrary entails increasing value the more it is applied or consumed. Packaging knowledge by using additional expertise is greatly enhancing the profitability of the product. Consultants therefore package their statements into beautiful graphics and slide shows so that the clients are convinced that they buy a valuable product. Constructing virtual realities is one of the specialties of consultants.

In analyzing problems they, in a way, sometimes create them in the first place. They then suggest solutions to the problems they have constructed beforehand. Constructing virtual problems and then offering real solutions appears to be the mainstay of the consulting business.

Consultancy in general and management consultancy in particular have to rely on theories and concepts that are regarded as valid. At least clients of consultants have to be convinced that they are being treated to the latest and most up-to-date knowledge. Management "gurus" appear to play a major role in this game by providing simple and easy to remember principles according to which a company should be "turned around" or "restructured". Lean administration, knowledge management, outsourcing, change management and similar terms are used to scale complicated procedures down to manageable and understandable pieces of information. It is, however, necessary to attach legitimacy to a concept by referring to its source, its pedigree and its context. It is important to turn a concept or strategy into a "tool", i.e., to make it applicable in a practical way.

This issue is of particular relevance to the practice of consultants in developing areas (Evers, Kaiser and Mueller, 2003). Development experts are used to transmit knowledge to underdeveloped countries to assist in the design and implementation of development projects. To this avail they first have to define and therefore "create" underdevelopment in fact finding missions, feasibility studies and project proposals.[5] A country becomes "least developed" if UNDP defines it as such; handicraftsmen and petty traders are defined as an "informal sector" and thus transformed into a target group for development assistance; women are transformed from "not gainfully employed" housewives to "women in development", thus enabling consultants to suggest adding a "women component" to a development project.

Experts and consultants use a special kind of language that contains key words and metaphors that are defined as legitimate. Imposing an "authorized way of seeing the social world helps to construct the reality of that world" (Bourdieu, 1991:106). Concepts and strategies used or advocated by consultants, emanate from centres of power as "authorized language", are propagated by spokespersons and eagerly marketed to, accepted by or forced upon experts as practitioners of knowledge. They, in turn, disseminate their knowledge to their target group or client. Evaluating the success or failure of a consultancy is often based on the elegance of report writing rather than the actual performance of the involved consultants. Choosing the right language and the appropriate concepts is an essential prerequisite for success.

7.4. Trends: Consultants in the New Economy

As the New Economy is taking shape and the demand for expert knowledge is, according to our analysis, rising, consultants are faced by a number of challenges, which can be briefly summarized as follows:

- Knowledge becomes easily available on the Internet. The question is therefore frequently asked whether expert knowledge is still necessary. In this case the value of the information available through the Internet is probably overestimated. It requires further specific

---

[5]We are here deliberately following a line of argument that was forcefully developed by Michel Foucault. In his study "Madness and Civilization" (1965) he had shown how knowledge and power were combined to define insanity. The language of psychiatry, he argues, is "a monologue of reason about madness" and a failure to listen to those labelled "mad" (Foucault, 1965:xii-xiii). If we substitute "madness" with "underdevelopment" and "psychiatry" with "development economics", we may reach similar conclusions as Foucault.

knowledge to combine various sets of data and information, to evaluate them through "best practices" in order to create new knowledge and solutions to new problems.

- Intelligent firms create their own proprietary knowledge. With the
growth of the "knowledgeable company" and knowledge management, the expertise of consultants might become obsolete. Empirical
evidence points into a different direction. Consultants have to live
up to the challenge and have to be one step ahead of competitors
and clients. They have to introduce structures and processes that are
superior and more intelligent than those in place at their client organizations. As this becomes increasingly difficult they have to resort to
impression management and to inventing new epistemic constructs
different from those known to clients. Strategic alliances and mergers
between consulting firms could be seen as another consequence of
the mounting pressure of the IT revolution. Larger units are able to
provide "one-stop-solutions" to engage in "butterfly collections" of
best practices and to "add value". Consultancy firms have to become
"intelligent organizations" themselves.

- Consultants have to give advice to clients by making them familiar
with new knowledge, but they also have to keep their knowledge a
secret. Once their experience and knowledge is commonly known,
their consulting services are no longer needed. Consultants need
networks to get access to new information, but have to keep this
information to themselves as long as possible. New tools have to
be invented or recycled. The fast development of information technology has decreased the survival time of management consultancy
tools and concepts. "Trade secrets" have become more important
but are more difficult to maintain. Intellectual property rights are
therefore emphasized by countries that produce knowledge. Franchising management concepts and tools can be seen as a move into
the direction of safeguarding or monopolizing knowledge.

- Consultants can no longer rely on "bench-marking" based on experience, but have to engage in knowledge production themselves.
This may in the long run be only feasible in larger consulting
corporations that are able to maintain their own research and development divisions.

We predict that the future of the consulting profession will to no small degree depend on the solution to these problems. As we have now successfully increased "ignorance" by posing questions we are not able to answer at this stage, we in true consultancy fashion may now plead that further research on the topic will be necessary.

References

Albrow, M. and E. King (eds.) (1981). *Globalization, Knowledge and Society*. London: Sage Publications.

Barber, W.H. and W.R. Nord (1977). Transactions between Consultants and Clients: A Taxonomy. *Group and Organization Studies*, 1(2), 198–215.

Beck, J.C. and M.N. Beck (1989). The Cultural Buffer: Managing Human Resources in an International Business Context. Paper presented at the International Conference on Personnel and Human Resource Management, December, Hong Kong.

Beck, U. (1992). *Risk Society: Towards a New Modernity*. London/Newbury Park, California: Sage Publications.

Bourdieu, P. (1991). *Language and Symbolic Power*. Cambridge: Polity Press.

Cheok, J. (1991). The Growing Management Consultancy Industry. *Productivity Digest*, 2–5 February.

Collis, D.J. (1998). The Management Consulting Industry. In *Career Guide Management Consulting*, A.R. Miller (ed.). Harvard Business School in association with the Harvard Business School Management Consulting Club.

De Guzman, D.S. (1993). The Management Consultant: Role and Opportunities. Paper presented at the Management Consultants Seminar held at Pinetree Town & Country Club from 7–9 October 1993 organized by the Institute of Management Consultants.

Drucker, P.F. (1994). *Postcapitalist Society*. New York: Harper Business.

Evers, H.-D. (2000a). Globalisation, Local Knowledge and the Growth of Ignorance: The Epistemic Construction of Reality. *Southeast Asian Journal of Social Science*, 28(1), 13–22.

Evers, H.-D. (2000b). *Epistemic Cultures: Towards a New Sociology of Knowledge*. Working Paper No. 151, Department of Sociology, National University of Singapore.

Evers, H.-D. (2003). Transition towards a Knowledge Society: Malaysia and Indonesia in Comparative Perspective. *Comparative Sociology*, 2(1), 355–373.

Evers, H.-D. and S. Gerke (1997). Global Market Cultures and the Construction of Modernity in Southeast Asia. *Thesis Eleven*, 50(August), 1–14.

Evers, H.-D., M. Kaiser and S. Mueller (2003). Entwicklung durch Wissen — Eine Neue Globale Wissensarchitektur. *Soziale Welt*, 54, 49–70.

Foucault, M. (1965). *Madness and Civilization*. Paris: Libraire Plon.

French, W.L. and C.H. Bell, Jr. (1978). *Organizational Development — Behavioral Science Interventions for Organization Improvement*. Englewood Cliffs, NJ: Prentice Hall.

Ginsberg, A. and E. Abrahamson (1991). Champions of Change and Strategic Shifts: The Role of Internal and External Change Advocates. *Journal of Management Studies*, March, 174–189.

Hitzler, R., Honer, A. and C. Maeder (eds.) (1994). *Expertenwissen, Die Institutionalisierte Kompetenz zur Konstruktion von Wirklichkeit*. Opladen: Westdeutscher Verlag.

Kennedy Information Research Group (2001). *The Global Consulting Marketplace: Key Data, Forecasts and Trends*. Peterborough, NH: Kennedy Information, Inc.

Knorr-Cetina, K. (1998). *Epistemic Cultures, How Science Makes Sense*. Cambridge, MA: Harvard University Press.

Lu, M. (ed.) (2002). *The Harvard Business School Guide to Careers in Management Consulting*. Harvard Business School in association with the Harvard Business School Management Consulting Club.

Mander, J. and E. Goldsmith (1996). *The Case against the Global Economy (and for a Turn Towards the Local)*. San Francisco, CA: Sierra Books.

McCune, J. (1997). The Consultant Quandary. *World Executive Digest*, December.

Menkhoff, T. (2001). Beyond the Asian Crisis — How Singapore's Small Entrepreneurs Manage Change. *Productivity Digest* (ed. by Singapore Productivity and Standards Board), 20(2), 22–26.

Menkhoff, T. and L. Kay (2000). Managing Organizational Change and Resistance in Small and Medium-Sized Family Firms. *Research and Practice in Human Resource Management*, 8(1), 153–172.

Menkhoff, T. and L. Kay (2003). Change Management and Consultants — New Challenges for Small Entrepreneurs in Singapore. In *Approaching Transnationalism: Transnational Societies, Multicultural Contacts, and Imaginings of Home*, B. Yeoh, C.K. Tong and M. Charney (eds.). Kluwer Academic Press.

Nahavandi, A. and S. Chesteen (1988). The Impact of Consulting on Small Business: A Further Examination. *Entrepreneurship Theory and Practice*, 13, 29–40.

Reddy, S.G. (1996). Claims to Expert Knowledge and the Subversion of Democracy: The Triumph of Risk over Uncertainty. *Economy and Society*, 25(2), 222–254.

Smircich, L. and C. Stubbart (1985). Strategic Management in an Enacted World. *Academy of Management Review*, 10, 724–736.

Smith, J.A. (1991). *The Idea Brokers, Think Tanks and the Rise of the New Policy Elite*. New York: The Free Press.

Tuggle, F.D. and W.E. Goldfinger (2004). A Methodology for Mining Embedded Knowledge From Process Maps. *Human Systems Management*, 23(1), 1–13.

Tung, L.-L. (2002). Information Kiosks: Singapore Users' Experience. *Human Systems Management*, 21(1), 21–41.

United Nations (1993). Management Consulting — A Survey of the Industry and its Largest Firms. In *UN Conference on Trade and Development, Programme on Transnational Corporations*. New York: UN.

Yoshihara, K. (1999). Building a Prosperous Southeast Asia. In *Ersatz* to *Echt Capitalism*. Richmond: Curzon.

Chapter 8

Building Vibrant Science and Technology Parks with Knowledge Management: Trends in Singapore[1]

Thomas Menkhoff, Hans-Dieter Evers, Marshall W. Meyer and Lionel Meng Huat Lim

8.1. Singapore: Towards a Knowledge-Based Economy

Singapore, a small city-state of over 4 million population, does not have any natural resources except its people. After an initial phase of export-oriented industrialization the Singapore government shifted its policy during the early 1990s to a state-led development of knowledge-based, high value added, high-tech industries and a knowledge-based service sector. A recent report on the state of the economy describes the road map to Singapore's future as follows: "As the Singapore economy develops it can no longer rely on the accumulation of capital and labor to sustain economic growth. Singapore needs to further develop its KBE (knowledge-based economy), deriving its growth from the production, dissemination and application of knowledge" (Toh, Tang and Choo, 2002). Earlier the foundation of a National Science and Technology Board in 1991 had marked the beginning of a massive government-led drive to improve the technology base of the Singaporean economy. A Strategic Economic Plan of 1991

[1]This is a revised version of an invited paper presented at the International Knowledge Management (KM) Challenge Conference (Theme: "Driving Performance through Knowledge Collaboration") in Sydney, Australia, 30th–31st March 2004. The conference was organized by Standards Australia International Limited (Sydney, Australia). The authors gratefully acknowledge the support they received from Ascendas Pte. Ltd., and other interviewees who took part in the exploratory research.

165

identified strategic clusters of manufacturing and services earmarked for government support. The Singapore Science Park was set up to facilitate research and development and to host the R&D activities of high-tech corporations and agencies. Various scholarship schemes were launched to train young scientists abroad. The National Information Infrastructure (NII), which was started in 1992 with the objective to employ a broad-band national network, has meanwhile been implemented (Low and Kuo, 1999).

During the Asian financial crisis it became clear that standard technology, like the production of mass storage devices, could no longer be sustained in the face of competition from China. Singapore has to concentrate on new, innovative technologies to maintain a competitive edge. This would only be possible, if the knowledge base of the economy would be further strengthened. The idea that knowledge had become the major factor of production was picked up quickly by Singaporean economists and the planners of the powerful Economic Development Board (EDB). The drive for a broader defined knowledge-based economy per se was outlined in government documents in 1999. A ten-year plan (Industry 21) showed the path to "develop Singapore into a vibrant and robust global hub of knowledge industries in manufacturing and traded services, giving new emphasis to knowledge-based activities as the frontier of competitiveness' (Chia and Lim, 2003). The situation became more urgent, when in 2001–2 the knowledge-intensive semiconductor producers experienced a severe downturn.

The Singapore government reorganized and re-named the statuary boards that had been responsible for the development of a high-tech industrial base. The National Science and Technology Board (NSTB) was re-organized and became the Agency for Science, Technology and Research (A*Star). This organization established two research councils, The Biomedical Research Council and the Science and Engineering Research Council, to support private sector research and development. It also formed Exploit Technologies Pte. Ltd. to safeguard and market intellectual property and the patents created by its research institutes. During the 1990s and into the new century a massive recruitment drive brought in foreign nationals that by 2001 made up about a quarter of the knowledge workers engaged in R&D (A*Star, 2002). The percentage of foreigners in the research institutes is even higher. This may be interpreted as an indicator of Singapore's high degree of globalization, but has also raised concern over Singapore's increased dependence on foreign talents.

There was also massive investment in institutions of higher learning. The two older universities NUS (National University of Singapore) and NTU (Nanyang Technological University) were complemented by a new government financed, but privately run institution, the Singapore Management University (SMU) with an undergraduate training programme modeled after the famous Wharton School (US) which had a management contract with SMU in the early stages. In 2003/4 the construction of a new complex named "Biopolis" (http://www.nstb.gov.sg/astar/biopolis/action/biopolis.do) was completed. This "biomedical city", situated at the Buona Vista Science Hub, will house the Genome Institute of Singapore (GIS), a research institute affiliated to A*Star, together with the Singapore Institute of Molecular Biology, the BioTechnology Centre, the Bioinformatics Institute, the Institute of Biomedical Engineering and other R&D organizations. Biotechnology will be one of the four pillars of a knowledge-based economy prioritized by the Singapore government.[2]

The GIS promises to develop a culture of excellence and innovation that is "conducive for collaboration between scientists from diverse cultural and social backgrounds" (Institute Prospectus). The multicultural environment is a theme that is emphasised in government position papers since the mid 1990s.

The output of the emerging knowledge-based economy of Singapore so far has been impressive. The number of patents filed has increased from 902 in 2000 to 1,096 in 2001; about half of them were filed in cooperation with other countries. 41% of the patents filed with others were the result of cooperation with the US (see Table 8.1), a country Singapore depends more and more in the sphere of knowledge governance.

In 2001 R&D expenditure has reached already 2.11% of Singapore's GDP, in comparison with Germany's 2.52% or Korea's 2.68%. Singapore is fast catching up with the OECD countries (see Tables 8.2 and 8.3).

---

[2]In the Singapore context, future growth industries include biotechnology/biological sciences, microelectronics, robotics & artificial intelligence, information technology, laser technology & electro-optics, and communications technology.

Table 8.1. Patents filed in cooperation with other countries, Malaysia and
Singapore, 2000.

Cooperation with	Malaysia		Singapore	
	Patents	%	Patents	%
France	2	1,9	19	4,6
Germany	14	13,1	64	15,4
Other EU	15	14,0	39	9,4
Australia	6	5,6	15	3,6
Japan	14	13,1	30	7,2
Switzerland	—		22	5,3
United Kingdom	15	14,0	46	11,1
United States	28	26,2	173	41,7
Others	13	12,1	7	1,7
Total co-operation with abroad	107		415	
Total Patents	211		975	

Source: Compiled from the OECD Data Base 2003.

Table 8.2. Research and development expenditures,
Singapore, 1992–2001.

Year	R&D expenditure, million S$	% of GDP
1992	949.3	1.19
1993	998.2	1.07
1994	1175.0	1.10
1995	1366.6	1.16
1996	1792.1	1.40
1997	2104.5	1.50
1998	2492.3	1.81
1999	2656.3	1.90
2000	3009.5	1.88
2001	3232.7	2.11

Source: A*Star (2002).

The register of Singapore's successes and challenges ahead in reaching knowledge-society status could be prolonged, but we shall rather
look at the role of the Singapore Science Park in achieving K-economy
status. In doing so we draw attention to the idea that the process

Table 8.3. R&D activities in selected countries, ranked by R&D expenditures.

Country	Expenditures on R&D as a percentage of GNP 1985–95	Number of RSEs per million people 1985–95	High — technology exports	
			$ millions	Percentage of manufactured exports
Sweden	3.4	3714	21969	34
Japan	2.9	6309	152431	38
Korea	2.8	2636	44433	39
Finland	2.5	2812	8797	26
US	2.5	3732	197657	44
France	2.4	2584	68655	31
UK	2.2	2417	95755	41
Denmark	1.9	2647	8174	27
Norway	1.8	3678	2703	24
Australla	1.7	3166	6415	1.7
Belgium	1.7	1814	—	—
Canada	1.6	2656	33608	25
Italy	1.1	1325	32747	15
Singapore	1.1	2728	74585	71
India	0.8	149	2654	11
Indonesia	0.8	—	4474	20
South Africa	0.7	938	—	—
Brazil	0.6	168	5175	18
China	0.5	350	33344	21
Argentina	0.4	671	1355	15
Malaysia	0.4	87	39490	67
Mexico	0.4	213	29692	33
Hong Kong (China)	0.3	98	7392	29
Phillippines	0.2	157	6249	56
Thailand	0.1	119	17758	43

Note: Not all countries are reflected in the table here as there are more than 250 countries in the original source.
Source: http://www.statistics.com; accessed in July 2002.
Source: Philips and Yeung (2003:715).

of knowledge governance and knowledge creation has *cultural* implications. The manufacture of knowledge cannot be explained and stimulated as a rational process alone as it rests as much on social interaction, life-world experience and culture. To develop a productive (epistemic) culture of knowledge production in Science Parks is challenging (Knorr, 1999; Evers, 2000). The preconditions for the development and growth of such knowledge cultures and their shape and contents should be investigated and understood to explain the morpohology of knowledge production, the mountains and valleys in the landscape of an emerging global knowledge society such as Singapore (Evers, 2004). This chapter seeks to contribute to this task by providing tentative answers to the following questions:

- What is going on at the Singapore Science Park and how does it support Singapore's development towards a knowledge–based economy?
- What is being done in terms of administrative processes to realize the vision of Singapore's policy-makers to create a culture of innovation in the Park and beyond, and how effective are these initiatives?
- How can knowledge management help to further transform the Singapore Science Park into a truly smart habitat for the intended cross-fertilization of talents and ideas as well as the creation of new knowledge, e.g. in the form of product innovations?
- What has been achieved? What are the challenges ahead?

8.2. Creating a Focal Point for Research, Development and Innovation: The Singapore Science Park

8.2.1. *What is a Science Park?*

According to the IASP International Board:

"A Science Park is an organisation managed by specialised professionals, whose main aim is to increase the wealth of its community by promoting the *culture of innovation* and the competitiveness of its associated businesses and knowledge-based institutions. To enable these goals to be met, a Science Park stimulates and manages the flow of knowledge and technology amongst universities, R&D institutions, companies and markets; it facilitates the creation and growth of innovation-based companies through incubation and spin-off processes; and provides other value-added services together with high quality space and facilities" (IASP International Board, 6 February 2002).

The Singapore Science Park is a specific state-initiated corporate entity to boost R&D in Singapore (http://www.singaporesciencepark. com/home/index.asp). Its origin can be traced back to the late 1970s when policy-makers and planners started to discuss the need for a national R&D programme and a more conducive R&D environment aimed at giving Singapore's industrialization a further boost and to enhance the country's competitiveness in an increasingly global economy (Rodan, 1989). As pointed out by Phillips and Yeung (2003:714), the successful development of the Jurong industrial zone (as vehicle for export-led growth) served as role model. In 1980, the Singapore Science Park was set up "as a place where R&D can converge and create synergies with institutions and firms alike, and researchers can work anytime, meet and share ideas" (NSTB spokesman interviewed by Phillips and Yeung, 2003:715). The active involvement of the powerful Economic Development Board (EDB) and the Jurong Town Corporation (JTC) in the planning and creation process of the Science Park underlined the strategic importance of R&D in Singapore's official economic policy. According to records from Ascendas,[3] the Park was literally a brainchild of the then chairman of the Jurong Town Corporation, Mr. Tang I-Fang.

In 1990 the management of the park — which is strategically located in Singapore's so-called Technology Corridor (see below) — was privatized as the erstwhile Technology Parks Pte. Ltd., since renamed as Ascendas Pte. Ltd., so as to achieve greater responsiveness to market conditions and to improve customer service quality. Ascendas is responsible for the Park's overall property development, marketing and management (amongst its other industrial and business parks in Singapore and other countries in Asia).

When the idea of establishing a science park in Singapore was first discussed in the late 1970s, it received mixed reactions just like the

---

[3]A wholly-owned subsidiary of JTC Corporation (JTC) since its incorporation, Ascendas is the developer and manager of the Singapore Science Park. It was originally known as Technology Parks Pte. Ltd. in 1990 and renamed as Arcasia Land Pte. Ltd. in April 1997. Subsequently it assumed a new identity as Ascendas Pte. Ltd. on 8 January 2001 following its merger with JTC International, the regional subsidiary of JTC.

National Technology Plan announced by the NSTB (now A*Star; see http://www.a-star.gov.sg) in 1991 or the recent expansion of the biomedical sciences cluster (Coe and Kelly, 2000; Koh, Koh and Tschang, 2004). Issues included cost concerns, the lack of a critical mass of knowledge workers, difficulties in transforming the educational system so as to promote greater risk-taking, entrepreneurial dynamism and creativity. Critics stressed that Singapore might fail in transforming itself into a knowledge-based economy and to replicate Silicon Valley or Hsinchu due to a limited talent pool, the dearth of energetic techno-entrepreneurs, innovative mindsets and supportive institutions such as venture capital firms. Looking back, the Park's track record looks pretty impressive.

The number of companies has grown from 117 in 1994 to a total of approximately 250 in 2004, including several "research facilities". Academic support is provided by its neighbor, the National University of Singapore (NUS). Comprising both local and non-local firms, the Park has attracted big MNCs such as Sony, ExxonMobil, Silicon Graphics, Seagate and Avaya (formerly known as Lucent Technologies) as well as small and medium enterprises (SMEs) and start-ups.

Local R&D facilitators include the Singapore Productivity, Innovation and Standards Board (SPRING) and the Infocomm Development Authority (IDA). The Economic Development Board provides various R&D benefits and incentives for tenants in form of the so-called Research and Development Assistance Scheme (RDAS)[4] or the Research Incentive Scheme for Companies (RISC). Another key player is the Agency for Science, Technology and Research or A*Star, the former National Science and Technology Board (NSTB), whose goal is to "create knowledge and to exploit scientific discoveries for a better world by fostering world-class scientific research and nurturing world-class scientific talent for a vibrant knowledge-based Singapore" (source: *http://www.nstb.gov.sg/astar/index.do*).

Many of the companies in the Science Park belong to the information technology sector, incl. electronics, telecommunication and life sciences. The tenants' profile is in line with the premises of the National

---

[4]Please refer to Appendix 8.1 on more details about the RDAS and RISC schemes provided by the EDB of Singapore.

Technology Plan which identifies various main R&D areas: information technology (IT), manufacturing and engineering technology, pharmaceuticals, telecommunications, chemicals, electronics and, lately, the life sciences.

8.2.2. *What is Going on Inside the Park in Terms of R&D and Innovation?*

What is really going on inside the Park in terms of R&D, knowledge creation, etc., and what are the outcomes?

To measure the breadth and depth of R&D activities in the Singapore Science Park is difficult due to enormous variations amongst the tenants and their respective research and/or development measures. Proxy input indicators include R&D expenditures, the number of knowledge workers (researchers, scientists, engineers), etc. as well as proxy output indicators such as major developments in form of products and services or patents. The measurement of such performance indicators and Science Park metrics in combination with an in-depth examination of success stories of successful networkers and innovators amongst tenants may enhance our understanding of the Park's productivity. Little is known about the social dynamics amongst tenant firms and their internal/external embeddedness, i.e., interactions both within the Park and with the outside world of science and technology.

A survey by Philips and Yeung (2003) of the Singapore Science Park suggests that creating R&D places and to enrich them by promoting and developing a culture of innovation is challenging. According to their analysis, there is a wide variation amongst the tenants[5] in terms of main activities and R&D, ranging from marketing, testing and inspection to applied R&D. Out of 34 firms surveyed by the authors (see Fig. 8.1), 16 (47%) were not engaged in R&D activities (of which 11 were foreign firms). As the representative of a small

---

[5]In 2000, about 50% of the tenants listed in the Park's tenant directory were foreign firms (27% American, 11% European, 9% Japanese and 3% from other countries). Most local firms were small and medium-sized establishments (70%); 23% were start-ups; and the rest were research institutes.

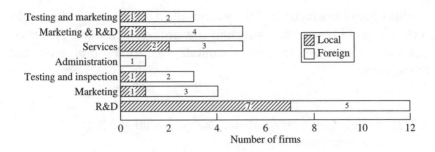

Fig. 8.1. Summary of tenant firms' main activities.

Source: Philips and Yeung (2003:721).

Japanese food/flavours sales office stressed: "There is only my boss and myself. R&D is done in Japan. Over here, we sell the R&D products' (Phillips and Yeung, 2003:721). A Japanese electronics firm was found to provide mainly software and support services to the parent firm in Japan. According to the authors, this finding is significant as it underlines a trend detected in other studies on R&D, namely that foreign subsidiaries of Japanese electronics and computer firms as tenants of science and technology parks do not necessarily drive the establishment of intimate *local* innovation networks due to their close ties to their parent firms abroad.

A representative of a pharmaceutical start-up described the firm's activity as the "organization of clinical research and testing of drugs to prove their effectiveness" (Phillips and Yeung, 2003:722). The actual testing, however, is done overseas while the Singapore office allows the firm to get in touch with customers. In the past, Singapore has attracted largely pharmaceutical business headquarters while R&D-based operations were difficult to set up due to the lack of a critical mass of experts such as researchers, scientists and engineers. However, it should be noted that the landscape of (innovative) R&D in the pharmaceutical sector is rapidly changing as shown by the rapid progress of the recent *Biopolis* initiative of the Singapore Government (http://www.nstb.gov.sg/astar/biopolis/action/biopolis.do).

As Phillips and Yeung (2003:722) have pointed out, national research institutes are more active and productive in terms of R&D as well as more embedded in the Park "because of their institutional origins" and availability of "Singapore government funds". The two institutes surveyed by the authors above employed more than 40 researchers, scientists and engineers and had received a number of benefits[6] from official incentive schemes and produced several "major developments" in form of product innovations. Rising expenditures, however, makes it increasingly difficult to make research pay for itself. The provision of testing and inspection services to private firms represent important income-generating activities but they can not be an *Ersatz* for sparkling business/product *ideas*, technological capabilities or the embeddedness in (vibrant) entrepreneurial and marketing/production networks.

8.3. Building a Vibrant Culture of Knowledge Transfer and Creation

8.3.1. *Singapore's Technology Corridor*

The construction of an effective and innovative culture of knowledge production or "knowledge habitat" is seen by many as a crucial precondition for the creation of new knowledge and product/service innovations (Keeble *et al.*, 1999). As Schrage (1997:173) puts it, it takes shared space to create shared understandings and hence to generate new knowledge, e.g. through the combination of various knowledge resources and competencies via knowledge transfer (Nonaka, 1995). In the case of Singapore, administrators, policy planners and technocrats have been proactive in promoting an "innovative milieu" and conducive R&D environment in certain spaces and areas. The establishment and continuous reinvention of institutions such as the National Science and Technology Board (NSTB)/Agency for Science, Technology and Research (A*Star) aimed at providing support for R&D and the exploitation of scientific knowledge as new factor of production in the resource-poor island republic or the development of challenging (stretch) master plans represent key measures in this respect.

---

[6]Please refer to Appendix 8.2 for a list of incentive schemes offered by the EDB of Singapore to the research institutes.

The central location of the Singapore Science Park can be traced back to the National Technology Plan (NTP) formulated in 1991 which mapped out a *technology corridor* along the south-western area of Singapore in line with the Strategic Economic Plan (Ministry of Trade and Industry, 1991). The blueprint for the technology corridor has contributed to the spatial integration of science habitats, business parks and tertiary institutions.

The Singapore Science Park (Fig. 8.2) is strategically located within this corridor in close proximity (1 km radius) to the National University of Singapore, the National University Hospital and such research institutions as the Institute of High Performance Computing etc. as well as national agencies like the DSTA (Defence Science Technology Agency). Proximity is the key, and there is no doubt that the tenant firms within the park can potentially benefit from such geographical

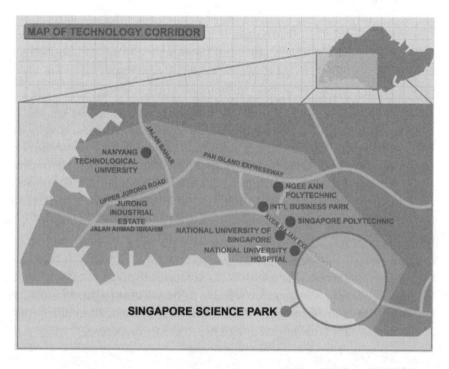

Fig. 8.2. Location of the Singapore Science Park and Technology Corridor.
Source: http://www.singaporesciencepark.com/about/where.asp.

advantages and agglomeration economies. Planners hope that networking among R&D companies, academia and research institutes will result in collaborative R&D projects (see Fig. 8.5).

8.4. "Craft, Create and Connect" — The Role of Ascendas Pte. Ltd.[7]

A key real estate player which is trying to promote a culture of innovation in the Singapore Science Park is Ascendas Pte. Ltd., a "synergistic merger" between Arcasia Land and JTC International's Business Parks and Facilities Group. The organization is a renowned provider of *total business space solutions* and develops, manages and markets science, business, industrial and hi-tech parks. Its office is located in Singapore Science Park I. Its mission is to *create total business environments that inspire people to excel*. Its vision is to *provide a focal point for R&D and innovation in Singapore and the region*. What can "crafting agencies" such as Ascendas as officially manager of the Singapore Science Park do to create an innovative climate in technology organizations (e.g. by connecting knowledge workers locally as well as regionally/globally) and how can knowledge management help?

The organization is renown in Singapore and beyond for their award-winning properties and high standards of real estate management. Ascendas pioneered the technology park concept with the Singapore Science Park, and has successfully exported this model to Asian markets. Its *total business space solutions* are categorized into IT, research, specialized, etc. space solutions, which include value-added amenities, business networking and even e-infrastructure services.

Science Park tenants can benefit from "broadband-enabled hi-tech facilities set in landscaped work-play environments" and can choose either "prepared land or ready-built fitted units" for their operations. With such physical space solutions (Fig. 8.3), Ascendas wants to provide a conducive environment for innovative research and development activities. Ascendas offers a wide array of e-services

---

[7]See Appendix 8.2 for an overview about the milestones of Ascendas.

| The Rutherford | The Aquarius | The Galen | Teletech Park |
| The Alpha | The Aries | The Capricorn | The Gemini |

Fig. 8.3. Examples of Ascendas' space solutions in the Singapore Science Park. Source: http://www.singaporesciencepark.com/bss/it.asp.

at competitive cost for their tenants located in science parks, business and industrial parks and commercial buildings. The goal is to offer tenants "one-stop business space-related services", including high quality broadband, telecommunication, and IT services. Tenants can benefit from "plug-and-play convenience, lower investment in office start-up cost and economies of scale". In terms of international networking with other science parks and incubation centres, Ascendas maintains partnerships with Sophia Antipolis Science Park (France), Heidelberg Technology Park (Germany), Alberta Research Council (Canada), Technopolis (Finland), Zernike (Australia) and International Business Incubator (US). This allows tenants to "explore synergies" and "network and collaboration opportunities" locally as well as overseas (source: http://www.ascendas.com/bss/networking.asp). Ascendas has also established ties with reputable tertiary institutions like the National University of Singapore (NUS) and the Nanyang Technological University, Singapore (NTU) with regard to "internships, job placements and business matching as a win-win value-add to the institutions and its tenants companies".

As part of the so-called "market access program", Ascendas maintains a network of "alliance partners" aimed at providing customers with "fee-based market access services" in form of "market research, business development, market entry strategies, market and financial planning, partner sourcing, capital fund raising, competitor benchmarking, regulatory, compliance and advisory services". Core of the "client promotion program" is an e-newsletter through which tenants can promote products, technologies, applications and services within the "Ascendas community of client companies and business associates". Other client promotion tools include print and broadcast media. The objective of the "business matching program" is to match customers with suitable business and/or technology partners to create new business opportunities and collaborations. Prospective clients can benefit from Ascendas' huge network of alliance partners in areas such as science and technology.

Ascendas can also help client firms in recruiting knowledge workers and experts due to its wide network of ties and links, e.g. with higher educational institutions in the region and beyond. The facilitation of cross-border internship opportunities enables tenant firms to tap on competencies of undergraduate and post-graduate students from various institutions of higher learning. Both participating companies and interns are stand to benefit as cost-effectiveness is crucial for business and students are provided with the opportunity to gather practical work experiences which might help them in securing a job later (source: http://www.singaporesciencepark.com/services/services.asp).

8.5. Creating a "smart" Science and Technology Park with Knowledge Management — Towards a KM Framework for Science Parks

The short summary of the various services and programmes provided by Ascendas (see above) suggests that "connecting" is a strategic element of STP business models which can add value to the operations of tenants. From a practical point of view, however, the question is whether connectivity options lead to actual collaborations and tangible outcomes such as product innovations.

Tenant firms are often selected by the management teams of science and technology parks with a view of generating a *communal* business environment in which on-site companies and K-based organizations interact, opportunities for technology transfer and development arise and activities between tenant companies and academic institutes will be possible. We argue that the challenges professional management teams of Science Parks are facing in building sparkling, intelligent parks where new knowledge is generated and exchanged, learning takes place and new ideas are brought to market are similar to that of knowledge (management) champions in corporations who make strategic use of knowledge management tools to enhance competitive advantage (see Chapter 10 in this book). Like in business organizations, the professional management teams of STPs who intend to transform these parks into true learning districts have to "enable" KM to use a popular phrase coined by management consultants. According to KM gurus such as Skyrme (1999; 2001), crucial enablers and factors include *leadership, culture, processes, explicit and tacit knowledge, knowledge hubs and centres, market leverage, measures, people/skills and HRM practices as well as technology*. A brief review of these components might be helpful in illustrating crucial "body parts" of an effective KM system for STPs as indicated in Table 8.4.

Our own interview data suggest that Ascenda's top management team is committed to the implementation of knowledge management within the Singapore Science Park and that it wishes to learn more about the determinants (and outcomes) of successful collaborations and networking activities. The evolving KM system is linked to its business *strategy* as indicated by the ongoing creation of a *tenant portal* as a platform to exchange information and knowledge amongst tenant firms. Interviewees referred to the intelligent business space provided by Ascendas as "exchange space aimed at knowledge sharing". The seamless integration of data and voice band with services represents a core competency of the firm.

Ascendas' leaders regard the establishment of conducive **culture practices** as very important so as to support learning and innovation within the park. In terms of the park's infrastructure and architectural design, great efforts were made to provide tenants and k-workers with attractive "shared space"/life-style options in form of modern gyms, nice swimming pools, trendy restaurants, etc. In its new Capricorn building in Science Park II (targeting the biotechnology, computer, E-services, life sciences, R&D, and software development companies),

Table 8.4. KM enablers of smart Science and Technology Parks (STPs): The case of the Singapore Science Park.

Enablers	Leadership	Culture	Processes	Explicit Knowledge	Tacit Knowledge	Knowledge Hubs and Centres	Market Leverage	Measures	People/Skills	HRM Practices	Technology
Implications for Practice	A compelling knowledge vision and strategy is actively promoted by the management team and other STP players (e.g. Hub of Technopreneurs Plan)	The establishment of conducive *culture practices* as precondition for creating new knowledge is seen as very important so as to support learning and innovation within the STP. Examples include the organization of regular business networking seminars (or the provision of transport services to "local" eateries).	Systematic gathering, organization, exploitation and protection of key knowledge assets within the STP is regarded as strategically important. Several tools (e-forum, business match-making services etc.) are provided.	The reuse of explicit knowledge in form of repositories, expert systems, etc. is crucial. The development and maintenance of relevant, needs-based information and knowledge inventories has been initiated.	The codification of tacit, experience-based knowledge takes place as far as Ascendas' own internal KM system is concerned.	Connectivity is strategy. Tenants have access to a one-stop shop to satisfy multiple knowledge needs. Knowledge resources have been categorized and will be further customized in future. Tenants are connected to other R&D centres, VCs etc.	Ascendas has packaged its knowledge and knowledge management capabilities into attractive looking products and services aimed at promoting and marketing the organization.	Attempts have been made to assess the value of the knowledge capital, which exists within the STP (e.g. in form of patents).	Top/middle managers have been tasked with the development of a KM system aimed at leveraging experience-based knowledge assets and learning capabilities.	There is an increasing recognition that people management practices are often more fundamental to knowledge management than the use of IT. Awareness building, training and appropriate performance management are crucial.	An effective information and communications network (incl. collaboration software solutions) is in place and will be further developed/rolled out in the future to ensure "connectivity" of people, information (and knowledge).
Challenges	To endorse this idea throughout the Park.	Spatial proximity does not guarantee "localised" interaction among tenants. To build a productive culture of a pursuit of knowledge.	Obtaining buy-in amongst tenant firms and to motivate them to share knowledge.	Prioritizing explicit knowledge needs. Knowledge transfer.	To motivate tenant firms to share (relevant) tacit knowledge. Codification of such knowledge.	Satisfying the various knowledge needs of tenant firms. Knowledge transfer.	Entrepreneurial atmosphere and mindsets of STP players.	Measurement of human capital assets and R&D outcomes beyond FDI: IC/IP, patents etc.	To obtain buy-in from all tenant firms and to promote KM.	Suitable incentives (e.g. for knowledge sharing) both within and between tenant firms and performance management system.	Connectivity may not automatically enhance collaboration and innovation. Culture is key!

for example, a wireless enabled coffee shop was installed to stimulate interactions between knowledge workers. Seminar rooms are equipped with the latest ICT such as the Ethernet local area network (LAN) technology, which links all businesses in the building into one entire network.

Knowledge workers such as R&D specialists can be "choosy".[8] To monitor the needs and desires of k-workers, Ascendas conducts regular opinion surveys. Respective survey data suggest that the aspirations of k-workers change over time. It is important to keep track of their needs so as to offer relevant services (such as bus transfers to nearby hawker centres) and products as well as attractive infrastructural facilities.

The systematic gathering, organization, exploitation and protection of key knowledge assets within the two STPs are of strategic importance. Concrete attempts to improve productivity of tenants by making *process-related (tacit and explicit) knowledge* readily accessible have been initiated.

Initially two on-line tools were available to enable tenants to interact with other tenants electronically via the Internet: (i) a so-called "*Electronic Forum*" (aimed at helping tenants to satisfy specific information needs — with regard to technology or seed financing — with the help of other Science Park tenants and to participate in expert discussions) and (ii) a dedicated virtual *Business Matchmaking* service to help tenants to find technology and/or business partners for joint projects. Subsequently, the two Internet online tools were removed from the Science Park website as they were found not to be very effective. For business matching, Ascendas now uses personalised matching which has been more effective in terms of a successful match. The organization also carries out successful matching through the use of elevator pitch events.

We assume that the identification, capturing, sharing and reuse of both *tacit and explicit knowledge* in form of strategic knowledge

---

[8]K-workers enjoy excellent leisure facilities at the Science Park in the form of a gym, swimming pool, tennis courts, restaurants, deli-bars, etc. The extent to which these facilities are used and inspire new ideas and collaborative innovations should be explored by future research.

repositories, best practice databanks, expert systems, etc. will be further developed in future in line with the expansion of the tenant portal. While this information and knowledge exchange platform will certainly enable technology-related companies to interact with each other "easily", the actual value added of interactions, collaborations and k-transfer between tenants will have to be further studied. A crucial benefit that the Singapore Science Park can offer both international investors and knowledge workers is the ability to connect them to other local R&D centres such as nearby Singapore's National University of Singapore (NUS) or Nanyang Technological University (NTU). Facilitation of business networking sessions, CEO meetings and short presentations by potential start-ups in front of VCs represents some of the current venues for interactions and the exchange of knowledge. Besides local connectivity, regional and global connectivity are further key strategy goals of Ascendas as outlined above.

Once fully established, the *knowledge hub* function of the planned portal will provide tenant firms and employees with an effective one-stop shop for multiple knowledge needs and the opportunity to create synergies in form of communities of interest and/or practice.

In terms of *achieving market leverage*, Ascendas has achieved great successes as evidenced by the range of e-infrastructure services including high quality broadband, telecommunication and wireless services for customers located in its science, business and industrial parks and commercial buildings.

Both the *measurement* of the knowledge capital, which exists in the Singapore Science Park, and the development of effective metrics are crucial.

People, skills and HRM practices: Ascendas has appointed internal managerial knowledge champions and provides various rewards to stimulate knowledge sharing. To what extent respective measures have been promoted amongst tenants has to be further explored.

Ascendas has put in place a sophisticated *technological infrastructure* to enable connectivity of people and tenant firms. As indicated above, technological leadership is one of Ascendas' strategic success factors. It is envisaged that the envisaged tenant portal will enhance virtual connectivity of tenants and effective, results-oriented collaborations.

8.6. Ascendas' Internal KM System: Ascendas' KM E-Portal (ASKME)

As a provider of *intelligent* business space, it is perhaps not surprising that Ascendas has invested considerable resources into the development of its very own, internal KM system. Top management is committed to KM and has appointed a member of the top management team as well as a senior executive to take care of it. At the core of its internal KM system is the so-called "Ascendas KM E-Portal", which was developed, in close collaboration with KM consultants from a well-known KM solution provider. The consultants developed the ASKME *knowledge tree* as well as the KM taxonomy and "guided" Ascendas staff through the development process on the basis of several meetings and interviews.

The e-portal ASKME has several main repositories (home, country news, customers, products and services, document library, search function, people directory, etc.) as illustrated in Fig. 8.4. Special features of the "*Home*" page include repositories such as "Let's Learn & Share" (see Fig. 8.4).

The spirit of sharing is regarded as a "core value" of the organization. The company rewards knowledge sharing activities and has instituted the so-called "Best Contributor/Adaptor Scheme", providing various tangible incentives for k-sharing. Knowledge sharing activities are also taken into account during performance appraisals.

An interesting feature of Ascendas' knowledge tree is the evolving best practice folder aimed at capturing and reusing experience-based knowledge of staff about core business products and services in form of fact sheets, maintenance-related lessons learnt, deal structuring knowledge, proposals, etc.

8.7. High-Tech Fantasy or Centre of Innovation? Challenges Ahead for Singapore's Science Park

More research is needed to assess the extent to which the substantial R&D investments have been of value in creating a truly "innovative R&D milieu" in the Singapore Science Park and producing significant R&D results in the form of product innovations, patents and

Fig. 8.4. Ascendas' KM e-Portal (ASKME).

so forth. A crucial factor is the "institutional thickness" (Keeble *et al.*, 1999), a term which refers to the degree of interaction between relevant institutions, tenant firms and so forth and the "mutual awareness of being involved in a common enterprise" (Phillips and Yeung, 2003:712). In theory, institutional thickness was enhanced through the set-up of several government-linked institutions aimed at promoting R&D activities in the Park and kick-starting collaborative ties between local universities and industries. In reality, however, relationships between tenants and these institutions may not always be compatible and synergistic. According to Phillips and Yeung's analysis (2003:707), it is a "myth that spatial proximity to R&D institutions and organizations automatically results in collaborative R&D efforts".

The managing director (MD) of a foreign software development company residing in the park whom we interviewed in the context of our research had mixed opinions about the culture of knowledge sharing and collaboration between the tenants. He argued that the "critical mass" might be lacking and that the main inhibiting factor promoting a knowledge sharing culture could be due to the diverse composition of the companies at the Science Parks as each company is basically more concerned with doing its "own" research and development. It was stressed that there is not always a "level playing ground" in terms of similar knowledge know-how among the companies due to the fact that Science Park I is basically a conglomerate of small companies each specializing in their own products and services. Though the developer and manager of the Science Park (Ascendas) had put in place sufficient infrastructure and technology to facilitate a sharing culture, there is minimal knowledge sharing, cooperation and collaboration among companies in creating shared understandings and opportunities for technology transfer in everyday life.

It was acknowledged that the Park's professional management team had made considerable efforts to promote bonding and interaction as well as enabling communication between the park's tenants through lifestyle sports and recreation events like the annual Healthy Lifestyle Week. But these rapport-building attempts were perceived as sometimes falling short in realizing inter-company collaboration and effective knowledge sharing. The interviewee stressed that due to the sheer size of Science Park II as compared to Science Park I and the fact that the majority of Life Sciences Research Companies are located in Science Park II, the latter might provide a richer culture of interaction and knowledge sharing. The interviewed CEO felt that one of the best strategies for promoting an effective knowledge sharing culture is to enable lots of free space for interaction so that employees of different tenant firms can become better acquainted with each other.

The good news: collaboration takes place. Asked whether his company has any particular ties to other tenants within the park, the company leader stated that his firm cooperates with a Japanese firm in software development and specific services. As he told us, he had actually seconded an engineer from his own firm to that particular company, stressing that both firms are engaged in joint consultancy efforts (he also collaborates with a company outside the Science Park).

Both the interview with the CEO of this particular foreign tenant in Singapore's Science Park as well as survey findings with regard to active collaborations among tenants (pertaining to R&D projects, product development and testing and inspection) as compiled by Phillips and Yeung (2003:726) suggest that the culture of collaboration[9] in the Singapore Science Parks is evolving and that geographical closeness and spatial proximity can make a difference. Of 34 Science Park tenants surveyed by the authors, 22 had collaborated on *R&D projects* (mostly on a one-off basis and confined to the sharing of facilities), 15 on *product development* and 18 on *testing and inspection*. Of 34 major developments identified by the researchers, 29 had been done in collaboration. Collaborations among firms occurred within and outside the Park. The extent to which Ascendas helped to facilitate such collaborations needs to be ascertained.

Connectivity and cultural challenges remain. Two short visits of the post-modern *Capricorn building* in Science Park II (which features a unique rainforest tree inside the building) produced interesting results. Observations and a short chat with specialists working there indicated that the modern infrastructure of the new building with its unique environment and "intelligent exchange space" is no automatic precondition for effective intra-organizational knowledge sharing and the creation of new knowledge. Bureaucracy and the existence of ethnically defined, more or less exclusive knowledge networks (communities of interest and practice) comprising many "foreign" K-workers from the People's Republic of China (who reach out to fellow ethnics in the US rather than to colleagues within the Science Park) were seen as certain barriers. The wireless enabled coffee shop was relatively empty and little interactions could be observed during our visits there.

However, in view of the dearth of representative, empirical studies about the inner logic of knowledge work within the Singapore Science Park, hasty generalizations should be avoided. Perhaps, the "missing"

---

[9]The institutional contours of (epistemic) knowledge creation cultures appear to be the following: There have to be a sizable number of persons who are relatively independent of outside control, who work closely together but are pitted against each other in competition for resources, recognition and excellence. In many aspects epistemic cultures resembles the culture of markets. There are stringent rules of conduct, but no undue regulation of values or prices; there is competition but no open conflict and there is a high degree of autonomy of decision making (Evers, 2004).

knowledge workers (e.g. high frequency computing experts housed in that building) were hard at work during the time of our visit, communicating and sharing knowledge with fellow researchers in the US due to the lack of synergetic expertise in Singapore at that point in time. Officials are convinced that this issue will be tackled in the mid-term as evidenced by the rapidly progressing Biopolis project and associated human capital development measures.

As stated at the beginning of the paper, Singapore does not have any natural resources except its people. Past, current and future human capital development measures and expenditures (e.g. in form of financial support for the education of 100 doctoral students in areas relevant for the Biopolis initiative) underline the ongoing commitment of Singapore's government to further transform the island republic into a fully developed, globally relevant knowledge economy. Singapore's public sector organizations and privatized entities such as Ascendas have embraced KM concepts proactively, and further positive spin-off effects with regard to research and innovation can be expected provided STP planners manage to create an organic culture of knowledge production with the "right" "ingredients of innovation" (Davis 2004). Greater entrepreneurial dynamism, intense linkages with Silicon Valley and other science parks (Koh, Koh and Tschang, 2004), "brokered technology" flows[10] (Burt, 2004:10), further development, utilization and exploitation of Singapore's *local* capabilities and cultural development[11] represent challenges which are currently being addressed by Singapore's policymakers head on at various fronts.

---

[10]According to Burt (2004:9), "organizations with management and collaboration networks that bridge structural holes in their markets seem to learn faster and be more productively creative". To what extent management companies of STPs can facilitate such knowledge networking activities needs to be examined.

[11]Davis (2004) has summarized the "common culture of innovation" in Silicon Valley as follows: risk taking attitude (failure is badge of honor), flexibility (test and probe), the dream of starting and running a business, dense concentration of people who have done this dozens of times and who question everything, excellent university involvement, high concentrations of capital, no formal mechanism forcing "meetings", relentless networking, conferences and events as well as multiple careers/companies.

8.8. Conclusion and Implications

In view of the globalization of R&D activities in an increasingly knowledge-driven world, policy-makers and planners in East and West have attempted to create specific places aimed at developing and embedding such activities locally. Singapore's Science Park is an interesting example in this respect. Both the Singapore government and the Park's management team (Ascendas) have invested significant financial, physical and human resources into this place so as to enhance the R&D capabilities of firms residing in the Park, to create a sparkling culture of knowledge sharing and innovation as well as to achieve trickle-down effects and significant outputs in form of new products, patents etc. The epistemic culture of the Singapore Science Park is evolving. Its facets, social knowledge transfer dynamics and effectiveness need to be further examined.

The provision of an excellent physical infrastructure and investment benefits is not always sufficient for the creation of a conducive culture of knowledge production (e.g. through R&D) and the generation of new ideas. As far as the Singapore Science Park is concerned, various strengths and inhibiting factors were highlighted in the paper. *Strengths* include the high quality space and facilities, its strategic location in a relatively thick landscape of relevant institutions, focused knowledge governance and knowledge management activities by its management team (as indicated by Ascendas motto "craft", "create" and "connect"), active collaborations between tenant firms and the existence of outputs in form of new product developments and patents. The relative "lack of a critical mass' in certain sectors, the insufficient local embeddedness of R&D measures, great variation amongst tenants and sometimes non-compatible motivations for occupying spaces within the Park were highlighted as *issues*. Some firms surveyed by Phillips and Yeung (2003) found it difficult to conduct cost-effective R&D activities and to bring ideas to market.

In terms of development, the Singapore Science Park is currently moving from its "institutional" phase to the "entrepreneurial" phase (Cox, 1985:20). The institutional stage is predictable and relatively easy to manage while the entrepreneurial phase can be unpredictable and risky. The sustainability of the Singapore Science Park depends on several factors. One key ingredient is its entrepreneurial dynamism which will be further enhanced in the future as indicated by the current policy discourse on technopreneurship and educational reforms to ensure a broader talent mix. Another element is the culture of knowledge sharing and innovation.

Further research is necessary to fully understand the social dynamics and cultural mechanics of successful knowledge creation in such parks and to formulate effective (best) knowledge governance practices which could be replicated by the management teams of other Science Parks in the region and beyond so as to actively support the development of a culture of innovation.

Whether Ascendas and STP tenants could benefit from k-creation facilitation services has to be examined.[12]

Singapore is keen to be part of the global knowledge society. There is hardly any attempt any more to localize knowledge production (see Chapter 4 in this book). Symbols of a global modernity abound. Multiculturalism is propagated in the sense that it is an expression of globality rather than an expression of a Southeast Asian identity. US-American business culture is favoured and propagated in the education system and in business. A large number of university professors and research scientists have been recruited from abroad thus creating a global culture within the sphere of business, research and development. Ethnicity is recognized as a fact of life but relegated to the realm of folklore and the earlier strict policy of dividing the population into four categories of Chinese, Malay, Indian and others is eroded. This, of course, is the virtual world of government policy and not the social reality of the Singapore way of life.

The intelligent "The Rutherford" building in Science Park I (see Figs. 8.3 and 8.5) expresses the cool culture of a globalized knowledge society and is perhaps symptomatic for the ongoing cultural change.

---

[12]There is evidence that companies such as HP do benefit from using facilitation and collaboration tools such as brainstorming sessions, bridge relations through which employees *broker* technology flows between projects, communities of interest, etc. The initiation of such practices amongst tenant firms by the management companies of STPs might have positive outcomes with regard to STP performance.

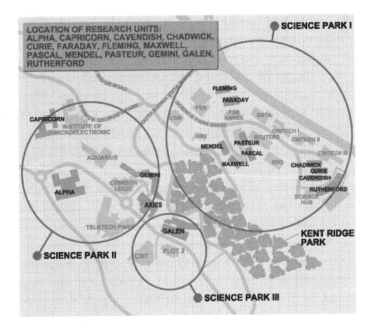

Fig. 8.5. Location of research units in the Singapore Science Park.
Source: http://www.singaporesciencepark.com/bss/research.asp.

Next to smart and properly equipped offices it contains a fitness club and an outdoor entertainment area. Its coffee house and restaurant serves "fast" food and constantly running CNN news, and is supposed to serve as a meeting point of minds where a multi-ethnic community of research scientists chat and share knowledge. In actual fact the restaurant is under-used at times and groups of ethnically homogeneous researchers saunter off to their respective favourite eating houses or hawker stalls outside the Science Park. Singaporean localism beats global knowledge society at least when it comes to subsistence behaviour, i.e., eating lunch.

Visitors to Science and Technology Parks are often impressed by symbols of globalized modernity, as expressed in the architecture of buildings, parks, signboards and logos. References to local culture are sometimes avoided and global corporate styles are preferred. Ethnically and culturally diverse knowledge workers in STPs do not necessarily accept this modernism as relevant. Modernist global symbols are sometimes rejected as cold, irrelevant and meaningless. The modernist milieu may decrease the feeling of belonging and identification with the work place and ultimately the effectiveness of the organization's epistemic culture of knowledge creation. Planners of STPs arguably appear to follow a rather bounded logic: modern technology, and world-class scientific research require a modern environment and a global symbolism. Obtaining patents, new ideas and effective research is, however, stimulated by a heterogeneous mix of alliance partners (Burt, 2004:10), diversity, contrasting life-styles and an "interesting" environment (Evers and Menkhoff, 2004). What knowledge workers think about such issues has to be examined by future research.

The global knowledge world extends around the world from the Silicon Valley through the Munich knowledge belt to Malaysia's Multimedia Supercorridor, the Science Parks of Singapore and beyond. It is dominated by "Western" corporate culture, which Singapore seems to accept, degrading local Singaporean multiethnic culture to "instant-Asia" folklore. The Asian values debate (Cauqulin and Lim, 1998) has died away.

References

A*Star (2002). *National Survey of R&D in Singapore*. Singapore: Agency for Science, Technology and Research.

Angel, D.P. and L. Savage (1996). Global Localization? Japanese Research and Development Laboratories in the USA. *Environment and Planning A*, 28, 819–833.

Burt, R.S. (2004). Structural Holes and Good Ideas. *American Journal of Sociology*, 110(2), 349–399.

Cauqulin, J. and P. Lim (eds.) (1998). *Asian Values: An Encounter with Diversity*. Richmond: Curzon Press.

Chia, S.Y. and J.J. Lim (2003). Singapore: A Regional Hub in ICT. In *Towards a K-based Economy: East Asia's Changing Industrial Geography*, S. Masyama and D. Vandenbrink (eds.), pp. 259–298. Singapore: ISEAS.

Coe, N.M. and P.F. Kelly (2000). Distance and Discourse in the Local Labour Market: The Case of Singapore. *Area*, 32(4), 413–422.

Coe, N.M. and P.F. Kelly (2002). Languages of Labour: Representational Strategies in Singapore's Labour Control Regime. *Political Geography*, 21(3), 341–371.

Cox, R.N. (1985). Lessons from 30 Years of Science Parks in the USA. In *Science Parks and Innovation Centres: Their Economic and Social Impact*, J.M. Gibb (ed.), pp. 18–24. Amsterdam: Elsevier.

Drucker, P.F. (1994). *Postcapitalist Society.* New York: Harper Business.

Davis, J. (2004). Fostering Creativity in Developing New Opportunities — Innovation in the Absence of Structure. Paper presented at the 2nd International Knowledge Management Symposium "Knowledge Governance in Science and Technology Parks", Singapore Management University, Singapore, 17 March 2004.

Evers, H.-D. (2000). Globalization, Local Knowledge, and the Growth of Ignorance: The Epistemic Construction of Reality. *Southeast Asian Journal of Social Science*, 28(1), 13–22.

Evers, H.-D. (2003). Transition Towards a Knowledge Society: Malaysia and Indonesia in Comparative Perspective. *Comparative Sociology*, 2(2), 355–373.

Evers, H.-D. (2004). Epistemic Cultures and the Production of New Knowledge. Unpublished MS., Singapore Management University.

Evers, H.-D. and T. Menkhoff (2004). Creating an Effective Epistemic Culture of Knowledge Production in Science and Technology Parks. Paper presented at the 2nd International Knowledge Management Symposium "Knowledge Governance in Science & Technology Parks", Singapore Management University, Singapore, 17 March 2004.

Florida, R. and M. Kenney (1994). The Globalization of Japanese R&D: The Economic Geography of Japanese R&D Investment in the United States. *Economic Geography*, 70(4), 344–369.

Goh, C.B. (1998). Creating a Research and Development Culture in Southeast Asia: Lessons from Singapore's Experience. *Southeast Asian Journal of Social Science*, 26(1), 49–68.

Keeble, D. *et al.* (1999). Collective Learning Processes, Networking and "Institutional Thickness" in the Cambridge Region. *Regional Studies*, 33(4), 319–332.

Knorr-Cetina, K. (1999). *Epistemic Cultures. How Science Makes Sense.* Cambridge, MA: Harvard University Press.

Koh, F., W. Koh and F.T. Tschang (2004). An Analytical Framework for Science Parks and Technology Districts with an Application to Singapore. *Journal of Business Venturing*, 20(2), 217–239.

Low, L. and E.C.Y. Kuo (1999). Towards an Information Society in a Developed Nation. In *Singapore, Towards a Developed Status*, L. Low (ed.), pp. 37–65. Singapore: OUP.

Ministry of Trade and Industry (1991). *The Strategic Economic Plan.* Singapore: SNP.

Nonaka, I. (1995). *The Knowledge-Creating Company: How Japanese Companies Create the Dynamics of Innovation.* New York: OUP.

NSTB (National Science and Technology Board) (1991). *Science and Technology: Windows of Opportunities, National Technology Plan.* Singapore: SNP.

Phillips, S.A.M. and H.W.-C. Yeung (2003). A Place for R&D? The Singapore Science Park. *Urban Studies*, 40(4), 707–732.

Polanyi, K. (1957). *The Great Transformation.* Boston: Beacon (1st Ed., 1944).

Rodan, G. (1989). *The Political Economy of Singapore's Industrialization: National State and International Capital.* London: Macmillan.

Schrage, M. (1997). Collaborative Tools: A First Look. In *Knowledge Management Tools*, R.L. Ruggles III (ed.). Boston, MA: Butterworth-Heinemann.

Skyrme, D.J. (1999). *Knowledge Networking: Creating the Collaborative Enterprise.* Butterworth Heinemann.

Skyrme, D.J. (2001). *Capitalizing on Knowledge: From E-business to K-business.* Butterworth-Heinemann.

Special Correspondent (1988). Singapore finds an Answer to Silicon Valley. *Asian Finance*, 78–79.

Tan, L.H. (1988). Hi-tech Vision Turns Industry Wheels. *Asian Finance*, 92–95.

Toh, M.H., H.C. Tang and A. Choo (2002). Mapping Singapore's Knowledge-based Economy. In *Economic Survey of Singapore* (3rd Quarter 2002), pp. 56–75. Singapore.

Appendix 8.1. The RDAS and RISC schemes of the Economic Development Board of Singapore

Research and Development Assistance Scheme (RDAS)

The RDAS Scheme is aimed at promoting commercially viable R&D work in Singapore. Grants of up to a few million dollars can be awarded for specific projects, depending on their merits. RDAS funds will cover up to 50% of the total costs of a particular R&D project, incl. R&D manpower, new R&D equipment, training etc. The scheme is open to Singaporeans or foreigners. Funds will only be provided where the R&D will bring clear economic benefits to Singapore.

Research Incentive Scheme for Companies (RISC)

The RISC scheme encourages companies to develop generic R&D capabilities and core competencies in Singapore. To qualify for the scheme, applicants must bring in or develop a specific R&D capability, which will enhance the company's sustainable competitiveness. In addition, the R&D programme should result in measurable benefits to the Singapore economy, lead to a substantial increase in R&D spending over a specified duration and involve the training of a significant number of knowledge workers (research scientists and engineers).

The EDB has a fund that invests in start-ups worldwide, with S$75 million available for investment in overseas companies intending to start businesses in Singapore. EDB's other venture capital funds include EDB Ventures, EDB Ventures 2 and Singapore Bio-Innovations aimed at making direct investments in companies, co-investing in projects with local companies and investing in venture capital funds.

The objective of EDB's *Innovation Development Scheme* is to assist Singapore registered companies and organizations in the manufacturing or services sector to develop capabilities in the innovation of products, processes and applications. Grants will typically cover 30–50% of the overall cost of specific projects.

The Government uses its resources directly to stimulate R&D and other high value added activities in key sectors (like electronics and ICT). These funds can be applied by way of grant to cover specific costs or by way of co-investment in start-up ventures. There are various Singapore governmental and quasi-governmental bodies that have funds for use in this way.

Source: http://www.tradepartners.gov.uk/text/education/singapore3/opportunities/opportunities.shtml.

Appendix 8.2. Milestones of Ascendas

2004	July 30	Ascendas secures a build-and-lease (B&L) project from Fortune 500 US multinational corporation, Hewlett-Packard (HP), to develop and manage a seven-storey industrial building, of which 70% will be leased back to HP over a 10-year period.
	April 28	Ascendas launches its first commercial building in China, Ascendas Plaza, a 30-storey office tower with a five-storey retail podium. It is located in Xujiahui, one of Shanghai's most vibrant business districts and retail belts.
	January 12	Ascendas steps up development of its India flagship, International Tech Park Bangalore, with the start of construction on the new US$15 million Inventor building, the fifth building in the Park.
2003	November 4	Ascendas to develop a 10,000 sq m facility within the business and commercial area in the new Hangzhou Modern Tele-Industrial Park (MTiP). This is Ascendas' first project in Hangzhou.
	July 11	Ascendas secures a 10-year contract for AREMS to be used in the 10 sq km Hunnan International Technopolis located in the Shenyang Hunnan New District.
	July 8	Ascendas launches the Ascendas Real Estate Management System (AREMS), a first-of-its-kind real estate management system, and enters into the Middle East with it first venture in Oman. Ascendas signs a 10-year deal with the Omani government-owned industrial developer, Public Establishment for Industrial Estates (PEIE), to adopt AREMS for the management of its six industrial parks and Oman's first technology park.
	June 17	Ascendas partners with Tamil Nadu Industrial Development Corporation (TIDCO) in India to develop an IT complex in Chennai.
	May 7	Ascendas and Tsinghua Science Park Development Centre, the commercial arm of Beijing's renowned Tsinghua University, enter into a broad-based partnership to undertake projects in real estate development, investment and related areas within China and the Asia-Pacific.
	April 30	Ascendas signs MOU with Pacific Healthcare Holdings to collaborate as preferred partners on expansion projects in the Asia-Pacific region.
	April 16	Ascendas is appointed by Infineon Technologies, German-based global leader in semiconductors, to develop its new Asia Pacific headquarters in Singapore under a 12-year Build and Lease agreement.
	April 6	Ascendas expands to Australia with a 25% stake in the Colonial First State Industrial Property Trust acquired from Macquarie Goodman.

Appendix 8.2 (Continued)

2002	December 20	Ascendas acquires Citicorp Centre in Seoul, marking its entry into the Korean market and the overseas office building sector.
	December 11	Ascendas' flagship in India, International Tech Park, Bangalore, named World Teleport Property of the Year 2002.
	December	Ascendas Real Estate Investment Trust (A-REIT) named Best New Structure Equity Deal in the Asset Asian Awards 2003 by leading Asian finance magazine, The Asset.
	November 19	Ascendas Real Estate Investment Trust (A-REIT) lists on the Singapore Exchange. As Singapore's first business and industrial property trust, A-REIT receives overwhelming demand at five times oversubscribed.
	October 10	Ascendas breaks ground for the S$45 million Cyber Pearl, a new IT complex in Hyderabad, India.
	July 4	Ascendas signs MOU with TIDCO to develop an IT complex in Chennai, India.
	June 5	Ascendas adopts Kent Ridge Park jointly with the National University of Singapore under the National Parks Board Adopt-A-Park scheme.
	May 24	Ascendas China wins US$5.5 million project to build-and-lease a customised manufacturing facility in Beijing for Germany's Friwo.
	May 20	Ascendas' incubator facility iAxil in Singapore Science Park joins the Technopreneurship Belt spearheaded by the Economic Development Board.
	January 17	Ascendas sets up S$30 million PACT (Partnership to Advance and Collaborate in Technology) Fund to invest in companies developing technology that have high synergistic fit with Ascendas' real estate business.
2001	November 30	Ascendas seals a joint venture with Australia's Macquarie Goodman Management (MGM) to explore real estate investment trust and property opportunities in Asia.
	November 28	Ascendas and Exel enter into a strategic Asia Pacific partnership to develop Xing Wang Logistics Centre.
	October 18	Ascendas signs a joint venture agreement with L&T Infocity to develop an IT complex in HITEC City, Hyderabad, India.
	October 3	Ascendas starts new subsidiary, Clear DataVoice, to provide e-infrastructure services to companies and property owners.
	September 26	Ascendas' Singapore Science Park partners Heidelberg Tech Park, Germany's leading BioPark, to explore synergies in providing network and collaboration opportunities for their respective customers.
	July 2	Ascendas completes S$30 million manufacturing complex for NH Technoglass within record 7 $1/2$ months in Singapore.

Appendix 8.2 (Continued)

May 31	Ascendas expands to Beijing with signing of a strategic alliance partnership with Beijing Economic and Technological Investment Development Corporation.
April 2	Ascendas sets up specialised carrier hotel arm with partner, Global Gateway.
March 5	Ascendas, F&N and CyberCity join hands in a consortium to acquire listed Hong Kong company Hing Kong (later renamed as Vision Century Corporation).
January 8	Merger of Arcasia Land and JTC International's Business Parks and Facilities Group to form Ascendas to create a stronger competitive advantage as an Asian real estate player.

Source: *www.ascendas.com.*

Chapter 9

Applying Knowledge Management in University Research

Benjamin Loh, Ai-Chee Tang, Thomas Menkhoff,
Yue Wah Chay and Hans-Dieter Evers

9.1. Introduction: Universities and New Markets of Knowledge Production

The development and transmission of knowledge has traditionally been seen as a central governing role and responsibility of universities. German education reformer Wilhelm von Humboldt advocated the idea of *akademische freiheit* (academic freedom) as the traditional ideal of the German university. He believed that the freedom to pursue knowledge is a fundamental principle of democracy that defines the existence of universities. A university's pursuit of knowledge, according to Humboldt, is inexhaustible and tireless: "One unique feature of higher intellectual institutions is that they conceive of science and scholarship as dealing with ultimately inexhaustible tasks: this means that they are engaged in an unceasing process of inquiry" (Humboldt, 1970:243). Similarly in John Henry Newman's classic *The Idea of a University* on the philosophy of higher education, he argued that the pursuit of knowledge is an end in itself, and that the university is a community of scholars, teachers and students devoted to the pursuit of truth. The "idea" which Newman referred to in his title work in 1851 was used in the sense of "ideal" — a focal point of how universities treated knowledge as an entity pursued for its own sake, regardless of cost or consequence. This ideal is most frequently exemplified by the university's role as the "critic and conscience of society".

While universities today still retain their role as the "critic and conscience of society", the critical function of universities has increasingly taken on a more pragmatic role in terms of staying "relevant" in an evolving techno-economic environment. We have often heard the lament that higher education is somewhat disconnected from society which it is supposed to serve, infamously represented by the Socratic metaphor of the "ivory tower" — a university perched on top of a hill amongst the clouds producing "useless" knowledge irrelevant to disciples descending down to the real world. The push for higher education to become relevant to the changing needs of society was echoed by a series of reports by the World Bank (World Bank, 1998; Stiglitz, 1999a; 1999b) as well as the Association of Commonwealth Universities (Gibbons, 1998) in the late 1990s. This call for higher education relevance, or pragmatization, arose out of various drivers and trends in the transition towards a knowledge-based economy — the heterogeneity of knowledge production, massification and democratization of higher education, and the integration and assimilation of information technology into the academic environment.

9.1.1. *Heterogeneity of Knowledge Production*

The transition from the old type of industrial society with its traditional dominance of manufacturing work and old industrial classes to an information and knowledge-based society has seen the emergence of knowledge as a factor of production that has grown in importance in relation to the other factors of labor and capital (Evers, 2000a; 2000b). In a knowledge-based society, there are distinct epistemic cultures of knowledge production, i.e., "different practices of creating and warranting knowledge in different domains" (Knorr-Cetina, 1999:246). Similarly Gibbons *et al.* (1994) have suggested that the trend of knowledge being produced in multiple sites has seen the heterogeneity of knowledge production where knowledge is no longer produced solely in the university setting but is produced increasingly in many other institutions such as government laboratories, industries and think tanks (Gibbons *et al.*, 1994; see also Etzkowitz and Leydesdorff, 1997). He predicted that "universities ... will comprise only a part, perhaps only a small part, of the knowledge producing sector" (Gibbons *et al.*, 1994:85) in the 21st century. In a study conducted by Godin and Gingras (1999) on the growth of non-university research in Canada, the authors found a visible trend in the diversification of the locus of science knowledge production between the years 1980 to 1995. While the rate of knowledge production of university research in the form of journal publications in those years has been stable, their study found a 68% growth of non-university contributions in relation to the total number of papers.

9.1.2. *Massification and Democratisation of Higher Education*

The second factor leading to the pragmatization of universities is the global massification and democratization of higher education in the past two decades. The development of mass higher education in modern industrial societies after World War II exhibited a rapid growth of enrolments in part through the expansion of elite universities and the creation of non-university vocational institutions in response to increasing occupational demands for post-secondary qualifications (Gibbons, 1998; Trow, 2000; Muthesius, 2001). In Europe, higher education access extended to almost a third or half of the population comprising mostly lower middle, middle and working class origins and, in recent decades, include increasing numbers of non-traditional students comprising matured, employed, part-time students and people aiming at employment in the rapidly growing semi-professions and knowledge-based service industries (Trow, 2000; Warner and Palfreyman, 2001).

Behind this great increase in participation in higher education were a number of more or less independent forces: the democratization of politics and society that followed World War II (Geiger, 1993; Fuller, 2002); the growth of the public sector that required more white collar workers (and university graduates); an expanding industrial economy that required more highly skilled and educated workers; and finally the widespread belief that further economic development depended on a supply of educated manpower, especially scientists and engineers. Among the most significant effects of mass higher education, of special significance for the production and distribution of knowledge, is the great increase in the market for continuing education in response to life-long learning as well as training and retraining. Continuing adult education today has become a high-growth industry that is worth an estimated 6% of GNP in the United States. Other developed countries are rapidly reaching this figure (Drucker, 2000) while the global executive education market offered by business schools is calculated to be worth in excess of $12 billion per annum (Crainer and Dearlove, 1998:170).

9.1.3. *Assimilation of Information Technology into the Academic Environment*

The emergence and use of IT in higher education has led to an increasingly virtual education system (Hailes and Hazemi, 1998; Jones and Pritchard, 1999; Rada, 2001; Tschang, 2001). A variety of Internet-based or World-Wide-Web-based distance-learning courses, such as Stanford's online master's degree in electrical engineering (developed in cooperation with Microsoft and Compaq) are now part of the universities' curricula. Online courses are also offered by, among others, Washington State University, Oklahoma State University, the University of Colorado, Regents College (New York), and the University of California. The continuous change, advancement and introduction of new information technologies had a destabilizing effect on traditional forms of higher education, and have put the survival of research universities, especially, at risk (Daniel, 1996). Trow (2000:14) noted that three American university presidents expressed that same view in almost identical words:

> "We cannot even be certain whether the university as we know it will survive at all, nor, if so, in what form... The existence of the university as it is now and as we know it is in doubt" (qtd. Muller, 1998: 222).

Members of the Association of European Universities (CRE) also stressed that:

> "It is not an exaggeration to say that the issue of new information and communication technologies questions the basic functions of the university" (qtd. Edwards, 1998:25).

The above drivers and trends towards university pragmatization have implications for the dynamics and conduct of university research. In the past, recognition of competence to carry out research arose out of an intense socialization into an academic discipline. Research was an elite activity conducted by people who themselves have had an elite higher education. The greater part of research still retains this character, but new patterns of research have emerged which involve collaboration with people from different industries and organizations who may not necessarily be academic researchers as evident in the "frequent interactions between [university based research scholars] and business people, venture capitalists, patent lawyers, production engineers, as well as research engineers and scientists located outside the university" (Gibbons, 1998:13). This has accelerated the commercialization of research and teaching in higher education, and the movement of both out of the tradition domain of higher education institutions.

Research results that were previously reported in peer-reviewed academic journals and conferences are increasingly confined to reports commissioned by commercial and industry sponsors. It may also involve shared use of academic and industrial facilities and technology, and is more likely to be trans-disciplinary and multidisciplinary as a result of the heterogeneous social distribution of knowledge production. Specialized knowledge no longer remains the domain of academia, but is increasingly produced and co-produced by public organizations and industry. Accordingly different patterns of research funding are emerging, and they are less dependent on funding within the university, central government or non-profit foundations, and more on the firms, industries and social lobbies directly involved (Geuna, 1999:18).

These developments imply that the conduct of contemporary research cannot remain easily within the confines of university departments or academic centres. This is prompting the emergence of a host of new institutional arrangements, linking government, industry, universities and private consultancy groups in different ways (Etzkowitz and Leydesdorff, 1997; Mills and Pumo, 1999; Peters, 2002). While traditional university-based research may be threatened by the encroachment of industry and the mentality and values of profit-making, researchers in countries with traditions of non-university research, on the other hand, may feel the need to link their research institutions more closely with universities so as to be more open to innovation and intellectual competition.

From a societal perspective, this movement and distribution of knowledge production, from and within university and non-university institutions, has important implications for a country's development towards a knowledge society (see Chapters 3–5 of this book). There are nodal points where knowledge is produced and from where it is globally distributed. Research on Indonesia, for example, may be carried out mostly by foreign scholars, affiliated to universities or research institutions around the globe, rather then Indonesian nationals or scholars attached to its local institutions. This unequal production and distribution of knowledge is widening the knowledge gap between highly productive and less productive countries which raises the issue of which knowledge is produced locally for local needs? The International Rice Research Institute (IRRI) in Los Banos, Philippines comes to mind as an example of "best practice". Most knowledge about the developing world and the transition societies is, however, still produced outside the region to which it pertains. The capacity to benefit from knowledge of various fields has two basic elements: the ability to acquire and to apply knowledge that already exists, and the ability to produce new knowledge. It is not enough to transfer knowledge, e.g. knowledge embedded in a particular technology, from one country to another. Instead, in order to achieve a sustained development, in this case the development towards a knowledge-based economy, it is necessary for the knowledge importing country to be able to acquire (i.e., absorb the knowledge, to understand it, to interpret) and to adapt it to local needs, and subsequently to produce knowledge endogenously along the same line (Cohen and Levinthal, 1990). Knowledge, therefore, has to be imported and adapted to local requirements, i.e., global knowledge has to be "localized". For any society and any nation state it will be crucial whether or not this will be achieved.

9.2. Knowledge Management in Universities and Research

Due to the appearance of new knowledge producers in the education sector, more and more universities are looking into the possibility of applying corporate knowledge management systems. Knowledge management can be defined as the task of developing and exploiting an organization's tangible and intangible knowledge resources (Menkhoff, Chay and Loh, 2004). KM refers to the totality of organizational strategies aimed at creating an intelligent organization, which is able to leverage upon its tangible and intangible assets, to learn from past experiences, whether successful or unsuccessful, and to create new knowledge.

Organizations progress from simple KM activities such as capturing existing knowledge to more sophisticated and complex ones such as the continuous creation of new knowledge. Core business driven knowledge processes of the KM event chain include: (i) locating and capturing knowledge; (ii) sharing knowledge; and (iii) creating new knowledge (see Fig. 9.1).

Universities are major players in the knowledge business (Goddard, 1998) and stand to benefit from knowledge management practices and solutions. An analysis of university mission statements, for example, shows that its aims and objectives are consistent with knowledge management principles: the discovery, acquisition or creation of knowledge (i.e., research), the transmission or dissemination of knowledge (teaching); the application of knowledge to human problems in the interests of public service; and the preservation of knowledge in libraries, museums and archives (Allen, 1988:66).

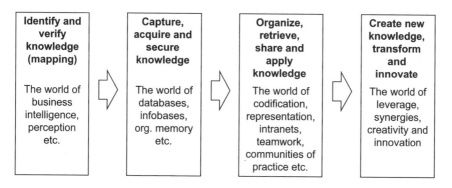

Fig. 9.1. The KM event chain.

Source: Adapted from Liebowitz (2000:6).

From an organizational learning point of view (Senge, 1990; Franklin *et al.*, 1998), a university seems to be well suited to the adoption of knowledge management/organizational learning practices as its environment puts a lot of emphasis on the exchange of ideas and knowledge sharing. The adoption of the scientific method of enquiry requires individuals within subject disciplines to be skeptical about one another's approaches and findings. With the common adoption of falsification as the dominant methodology both in the sciences and social sciences, we see a constant quest for new discoveries and advancement of knowledge (Franklin *et al.*, 1998:232). The sharing of this knowledge in conferences and academic journals is part of the knowledge culture of universities, a feature much less pronounced or even absent in business corporations. The division of university research into disciplines creates, however, boundaries that are difficult to transcend. Though it is well known that new scientific discoveries are often made in areas between disciplines, interdisciplinary research is still difficult to institutionalize.

As universities today thrive to stay relevant in a knowledge society characterised by the emergence of new knowledge markets and the entrance of new market players, knowledge management in higher education is becoming a vital competitive weapon. Besides the application of knowledge management to intra-organizational processes and strategy (Pornchulee, 2001), the university's research process represents a key area which can be enhanced through the application of knowledge management. For example, Kidwell, Linde and Johnson (2000:32) explored how repositories of research interests and results as well as portals for research administration procedures and best practices can bring associated benefits such as increased competitiveness and responsiveness for research grants, contracts, and commercial opportunities, reduced turnaround time for research, minimised devotion of research resources to administrative tasks, facilitation of interdisciplinary research, leveraging of previous research and proposal efforts, improved internal and external services and effectiveness, and reduced administrative costs.

However, to reap the benefits from the application of knowledge management, there are issues and challenges that need to be addressed.

In a study assessing the challenges that higher education institutions face in implementing knowledge management, Rowley (2000) examined the characteristics and features of successful knowledge management projects (see Davenport, DeLong and Beers, 1998) and suggested that universities need to address four key KM objectives: (i) creating and maintaining knowledge repositories; (ii) improving knowledge access; and (iii) enhancing the knowledge environment; and (iv) valuing knowledge.

In terms of *knowledge repositories*, Rowley found that universities abound in potential knowledge repositories, from the corporate financial and library databases to the individually-owned databases of faculty members which hold their collection of both electronic and print documents. These various databases often provide access to internally generated data about the university's operations. However, few universities have an integrated collection of knowledge, embedded either in one knowledge repository, or in a series of linked repositories. Knowledge essential to the research process is often located in multiple sources that takes time and effort to locate, consolidate and utilize. In order to facilitate the operation of a knowledge-based operation, such repositories need to encompass both internal and external knowledge, and explicit and elicited tacit knowledge. According to Rowley, universities are still a long way from a scenario in which each member of the community, that is the university, has access to the combined knowledge and wisdom of others in the organization, and has access to that knowledge in a form that is packaged to suit their particular needs. While many institutions have taken the first step, and have created converged library and information systems departments, this restructuring is often more systems driven than knowledge driven.

In the area of *knowledge access*, Rowley found that universities have well established access to published knowledge sources across and within the academic community. Internet connectivity has been an invaluable resource where researchers and academic staff have access to public knowledge including a host of electronic documents and electronic journals. Within universities, networks based on intranet technology have supported internal communication through e-mail, and access to databases and electronic documents. Most libraries in higher education also have a good coverage of selected sources of information, including databases, and lists of experts. In summary, universities have been proactive in the area of knowledge access, especially with respect to explicit and public knowledge. Further improvements can encompass issues of security, and access rights for different categories of staff and students.

Thirdly, the creation of a *knowledge environment* in which knowledge management activities such as knowledge creation, transfer and use can strive have traditionally been embedded within the academic reward structure of research and scholarship. Rowley argues that rewards are a central element of higher education where high value on evidence of individual achievement in research and scholarship are key in the award of academic achievements such as the accolade of "Professor". Reputation, salary, and opportunities to participate in the further creation and dissemination of knowledge depend significantly upon individual performance. The transfer market for professors with international reputations suggests that the knowledge bases are integrally associated with individuals. While universities have traditionally been considered as the archetypal learning organization or community where there is substantial knowledge sharing in terms of academic knowledge and expertise in the form of journal publications and teaching, these forms of knowledge sharing are paradoxically induced more by peer-competition than altruistic sharing. This has potential implications for the formation of KM groups such as communities of practice or interest groups where members are informally bound by a common interest (e.g. engaging in lunchtime discussions to solve difficult problems) and by what they have learned through their mutual engagement in these activities.

Finally, *valuing knowledge* is concerned with viewing knowledge as an asset. However, Rowley argues that universities have no experience of valuing their intellectual capital and entering those values on their balance sheets. The challenge of such valuation and representation of intellectual capital is a result of the current lack of an established methodology for assigning values to knowledge assets (Firer and Williams, 2003). Such valuation, when established, will have two valuable outcomes: enhanced and shared understanding of the role of knowledge in the university, and the opportunity to monitor the increases and decreases in the knowledge assets embedded in the organization.

Although knowledge management has found much favour in knowledge-based organizations, there is one respect in which such organizations are very different from universities. Consultancy and other organizations that have embraced knowledge management are global organizations, and implicit in their global nature is the sense in which they constitute international communities, independent of state or national and cultural agendas. How might universities move from the collegially networked institutions, with some international student base, towards an era in which strategic alliances allow the creation of a shared, global knowledge base? Is it possible to create a global university? Quite apart from the role of the state in such an endeavour, and the implications for the sharing of knowledge and the basis for learning across national boundaries, there is a real challenge associated with the concept of a "university". Universities have traditionally been defined by their diversity and their role in relation to knowledge and learning across a range of different disciplines. Rowley suggests that such a lack of focus makes it difficult for universities to be at the leading edge in all areas of knowledge.

9.3. Applying KM in the Area of Research: The Case of the Singapore Management University (SMU)

In the following section we will illustrate how knowledge management principles have been put to practice in the area of research exemplified by the approach adopted by the Singapore Management University (SMU). SMU is the country's first private university funded by the government of Singapore and is modelled after one of the world's leading business schools, the Wharton School of the University of Pennsylvania. SMU's curriculum and programmes adopt a flexible, multidisciplinary approach towards managing the increasingly complex demands of modern businesses, notably with an emphasis on computer literacy and technology, company internships, business visits and student exchange programmes. The objective is to develop well-rounded students with the ability to focus on specialized careers.

Research is of strategic importance at SMU as reflected in its mission to create and disseminate knowledge and aspirations to generate leading-edge research with global impact. Based on a survey that investigated IT needs and requirements of SMU faculty, five primary areas have been identified in the university as important to the conduct and advancement of research in SMU: (i) long term institutional commitment for Faculty research; (ii) the need for more open communication channels; (iii) the need for standardization of policies, tools and standards; (iv) the need to amplify IT infrastructure and tools for research; and (v) dedicated IT support for Faculty research.

In order to assess the achievements and challenges of embedding knowledge management in SMU's research agenda, we use Rowley's (2000) four types of knowledge management objectives of higher education institutions as a lens through which to view SMU: (i) creating and maintaining knowledge repositories; (ii) improving knowledge access; (iii) enhancing the knowledge environment; and (iv) valuing knowledge. The illustrations and findings are based on an online questionnaire survey and focus group discussions conducted as part of a SMU-funded research study "Building An Intelligent Organization: A Knowledge Management Framework for the Singapore Management University (SMU)".

9.3.1. *Creating and Maintaining Knowledge Repositories in Research*

Technology has been exploited through the design and building of a critical IT infrastructure, since SMU started operations in 2000, catering to fundamental needs such as the availability of the communications infrastructure, ensuring the reliability, security and availability of computer hardware and software, setting up SMU's "bread and butter systems", classrooms, etc. Data accumulated are mostly in the areas of student and corporate information. IT support services are centrally provided and are mostly operational. However, they are system driven rather than knowledge driven, something which has been highlighted by Rowley (2000) as a common inadequacy of educational institutions dealing with large amounts of accumulated data. While information has been readily captured in documents and databases through the various IT systems available, there have been less ready efforts to capture and disseminate knowledge, i.e., information combined with experience and judgement (Nonaka and Takeuchi, 1995). Related issues and questions include: "Are people willing to share knowledge or do they hoard it?" or "To what extent can experience-based knowledge be codified and how difficult is it to transfer?" Indeed, a survey on effective knowledge management practices within the university revealed that knowledge hoarding may cause members to be excluded from information, negatively affect their status and reputation, and difficulty in creating new knowledge (see Fig. 9.2 and Chapter 13 of this book).

Knowledge sharing often stops at copyright. Often data and information are only accessible to authorized personnel, and it is not uncommon to hear remarks such as "our communication policy is based on a need to know basis" or terms such as "data owners", "privacy issues", "disclaimers" and the like. To encourage more transparency and sharing of knowledge, work is in progress in SMU to create a repository of research results so that faculty can tap on information in the repository for combined efforts. Applications such as an online "Research Grant Application System" and a "Research Publication System" have been set up so far to provide faculty with information on research

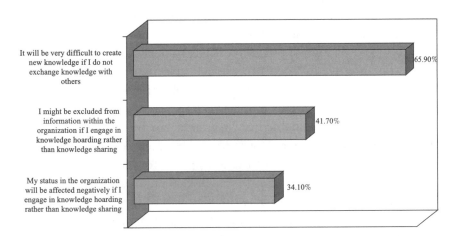

Fig. 9.2. Expected costs of knowledge hoarding.
Source: SMU survey (multiple response question; n = 132).

done and works-in-progress of their colleagues so that communities of researchers can be identified. This will benefit researchers by leveraging previous research and proposal efforts, as well as reduce the turnaround time for research to be completed. Another emerging repository is the Faculty Information System (FIS) which enables the coordination of sharing of academic IT strategies, innovations and solutions, cross faculty programs, as well as to facilitate research collaboration and to provide faculty-centric information for Faculty, Deans, Provost and the President.

Future KM-related projects in the area of research include: (i) the creation of a central repository of research results and research efforts in SMU where contributions by faculty, students and staff are stored and accessed. The idea is to have a digitized archive of research efforts in SMU for reference and for future generations; and (ii) constant evaluation and testing for cheaper, better and faster tools, both in terms of technological methods, hardware and software for research purposes in the various stages of the research processes.

9.3.2. Improving Knowledge Access

To position SMU research in the global arena, the university constantly seeks to invest in information and infrastructure resources as well as to make use of collaborative tools, shared resources and communication channels. Covered by a comprehensive wired and wireless network, SMU is linked via high-speed connectivity to next generation networks (based on Internet Protocols to carry all telecommunication services as opposed to legacy networks that are a collection of specialized networks overlaid on a circuit-switched PSTN) locally and internationally. This technology-enabled environment has benefited research in terms of high-speed connectivity to the research hubs of the world (see Fig. 9.3). SMU is part of the Singapore Advanced Research and Education Network (SingaREN) which is a national initiative to create a high-speed broadband network platform to support and connect research and education (R&E) and advance network technology development in Singapore to partners in the US/Korea/global participating institutions, serving users from academia, research organizations and industry.

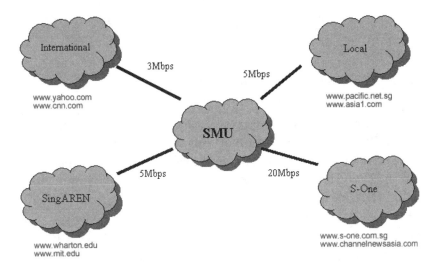

For research and academic oriented access, SMU is connected to Singapore Advanced Research and Education Network, or SingAREN. This in turn connects SMU to a multitude of next-generation Internet initiatives, including Internet2, vBNS and STAR TAP in the North American Continent.

Fig. 9.3. Linking SMU locally and to educational and research centers of the world.

Source: Office of Communications and IT, SMU Intranet 2002.

There is also a fair amount of workspace freedom, where users are given a fair degree of control on what they can store on their PCs, as compared to other education institutions. Faculty, staff and students have the freedom to make use of any other tools they feel that will increase their personal and research productivity, with the recognition that some tools are more productive than others depending on the frequency and relevance of the tools for daily work. SMU provides a standard suite of tools and software (e.g. Microsoft Office, Adobe Acrobat, SPSS, SAS, etc.) for effective and (inter) disciplinary research work. Various funding schemes such as research grants and a DART fund (a fund at the disposal of faculty to initiate research) may be drawn upon for encouraging research endeavours. In addition, faculty members can request for technical help and draw from a comprehensive and growing suite of research software that are relevant to their research needs in areas such as data modelling, psychology, programming, mathematics and statistics, bibliographic citations, as well as design and drawing applications.

9.3.3. Enhancing the Knowledge Environment and Valuing Knowledge

An effective knowledge culture is a key knowledge management enabler. While technology is important in facilitating knowledge management, it is the people who, if they are willing to share and participate in various knowledge exchanges, can create an ideal environment and culture for knowledge and innovation to thrive. Our survey on effective knowledge management practices within the university revealed that engaging in knowledge sharing would help members to avoid costly mistakes, make innovation easier, save time by not "reinventing the wheel", and make more informed decisions with the inputs from colleagues (see Fig. 9.4 and Chapter 12 of this book).

SMU research is making progress towards this direction and more will be done in future to create a conducive environment for knowledge creation, and much more in terms of the valuation of knowledge. A headway towards this direction has been the creation of communities

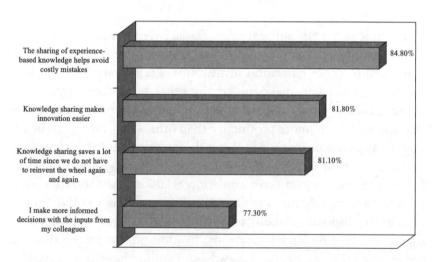

Fig. 9.4. Expected benefits of knowledge sharing.
Source: SMU survey (multiple response question; n = 132).

of interest or practice, defined as "groups of people who share a concern, a set of problems, or a passion about a topic, and who deepen their knowledge and expertise in this area by interacting on an ongoing basis" (Wenger *et al.*, 2002:4). One example is SMU's "Knowledge Force", a newly formed community of interest comprising scholars from various local and international institutions. The Knowledge Force is concerned with the development of theoretical knowledge management (KM) models and practical KM solutions through research and collaboration with other KM specialists and industry partners. Besides conducting theoretical and applied research studies on KM, its members are also active in teaching and consultancy. Their interaction and collaboration have enabled them to explore new and interdisciplinary topics relating to the knowledge society, k-leadership, change management practices in private and public sector organizations, and the development of collaborative culture for results-oriented knowledge sharing.

It is envisioned that more of these communities of interest will be formed in the future. Other routine measures aimed at building a culture of knowledge sharing in the area of research include the organization of regular research workshops and seminars as platforms for the discussion of research findings as well as regular information sharing sessions, e.g. with a focus on new research software and tools.

Within SMU, the Centre for Academic Computing (CAC) was set up to advance university research through information technology and to provide faculty research support throughout the entire research process. Drawing information from various CAC support systems and past experiences, CAC classified SMU's faculty in relation to their research support needs and types (Table 9.1). The respective classification was termed *faculty group mix* and is being used to draft concrete support plans. With information on its clients, CAC is able to map its strategic plans more effectively and to provide relevant and needs-based research resources and support. As the analysis in Table 9.1 suggests, there are some faculty segments (e.g. new researchers who work quantitatively or those with a cross-disciplinary orientation) who need "personalized help" from CAC staff who are familiar with their specific type of work and requirements. To minimize the problem of over-dependency on

Table 9.1. Faculty group mix and support matrix.

Faculty Group Mix (FY2002/03)	Description	Forms of IT Support Needed
Established researchers (both qualitative and quantitative)	Independent • Require minimum help • Know the ropes of doing it • Likely to be mentors	• Relief from research administrative hassle • Research Assistants (RAs) • Research software
New researchers (qualitative)	Independent • Require minimum help • Prefer tested research tools • Likely to be on tenure track	• Research software (if any) • Basic desktop/research software support
New researchers (quantitative)	Independent • Know what they want • Willing to try new tools and committed time and effort into using IT for research (with or without success) • Normally work alone or with undergrads as RAs, rather than Graduate RAs • Likely to be on tenure track	• IT support required is more complex and diversified — hardware set up and repair, software patches, database issues, system design issues, storage and backup issues • High performance computing support • Relief from research administrative hassle • RAs • Research software
Cross-disciplinary researchers and/or "re-born" researchers	Independent • Sometimes do not know what they want • Willing to try new tools but frustrated with steep learning curve • Less willing to commit more time and effort into using IT for research • High expectations with regard to IT and IT support • Most use RAs (undergrads) • Likely to be mature faculty	• Lots of hand-holding especially on newer technologies • Relief from research administrative hassle • Assistance to RAs (if any) • Research software • Faculty IT learning needs

Table 9.1. (*Continued*)

Faculty Group Mix (FY2002/03)	Description	Forms of IT Support Needed
Risk aversive researchers	Interesting group • Committed to doing research whether they are or not on research track • Lack of technical expertise • Afraid of not doing research • Need significant IT support	• New software and IT techniques • IT help to reduce learning curve — some expect help in basic statistics, too. • Range of IT support required is wide — hardware, software and programming, etc. • Faculty IT learning needs
Self-sufficient		• No help needed

particular CAC experts, CAC is in the process of setting-up a knowledge base which contains case histories and solved problem-logs so that other members in CAC can help faculty members whenever their "preferred" support staff is absent.

CAC provides research support throughout the entire research process. During the start-up phase of a new research initiative, for example, it provides matchmaking services to link researchers with similar interests as well as training in statistics. During the preparation phase, the "Research Grant System Website" enables online research grant applications. The site also enables users to track the status of applications, to submit reimbursements and claims, to monitor approved budgets and to upload research output. The actual research work of researchers is supported by the provision of various online survey, library and other services (Fig. 9.5).

CAC's approach is to understand the aspirations and motivations of research faculty and to customize solutions. The mentality of tenure track faculty is often influenced by the "publish or perish syndrome". CAC conducts needs surveys to establish what each faculty requires throughout the research process so as to produce good results. CAC's

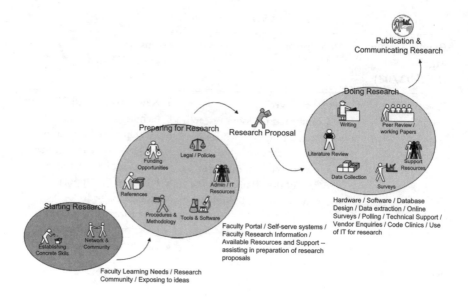

Fig. 9.5. Research support services provided by CAC.

strategy is to be a strong advocate for IT-enabled, "smart" research as well as respective needs. Its support includes:

1. Setting up and supporting a good research IT architecture including resources for numerically intensive computing, large databases, standard compilers, subroutine libraries and other software applications.
2. Sourcing, directing and informing research faculty for/to/about available resources in SMU, offering support services in general consulting, code clinics, training classes, technology searches and reviews.
3. "Jump starting" younger faculty members and returning Faculty Development Scheme (FDS) members as these are the ones that require most help as they have an urgency to publish so as to achieve tenure.
4. Providing certain levels of commitment to IT support and the technologies available for un-sponsored or self-sponsored research.
5. Assisting faculty to publish their work, e.g. in SMU's online working paper series, etc.

If SMU is to produce research of the highest quality and to compete effectively in an increasingly competitive funding environment, administrative or support deficiencies that might hinder faculty to do research have to be minimized. Another key ingredient is the development of a supportive research culture.

A recent brainstorming session about this topic with a focus group of selected members of SMU's faculty produced some concrete KM suggestions and measures that could enhance the quality and conduct of research in SMU. Domains such as leadership, strategy, culture, rewards, technology and processes were identified as key enablers of KM in research (Table 9.2). Two themes surfaced during the focus group session: (i) the importance of trust and support from both peers and top management; and (ii) the need to promote regular knowledge sharing activities such as informal/formal gatherings, workshops and tea/coffee breaks in an attractive environment so as to intensify communication and research-related dialogues both within and beyond the SMU community. The latter included suggestions to appoint internal mentors/referees/reviewers for researchers and potential journal contributions *before* research outputs are submitted to premier journals. It was argued that this would eventually lead to a better understanding of the international review process, the fostering of a culture of peer-review knowledge sharing and impressive publication records.

9.4. Conclusion

Universities are (still) part and parcel of the thriving knowledge business as their core activities are associated with knowledge creation, dissemination and learning. Unlike Rowley (2000), Drucker and others who have predicted that the brick and mortar institutions of higher education will cease to exist in the future due to their inability to reinvent themselves and to catch up with more intelligent, knowledge-creating organizations such as professional consulting firms, we are confident that universities will live up to the challenge and become "smart(er)" organizations with the help of KM. In this paper, we endeavoured to illustrate the applicability of knowledge management to higher education institutions with special reference to university

Table 9.2. KM initiatives to enhance research in SMU: Some brainstorming results.

LEADERSHIP	STRATEGY	CULTURE	HRM/REWARDS	TECHNOLOGY	KM PROCESSES
• Ensure KM support from top management to: (a) allow faculty to fail; (b) allow faculty to experiment; (c) provide sufficient time for research • Find a leader who is acceptable to (almost) everyone to champion research (and KM) • Appoint internal referees for papers written by staff • Conduct peer review of research results "internationally" before submission to top journals	• Formulate strategic research program/agenda to gain competitive advantage • Incorporate KM into school's research policy • Set up study groups (thematic research groups) in line with research strategy • Develop units/"cells" that can stimulate interest groups using KM network • Draw visiting staff into SMU's research activities • Make ownership of research/output known explicitly and provide recognition	• Build a culture conducive to learning and research (e.g. through regular exchange of research results, seminars etc.) • Actively promote an epistemic culture • Build trust among colleagues for cohesiveness • Ensure social facilitation and social interaction • Institute a research-oriented mentor-mentee scheme (e.g. to produce "quality" articles) • Enable coaching of junior staff by experienced (not necessarily senior) staff • Beef up faculty's KM skills and provide respective training • Conduct research workshops so as to share "secrets" of how to conduct top quality research • Have more tea breaks to promote knowledge sharing in research	• Institute an effective reward structure for knowledge *sharing* and research collaboration/facilitation (e.g. coaching others)	• Streamline admin matters to allow researchers to focus on core activities (research) rather than the mundane (research admin) • Provide data-analysis services (e.g. stats) • Provide effective/state-of-the-art search engines • Provide infos about specific research interests and knowledge of academic staff → repository • Enable the sharing of individual KM/research systems → best practice identification • Make effective use of IT so as to enable effective collaboration and to overcome distance • Build up and use a repository of cases to recycle, reuse and rebuild knowledge	• Provide an answer to the question: "If we would only know what we know" • Capture research results • Share and disseminate research results/knowledge • Make/effective use of existing "Rolodex" • Provide a top (thematic) research conference repository

research. Based on the case of the Singapore Management University, we argued that knowledge management concepts and tools can indeed benefit and have the potential to advance the cause of research in the university. Based on Rowley's (2000) typology of knowledge management objectives in universities, we found that KM-led activities and tools in the areas of knowledge repositories and knowledge access have been sufficiently addressed to advance research in SMU. In tandem with the rapid expansion of SMU, more emphasis will be put on the cultivation of a knowledge-sharing environment and knowledge valuation. To become a KM-enabled organization and to implement a KM-led research focus, the following results will have to be achieved.

Firstly, SMU will continue to promote and cultivate a knowledge-sharing culture amongst its members so as to enable and support the exchange of tacit knowledge between individuals and groups/teams, not just at the level of sharing of research results but also with regard to the know-how of producing desired end-results such as top-tier publications. As the story of SMU's Knowledge Force suggests, it might be worthwhile to hatch more communities of interest so that more individuals and groups can create synergies, share knowledge and achieve results. SMU's supportive knowledge-sharing culture will allow its members to share information and knowledge openly, to learn from each other and the past, to act as mentors and to grow professionally.

Ideally, *internal* knowledge-sharing should be proclaimed as a corporate value by universities that is recognized by senior members of the university administration, including board members. Barriers and challenges that need to be addressed in this area include how tacit knowledge can be captured and shared for the good of the university — e.g. to do things, better, faster and cheaper (the know-how). The sharing of know-how plays a key role in many strategic activities and processes such as recruitment and training. As the complexity of SMU's knowledge base increases, the need to cooperate, coordinate and share experience-based knowledge between organizational units will further increase. Eventually this might lead to the need to transfer best practices quickly from one unit to another, a standard KM tool in large organizations. Indirectly, CAC is already heavily involved in such best practice transfer activities as it constantly is on the look out for "tricks and tips" to share with faculty. Once CAC has "wind" of a useful tool, it evaluates, secures, and shares it with faculty. One example is the recent dissemination of knowledge and competencies with regard to Endnotes, a bibliography software that helps to organize references and citations in the course of writing, through sharing and informa- tion sessions for faculty and research staff. It would be ideal that such internal knowledge sharing activities be formalized as a corporate value in the university.

The need to share know-how effectively is of increasing importance in this era of globalization which brings about not only a vast increase of what we know, but an even greater amount of ignorance, i.e., of what we know that we don't know (Luhmann, 1971; Lyotard, 1984; Stichweh, 1995; Evers, 2003b; Evers and Menkhoff, 2004). While knowledge is rapidly increasing, the knowledge about what we do not know is increasing at an even faster pace. The social ability to co-operate and communicate with different kinds of people and experts to share and create knowledge through informal learning and mutual engage- ment will become a key in the fostering of a knowledge-sharing culture in universities and organizations.

In many organizations a "need to know culture" prevails that works against knowledge sharing and innovation. Competition in academia has made works-in-progress confidential and often inacces- sible. Researchers are not rewarded based on the extent of internal knowledge sharing activities but rather based on the number of pub- lications in internationally refereed top journals. Often there are little incentives for university lecturers to share knowledge about effective research strategies and know-how other than participating in research seminars and conferences. The knowledge of doing quality research is normally passed on via mentors/gurus/doctoral supervisors or within trusted informal groups (COI). One of the related challenges is to capture knowledge about best research practices (which usually comes in the form of tacit knowledge, learned through hours of painstak- ing efforts) and to share that amongst other organizational members. Overcoming such challenges requires appropriate incentives and recog- nition for knowledge sharing (e.g. during performance appraisals), mutual trust, suitable mechanisms (e.g. regular share fairs) and a caring organization.

As knowledge no longer remains the domain of academia but increasingly is produced and co-produced by public organizations, industry and think tanks, universities are now confronted with very smart competitors who can generate knowledge quickly as well as the challenge of how to participate and accommodate "different practices of creating and warranting knowledge in different domains" (Knorr-Cetina, 1999:246). As university research becomes increasingly an outcome of collaborative dialogues between researchers and the researcher's target audience and sponsors, there is a trend towards more participative research involving many actors and experts who move less according to the dynamics of their original disciplines and more according to problem and application interests (Gibbons, 2000:41). Gibbons suggests that important intellectual problems are emerging in a "context of application", and pursuing problem interests means that academics may be away from the university, working in teams, with experts from a wide range of intellectual backgrounds, in a variety of organizational settings. As a result, researchers must adopt a different set of research practices to participate in cross-industry collaborative knowledge sharing.

To sum up, the university community and its major stakeholders stand to gain through effective knowledge management and the further development of its knowledge sharing culture based on top management support and allocation of sufficient resources, suitable organizational structures (e.g. the appointment of a chief knowledge officer as head of a KM unit), a reward system which puts a premium on knowledge sharing and innovation rather than knowledge hoarding, top notch KM software solutions and effective KM processes.

References

Allen, A. (1988). *Missions of Colleges and Universities.* San Francisco: Jossey-Bass.

Bennis, W. (1973). *The Learning Ivory Tower.* San Francisco: Jossey-Bass.

Cohen, W.M. and D.A. Levinthal (1990). Innovation and Learning: The Two Faces of R&D. *The Economic Journal*, 99, 569–596.

Crainer, S. and D. Dearlove (1998). *Gravy Training: Inside the Shadowy World of Business Schools.* United Kingdom: Capstone Publishing Limited.

Daniel, J. (1996). *Mega-Universities and Knowledge Media: Technology Strategies for Higher Education.* London: Kogan Page.

224   B. Loh et al.

Davenport, T.H., D.W. DeLong and M.C. Beers (1998). Successful Knowledge Management Projects. *Sloan Management Review*, 39(2), 443–57.

Drucker, P.F. (2000). Into Knowledge. *Forbes Global*, 15 May 2000.

Edwards, K. (1998). *Restructuring the University: New Technologies for Teaching and Learning.* Paris: CRE Association of European Universities.

Etzkowitz, H. and L. Leydesdorff (1997). *Universities and the Global Knowledge Economy: A Triple Helix of University-Industry-Government Relations.* London: Pinter.

Evers, H.D. (1999). The Global Context of Development Anthropology: Social and Cultural Dimensions of Market Expansion. *Development Anthropologist*, 17(1), 108–116.

Evers, H.D. (2000a). Globalisation, Local Knowledge and the Growth of Ignorance: The Epistemic Construction of Reality. *Southeast Asian Journal of Social Science*, 28(1), 13–22.

Evers, H.D. (2000b). Epistemic Cultures: Towards a New Sociology of Knowledge. Working Paper No. 151, Department of Sociology. National University of Singapore.

Evers, H.D. (2003a). Malaysian Knowledge Society and the Knowledge Gap. *Asian Journal of Social Science*, 31(1), 383–397.

Evers, H.D. (2003b). Transition Towards a Knowledge Society: Malaysia and Indonesia in Comparative Perspective. *Comparative Sociology*, 2(2), 355–373.

Evers, H.D. and T. Menkhoff (2004). Expert Knowledge and the Role of Consultants in an Emerging Knowledge-based Economy. *Human Systems Management*, 23(2), 137–149.

Firer, S. and S.L.M. Williams (2003). Intellectual Capital and Traditional Measures of Corporate Performance. *Journal of Intellectual Capital*, 4(3), 348–360.

Franklin, M. Hodgkinson and J. Stewart (1998). Towards Universities as Learning Organizations. *The Learning Organization*, 5(5), 228–238.

Fuller, S. (2002). *Knowledge Management Foundations.* Boston and Oxford: Butterworth Heinemann.

Geiger, R. (1993). *Research and Relevant Knowledge: American Research Universities since World War II.* New York and Oxford: Oxford University Press.

Geuna, A. (1999). *The Economics of Knowledge Production: Funding and the Structure of University Research.* Cheltenham: Edward Elgar.

Gibbons, M. (1998). Higher Education Relevance in the 21st Century. *World Bank Working Paper No. 19717.* Washington: World Bank Group.

Gibbons, M. (2000). Universities and the New Production of Knowledge: Some policy Implications for Government. In *Changing Modes*, A. Kraak (ed.). Cape Town: Human Sciences Research Council Publishing.

Gibbons, M. *et al.* (1994). *The New Production of Knowledge: Science and Research in Contemporary Societies.* London: Sage.

Goddard, A. (1998). Facing Up to Market Forces. *Times Higher Education Supplement*, 13 November 1998, 6–7.

Godin, B. and Y. Gingras (1999). The Place of Universities in the System of Knowledge Production. *Research Policy*, 28(2), 273–278.

Hailes, S. and R. Hazemi (1998). Reinventing the Academy. In *The Digital University: Reinventing the Academy*, R. Hazemi *et al.* (eds.). London: Springer.

Humboldt, W. (1970). On the Spirit and the Organizational Framework of Intellectual Institutions in Berlin. *Minerva*, 8(2), 242–250.

Jones, D.R. and A.L. Pritchard (1999). Realizing the Virtual University. *Educational Technology*, 39(5), 56–59.

Kidwell, J., K. Linde and S. Johnson (2000). Applying Corporate Knowledge Management Practices in Higher Education. *Educause Quarterly*, 4, 28–33.

Knorr-Cetina, K. (1999). *Epistemic Cultures: How Sciences Make Knowledge*. London: Harvard University Press.

Liebowitz, J. (2000). *Building Organizational Intelligence: A Knowledge Management Primer*. Boca Raton: CRC Press.

Luhmann, N. (1971). Die Weltgesellschaft. *Archiv für Rechts- und Sozialphilosophie*, 57(1), 1–35.

Lyotard, J.F. (1984). *The Postmodern Condition: A Report on Knowledge*. Manchester: Manchester University Press.

Menkhoff, T., Y.W. Chay and B. Loh (2004). Notes from an "Intelligent Island": Towards Strategic Knowledge Management in Singapore's Small Business Sector. *International Quarterly for Asian Studies*, 35(1–2), 85–99.

Mills, Q. and J. Pumo (1999). Managing Change in Higher Education. In *Renewing Administration: Preparing Colleges and Universities for the 21st Century*, D. Oblinger and R. Katz (eds.). Bolton, MA: Anker.

Muller, S. (1998). The Management of the Modern University. In *University in Transition*, D. Muller-Boling *et al.* (eds.). Guetersloh: Bertelsmann Foundation Publishers.

Muthesius, S. (2001). *The Post-War University: Utopianist Campus and College*. Boston, MA: Yale University Press.

Nonaka, I. and H. Takeuchi (1995). *The Knowledge Creating Company*. New York: Oxford University Press.

OECD (2000). *Knowledge Management in the Learning Society*. Paris: OECD.

Peters, M. (2002). Education Policy in the Age of Knowledge Capitalism. *Keynote address to the World Comparative Education Forum on Economic Globalization and Education Reforms*, 14–16th October 2002, Beijing Normal University, China.

Pornchulee, A.A. (2001). Knowledge Management in Higher Education. *Proceedings of the 1st SEAMEO Education Congress*, Bangkok, March 2001, Thailand.

Rada, R. (2001). *Understanding Virtual Universities*. Bristol: Intellect.

Rowley, J. (2000). Is Higher Education Ready for Knowledge Management? *The International Journal of Educational Management*, 14(7), 325–333.

Senge, M. (1990). *The Fifth Discipline: The Art and Practice of the Learning Organization*. New York: Doubleday/Currency.

Stichweh, R. (1995). Zur Theorie der Weltgesellschaft. *Soziale Systeme*, 1(1), 29–46.

Stiglitz, J. (1999a). April 3 — Last Update Public Policy For a Knowledge Economy. *Remarks at the Department for Trade and Industry and Center for Economic Policy Research*, 27 January 1999, London. Available: *http://www.worldbank.org/html/extdr/extme/jssp012799a.htm* [Accessed 3 April 2003].

Stiglitz, J. (1999b). April 3 — Last Update On Liberty, The Right To Know, and Public Discourse: The Role of Transparency in Public Life, *Oxford Amnesty Lecture*, 27 January 1999, Oxford, U.K. Available: *http://www.worldbank.org/html/extdr/extme/jssp012799.htm* [Accessed 3 April 2003].

Trow, M. (2000). From Mass Higher Education to Universal Access: The American Advantage. *Minerva*, 37, 1–26.

Tschang, T. (2001). Virtual Universities and Learning Environments: Characterizing their Emergence and Design. In *Access to Knowledge: New Information Technologies and the Emergence of the Virtual University*, T. Tschang and D. Senta (eds.). Oxford: Pergamon.

Warner, D. and D. Palfreyman (2001). *The State of UK Higher Education: Managing Change and Diversity*. Buckingham: SRHE/Open University Press.

Wenger E., R. McDermott, and W.M. Synder (2002). Cultivating Communities of Practice. Boston: Harvard Business School Press.

World Bank, The (1998). *World Development Report: Knowledge For Development*. Oxford: Oxford University Press.

Part IV

KM Applications and Challenges

Chapter 10

Notes from an "Intelligent Island": Towards Strategic Knowledge Management in Singapore's Small Business Sector[1]

Thomas Menkhoff, Yue Wah Chay and Benjamin Loh

10.1. Introduction

Singapore is successfully transforming itself into a knowledge-based economy. As a response to the country's rapid development progress on the basis of export-led growth and the inputs by multinational companies, Singapore's government unveiled a new policy framework in 1991 that would take the country to the "next lap" of its development trajectory. The next lap strategy called for more ambitious industrialization programs in order to take Singapore to a higher level of technological sophistication and a shift towards knowledge-intensive industries. The computerization of Singapore's civil service which can be traced back to 1981, the remarkable IT literacy of local students, the systematic recruitment of foreign talents for new growth areas such as biotechnology and life sciences or the wireless technology-enabled lecture rooms of local universities such as the Singapore Management University (SMU) underline the commitment and gravity of respective policy implementations.

[1] This is a revised version of a paper presented at the International Conference on Globalization, Innovation and Human Resource Development for Competitive Advantage. Bangkok, Thailand, 17th–19th December 2002. The authors gratefully acknowledge the support of the management and staff of Origin Exterminators Pte. Ltd., and other informants who participated in the research. The Arnold–Bergstraesser Institute in Freiburg, Germany, kindly allowed us to reprint this essay which was first published in the *International Quarterly for Asian Studies*, Vol. 35, Nos. 1–2 (2004), 85–99.

Singapore's vision of the city-state as an intelligent island was spelled out in the National IT Plan (1986) and the IT2000 blueprint, a rolling plan developed in 1992. Due to continuous IT investments, an increasing number of households have a PC. Singapore's Internet penetration rate is very high, and more and more Singapore homes have access to the republic's nationwide broadband network. The World Competitiveness Yearbook has ranked Singapore among the top nations in the world for strategic exploitation of IT (National Computer Board, 1997a; 1997b; Mah, 1999).

The K-economy policy goals of Singapore's government represent both opportunities and challenges for the local small- and medium-sized enterprise (SME) sector which has been recognized as "an indigenous base [that] is more permanent and durable than a foreign one" (Lee and Low, 1990:23). SMEs are increasingly seen as important vehicles for increasing the economy's competitiveness in the global market system and essential for sustained long-term economic stability. In April 2000, a 10-year strategic SME 21 Plan was set up to prepare Singapore's SMEs for the new paradigm of the knowledge-based economy and to enable these companies to gain the required expertise to undertake knowledge-intensive activities (Singapore Productivity and Standards Board, 2000:4). In line with the ongoing transition towards a truly knowledge-based society, more and more private sector companies in the lion city (following the lead of Singapore's public sector organizations) are proactively embracing knowledge management concepts.

A recent survey of change management practices of 101 local SMEs conducted by the authors (Menkhoff, Chay and Loh, 2002) revealed that Singaporean SME owners implement organizational change measures on a routine basis. Changing the firm's strategic direction and technology, IT-related changes, and changes related to people and their task behaviour were the most frequently adopted measures (see Fig. 10.1).

Further evidence for the increasing attractiveness of KM is provided by numerous case studies of organizations published in Singapore's local media such as the *Straits Times/Computer Times* that succeeded in learning from past experiences and leveraging upon human capital

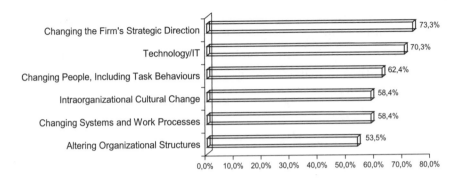

Fig. 10.1. Most frequently adopted change measures.

assets through effective KM systems built upon conducive cultures of interaction, collaboration, and mutual enrichment.

This essay outlines some of the potential benefits and challenges of implementing strategic knowledge management systems in SMEs. Research questions include: What is knowledge management and why has it become an issue? Why should SMEs adopt strategic KM? What are the potential benefits and pitfalls of KM in SMEs? What are the main drivers and tools of KM? How do KM systems for SMEs look in reality? The latter will be illustrated by a local case-study, namely a small pest control firm whose owners implemented various smart KM tools aimed at increasing operational effectiveness and customer service quality.

10.2. What is KM?

Knowledge management can be defined as the task of developing and exploiting both tangible and intangible knowledge resources of an organization. Tangible assets include information and experience-based knowledge about customers, suppliers, products, competitors etc. Intangible assets include the competencies and knowledge resources of people within the organization. In brief, KM refers to the totality of organizational strategies aimed at creating a *smart* organization, which is able to derive maximum benefit from its tangible and intangible assets, to learn from past experiences, whether successful or unsuccessful, and to create new knowledge. According to KM gurus, KM should be business driven and strategic in outlook so as to maximize return on (intellectual) capital and to sustain business success in an era of turbulent markets and global market expansion (Nahapiet and Ghoshal, 1998).

10.3. Why KM has Become an Issue?

The process of globalization — driven by the explosive growth of new information and communication technologies — has increased competition and thereby the need to make more effective use of both individual and organizational knowledge assets. Another factor in the emergence of KM concepts is the continuous "rightsizing" trend. Starting in the 1980s, corporate downsizing measures led to the loss of valuable information and knowledge resources and subsequently to the emergence of KM as a strategic countermeasure. These developments saw an increased emphasis on technology and KM systems to capture knowledge residing in employees' minds (tacit knowledge) and to turn it into explicit knowledge. In view of the explosive growth of information sources (e.g. Internet) and the accelerated pace of technological change, KM was propagated as an effective coping strategy. KM gurus often regard technology as a crucial "enabler" of information and knowledge sharing across platforms and continents. Within an organization it enables the more effective use of knowledge. Enlightened leadership and a strategic outlook, a "high care culture" (Von Krogh, 1998), supportive human resource management practices and reward systems represent other important KM constituents.

10.4. How SMEs can Benefit from KM?

Core business-driven knowledge processes in organizations include: (i) locating and capturing knowledge; (ii) sharing knowledge; and (iii) creating new knowledge (see Fig. 10.2). Many benefits can be derived by both small and large firms from the implementation of KM systems as illustrated below.

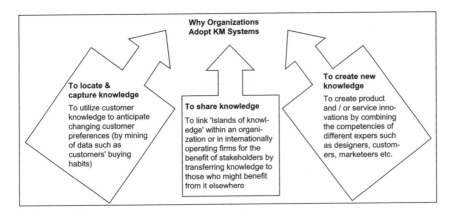

Fig. 10.2. Steps in the KM event chain and benefits of KM systems.
Sources: Von Krogh (1998); Von Krogh, Ichijo and Nonaka (2000); Von Krogh, Nonaka and Nishiguchi (2000).

By locating and capturing innovative ideas and other types of strategically important knowledge such as best practices used by technicians to solve maintenance problems, small entrepreneurs can improve innovativeness, service quality and response time. The documentation of "war stories", yellow pages and data mining are useful KM tools for locating and capturing knowledge.

By sharing knowledge and experiences about cost-effective procedures and operational approaches, SME owners can achieve substantial savings. Tea gatherings, TGF meetings, intranet systems and groupware platforms represent suitable "technological" enablers of knowledge sharing and collaboration.

Through the analysis of completed projects and the generation of new knowledge in the form of lessons learned through so-called after-action reviews, small entrepreneurs can avoid potentially costly future mistakes (Carlsen and Skaret, 1999; Groom and David, 2001). Creating new knowledge, for example within small teams whose members share a mutual context of experience and collaborate on a joint task bonded by a common sense of purpose and the need to know what the other "community members" know, can lead to profitable product and service innovations.

10.5. Knowledge Management Challenges in SMEs

10.5.1. *Challenge No. 1*

One of the objectives of KM is to maximize return on an organization's tangible and intangible knowledge assets and resources such as customer-related information or the tacit knowledge, competencies and experiences resident in the minds of employees. KM aims at creating a "smart" organization, which is able to learn from experience-based knowledge and to transfer it into new knowledge in the form of product and/or service innovations. One example is the set-up and use of computerized files to record and keep track of customers' preferences, as well as inquiries, etc. aimed at improving customer relationships. Many firms integrate such KM strategies into their CRM systems.

Many SME owner-managers, however, are not familiar with the conceptual basis and potential benefit of KM models, the latest KM software tools and so forth. To develop people's capacity to learn as well as the collective intelligence of an organization requires KM competencies, visionary leadership, a "high organizational care culture" (Von Krogh, 1998) so that they are willing to share ideas, information, knowledge and space (Schrage, 1997) and, last but not least, an efficient and suitable communication and information infrastructure. A survey of KM practices adopted by SMEs in the Netherlands by Beijerse (2000) revealed a surprisingly long list of knowledge sharing practices but also significant gaps as shown in Table 10.1.

10.5.2. *Challenge No. 2*

SMEs do make use of various KM tools (see Fig. 10.3) in their day-to-day business such as maintaining CV databanks, having discussions with customers, conducting market inventories and so forth. However, the development of a truly visionary KM strategy and creation of a business-driven, IT-based knowledge information system are often neglected. SMEs seldom have a systematic KM policy on the strategic level with regard to the monitoring and evaluation of available, "nice to have" and "must have knowledge" or the development, acquisition, organization, sharing, utilization and/or creation of (innovative) knowledge.

Table 10.1. Knowledge sharing gaps in SMEs.

KM instruments found in KM literature	Found in SMEs?
Appointment of information agents	No
Facilitation of a "consultation culture"	No
Facilitation of private chats	No
Holding internal (information and/or knowledge) audits	No
Internal secondment	No
Knowledge management system	No
Job rotation	No
Theme and task groups with various employees	No
Working in autonomous work groups	No

Source: Beijerse (2000).

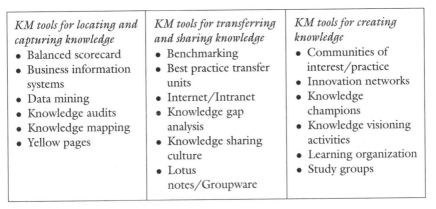

KM tools for locating and capturing knowledge	KM tools for transferring and sharing knowledge	KM tools for creating knowledge
• Balanced scorecard • Business information systems • Data mining • Knowledge audits • Knowledge mapping • Yellow pages	• Benchmarking • Best practice transfer units • Internet/Intranet • Knowledge gap analysis • Knowledge sharing culture • Lotus notes/Groupware	• Communities of interest/practice • Innovation networks • Knowledge champions • Knowledge visioning activities • Learning organization • Study groups

Fig. 10.3. Knowledge management tools.

Sources: Schrage (1997); Von Krogh (1998); Von Krogh, Ichijo and Nonaka (2000); Von Krogh, Nonaka and Nishiguchi (2000).

10.5.3. *Challenge No. 3*

SME owners do not always create facilitative structures for simple KM activities such as capturing existing knowledge or more complex ones such as the continuous creation of new knowledge. Very often cultural barriers such as distrust, lack of recognition and communication, "knowledge is power" mindsets, retrenchment concerns and so forth act as demotivators with regard to effective knowledge sharing and utilization of "what we know".

10.6. Strategic Imperatives of KM in SMEs

The particular implementation needs of a SME depend on the size, needs, market position, strategic outlook and resources/assets of the respective firm. Potential strategic business objectives of KM include risk management, improvement of operational efficiency and innovativeness, customer-driven learning through fully integrated customer feedback systems etc. (Von Krogh, 1998; Von Krogh, Ichijo and Nonaka, 2000; Von Krogh, Nonaka and Nishiguchi, 2000).

Firms which put emphasis on risk management and uncertainty reduction, often integrate KM into scenario planning activities aimed at assessing the impact of external factors such as changing government policies and regulations on the particular business. SWOT analyses are suitable means to generate knowledge about competitors' behaviour, possible reactions and counter strategies.

Most organizations are eager to improve operational efficiency. KM can be a great help here by initiating activities aimed at sharing knowledge about intra-organizational best practices (e.g. in the field of sales and marketing or technical support), e.g. through institutionalized best practice forums, share fairs etc. In many organizations, islands of knowledge (silos) exist that could be effectively linked with the help of a KM system so as to improve knowledge exchange, learning and performance.

Strategy goals with regard to innovation can be attained through the proactive creation of new knowledge (e.g. in the form of new ideas, service forms, etc.) by exploiting potential synergies between different types of experts and their tacit knowledge assets in the context of communities of interest, dedicated study groups etc. Very often management does little to facilitate such endeavours. According to the Japanese KM gurus Nonaka and Takeuchi (1995), the "combination" of different knowledge resources is a key modus for the generation of new knowledge. Innovations on the basis of real collective learning are often created in small teams whose members share a mutual context of experience and collaborate on a joint task bonded by a common sense of purpose and the need to know what the other "community members" know.

10.7. Do Small and Large Firms Require Different KM Approaches?

Whether firms require specific KM systems depends on their size and other issues which have to be systematized during a "KM needs assessment exercise". By default many SMEs already have in place what experts call "facilitating structural requirements for successful KM implementation" such as a flexible and flat organizational structure. Real challenges for SMEs in the field of KM include delegation of decision-making authority, the creation of an open culture, the use of more sophisticated KM tools such as knowledge mapping techniques, benchmarking, scenario planning, IT-based KM tools etc. on the basis of a pro-active KM strategy embedded in a motivating culture (Von Krogh, 1998). Many large organizations cannot be classified as intelligent organizations. Size matters but is not the main issue. E-learning, for example, is a valuable option for both small and large firms. SMEs which want to "go shopping" for the right vendor or tool should consult business associations, IT promotion agencies, Chambers of Commerce, etc. in order to contact vendors and consultants who have successfully implemented KM systems in small firms. Before purchasing any specific KM system, KM needs should be assessed thoroughly (e.g. with the help of a consultant). SMEs should also check whether they are eligible for IT/KM-related SME grants.

In Singapore, assistance for the setting up of corporate KM systems comes under the Local Enterprise Computerization Programme (LECP), which is administered by the Singapore Productivity and Innovation Board (SPRING). This program aims at encouraging local enterprises to achieve a higher level of competitiveness through more effective use of information technology (IT). SMEs can obtain assistance under LECP to defray the cost of engaging qualified and reputable IT consultants for their computerization project in the following areas:

- Feasibility Study: includes fact-finding, definition and documentation of user requirements, short-listing of computer vendors and preparation of "Request for Proposal" (RFP), evaluation and recommendation of hardware and software as well as the development of an implementation plan.

- Implementation Consultancy: includes initial fact finding, definition and documentation of user requirements, initial project schedule planning, project monitoring and control, procedure streamlining and formalization, assistance in data conversion, planning and conduct of user acceptance test, planning for post-implementation review, etc.

The LEC program subsidizes the costs of a feasibility study and implementation consultancy but does not cover the cost of the KM software.

10.8. Towards Effective KM in SMEs

Beijerse's (2000) survey of KM practices of SMEs in the Netherlands found that SMEs lack: (i) systematic KM policies on a strategic level with regard to the monitoring of available/necessary knowledge or the development, acquisition, locking, sharing, utilization or evaluation of knowledge (strategy); (ii) policies on a tactical level to make the structure facilitative of development, acquisition and locking of knowledge (structure); and (iii) policies to enable a motivating culture with regard to sharing and utilizing knowledge (culture).

As in the context of change management, the mindset of small entrepreneurs is often a major hindrance for implementing new KM systems (Menkhoff, Kay and Loh, 2002). Based on research on change management practices of SMEs in Singapore, we argue that entrepreneurs with a tertiary education in business management or engineering and certain personality traits such as change propensity will find it easier to appreciate and embrace KM concepts, provided they are not too impatient when it comes to measuring the return on investment (ROI) in KM systems. With a good strategy, suitable KM policies, caring leadership behaviour and a proper performance management system as well as the right KM tools, it can be expected that more and more SME owners will succeed in making internal/external knowledge assets more productive so as to leverage organizational core competencies.

We will now examine the case study of a Singaporean SME, which overcame these challenges and implemented a knowledge management solution for its business operations.

10.9. Case Study: Pest Control Knowledge Management at Origin Exterminators (Singapore) Pte Ltd

Origin Exterminators Pte. Ltd. is a Singapore pest control firm that uses knowledge management technology to improve its pest control methods and operations. The small and medium-size enterprise (SME) provides an array of pest management and consultancy services such as subterranean termite inspection and treatment, rodent baiting and trapping, mosquito larvaciding and fogging, and specialized termite management programs. It serves over 2000 clients in hotels, condominiums, commercial properties, industrial estates, residential homes, restaurants, clubs, schools, places of worship and government sites.

Recognizing the imperatives and benefits of adopting IT in order to retain a leading position in the knowledge-based economy, Origin's director Carl Baptista teamed up with an Internet business solutions provider, iBase Technology Pte. Ltd., to develop and implement a web-based Enterprise Resource Planning (ERP) solution to integrate information between major functions such as human resources, operations and sales. Previously loaded with manual paperwork and discontinued knowledge flows between front-end and back-end operations, Origins is now web-enabled with a customer-oriented online interface where clients can log in to check the status of pest control, make online payments, and obtain cost estimates for other services.

A wireless and convergence technology system was also part of the ERP solution at Origins. Armed with a wireless GSM-enabled Palm handheld with barcode reader, each of Origin's field operators is able to coordinate concurrent task operations at the pest control site. For example, after laying down several baits in a large rat-infested area, the field operators subsequently scan the tags attached to the bait and input information on how much bait has been consumed. The information is then transmitted to the base-station at Origin's headquarters where the data can be processed by pest management experts who now have real-time and consolidated knowledge of the infestation condition of the entire site. This allows the experts to react and rectify problems, issue detailed and customized procedures, and communicate with their teams on the field.

This wireless solution also saw an increase in productivity and efficiency in scheduling and operations. Previously Origin's management had no control over staff activities on the field and could therefore not ensure their clients of a uniform quality service. The only mode of communication upon completion of a job was by public telephone. With the wireless convergence system in place, a Short-Message-Service (SMS) is sent through the Palm handheld when a job is begun, and another when it is completed. This allows Origin's management and pest experts at the headquarters to track the precise duration of the job, how well it was accomplished, and to issue subsequent job orders.

Over 70% of the cost of implementing the ERP and wireless solution was subsidized by a LETAS grant from the then Singapore Productivity and Standards Board (now the Singapore Productivity and Innovation Board). With such positive endorsement of knowledge and IT-led upgrading for SMEs, Origins is now considering plans to introduce Global Positioning Satellite (GPS) technology into its knowledge-enabled pest-control business.

10.10. Conclusion

SMEs can benefit from knowledge management concepts and tools. As economies and businesses shift towards a new world configuration of digital information and knowledge-based work, SME owners need to take on this challenge and find out how information and communication technologies as well as KM solutions can assist them. To assist the SME sector to keep pace with the emerging knowledge-based economy, government agencies, chambers of commerce, industrial and private sector organizations will need to commit more resources and provide more assistance in order to make the implementation of KM in SMEs more tangible and economically viable. Owners and managers of SMEs must be willing to break away from practices that had worked well for them in the old economy, and embrace the changes now associated with the new economy. Contrary to trends detected in our own study on the change propensity of (Chinese) SME owner-managers in Singapore (Menkhoff, Kay and Loh, 2002), a recent survey (Chua, 2001) of 158 Chinese enterprises in Singapore showed that a relatively large proportion of these firms paid insufficient attention to IT skills upgrading, innovation as a source of competitiveness, product customization, customer satisfaction and e-commerce operations. Based on these indicators, the author concluded that many SMEs in Singapore are not yet ready for the new economy. Predictors and key ingredients of entrepreneurial "new economy compliance" remain, however, unclear.

Singapore's SME policy makers do hope that new economy related assistance schemes will motivate more local small entrepreneurs to embrace related changes proactively. To increase online transaction capability of local SMEs and to encourage small entrepreneurs to adopt "ready-made" e-commerce solutions, both Singapore's SPRING and the Infocomm Development Authority (IDA) have implemented various new economy related SME upgrading schemes during the past few years. As illustrated above, Origin Exterminators represents a dynamic beneficiary of these policies. The characteristics of those small entrepreneurs who take up the challenge (and those who do not) have yet to be ascertained by empirical research (Menkhoff and Gerke, 2002). Many analysts are excited about the challenges and economic dynamism that KM will bring, and research is currently being conducted by the authors of this essay to examine KM practices in Singaporean and German organizations. We seek to examine how knowledge is created and utilized in business organizations, and to understand the process whereby individual and organizational learning is transformed into key competencies and practices. National cultures matter. But in what ways? It is hoped that the study will help to identify some of the drivers of effective KM processes in small firms and to establish what it takes to improve firm performance through KM systems.

References

Albrow, M. and E. King (eds.) (1981). *Globalization, Knowledge and Society*. London: Sage Publications.

Baber, Z. (ed.) (1998). Science, Technology and Society in the Asia-Pacific Region. *Southeast Asian Journal of Social Science*, 26, 1.

Beck, U. (1992). *Risk Society: Towards a New Modernity*. London and Newbury Park: Sage Publications.

Beijerse, R. (2000). Knowledge Management in Small- and Medium-sized Companies. *Journal of Knowledge Management*, 4(2), 162–179.

Carlsen, A. and M. Skaret (1999). Practicing Knowledge Management: Lessons from Processes in Small Firms. In *Knowledge Management: Enterprise, Network and Learning* J. Schreinermakers and J. Barthes (eds.), pp. 47–55. Würzburg: Ergon Verlag.

Chua, S.E. (2001). The New Economy and Chinese Enterprises in Singapore. Unpublished MS., Faculty of Business Administration, National University of Singapore.

Collis, D.J. (1998). The Management Consulting Industry. In *Career Guide Management Consulting*, A.R. Miller (ed.). Harvard Business School in association with the Harvard Business School Management Consulting Club.

Delanty, G. (1999). *Social Theory in a Changing World: Conceptions of Modernity*. Malden: Polity.

Drucker, P.F. (1994). *Postcapitalist Society*. New York: Harper Business.

Dutrenit, G. (2000). *Learning and Knowledge Management in the Firm: From Knowledge Accumulation to Strategic Capabilities*. Cheltenham and Northampton: Edward Elgar.

Evers, H.-D. (2000a). Globalization, Local Knowledge and the Growth of Ignorance: The Epistemic Construction of Reality. *Southeast Asian Journal of Social Science*, 28(1), 13–22.

Evers, H.-D. (2000b). Epistemic Cultures: Towards a New Sociology of Knowledge. Working Paper No. 151, Department of Sociology, National University of Singapore.

Evers, H.-D. (2003). Knowledge Society and the Modernization of Southeast Asia (Interview with Prof Evers). *Harvard Asia Quarterly*, Winter Issue.

Evers, H.-D. and T. Menkhoff (2004). Reflections about the Role of Expert Knowledge and Consultants in an Emerging Knowledge-based Economy. *Human Systems Management*, 23(4), 137–149.

Groom, J. and F. David (2001). Competitive Intelligence Activity among Small Firms. *SAM Advanced Management Journal*, 66(1), 12–20.

Kennedy Information Research Group (2001). *The Global Consulting Marketplace: Key Data, Forecasts and Trends*. Peterborough: Kennedy Information, Inc.

Knorr-Cetina, K. (1998). *Epistemic Cultures: How Science Makes Sense*. Cambridge: Harvard University Press.

Lee, T.Y. and L. Low (1990). *Local Entrepreneurship in Singapore: Private and State*. Singapore: Times Academic Press.

Lu, M. (ed.) (2001). *The Harvard Business School Guide to Careers in Management Consulting*. Harvard Business School in Association with the Harvard Business School Management Consulting Club.

Luhmann, N. (1971). Die Weltgesellschaft. *Archiv für Rechts- und Sozialphilosophie*, 57(1), 1–35.

Lyotard, J.-F. (1984). *The Postmodern Condition: A Report on Knowledge*. Manchester: Manchester University Press.

Mah, B.T. (1999). Towards an Information Society. *The World Paper Online*, January.

Menkhoff, T., Y.W. Chay and B. Loh (2002). Change Leadership in Organizations: The Case of Singapore's Small- and Medium-Sized Enterprises. *International Small Business Series*, W. Koenig, K. Mueller and R. Strohmeyer. Institute of Small Business, University of Goettingen, Federal Republic of Germany.

Menkhoff, T. and S. Gerke (eds.) (2002). *Chinese Entrepreneurship and Asian Business Networks*. London and New York: Routledge Curzon.

Menkhoff, T., L. Kay and B. Loh (2002). Worlds Apart? Reflections on the Relationship Between Small Entrepreneurs and External Change Advocates in Singapore. *Journal of Asian Business*, 18(1), 37–65.

Nahapiet, J. and S. Ghoshal (1998). Social Capital, Intellectual Capital, and the Organizational Advantage. *Academy of Management Review*, 23(2), 242–266.

Nonaka, I. and H. Takeuchi (1995). *The Knowledge-Creating Company*. Oxford: Oxford University Press.

National Computer Board (1997a). *IT 2000. A Vision of an Intelligent Island*. Singapore.

National Computer Board (1997b). *Transforming Singapore into an Intelligent Island*. Singapore.

Schrage, M. (1997). Collaborative Tools: A First Look. In *Knowledge Management Tools*, R.L. Ruggles III (ed.). Boston: Butterworth-Heinemann.

Singapore Productivity and Standards Board (2000). *SME 21: Positioning SMEs for the 21st Century*. Singapore: SPSB.

Stehr, N. (1994). *Knowledge Societies*. London: Sage.

Von Krogh, G. (1998). Care in Knowledge Creation. *California Management Review*, 40(3), 133–154.

Von Krogh, G., K. Ichijo and I. Nonaka (2000). *Enabling Knowledge Creation — How to Unlock the Mystery of Tacit Knowledge and Release the Power of Innovation*. New York: Oxford University Press.

Von Krogh, G., I. Nonaka and T. Nishiguchi (2000). *Knowledge Creation — A Source of Value*. London: McMillan Press.

Chapter 11

Collaboration and Competition: The Knowledge Research Institute of Singapore as a Model KM System[1]

Patrick Lambe

11.1. Introduction

The following case study describes KM implementation challenges in Singapore. While the case is fictional, the study is solidly research-based, and addresses commonly-encountered KM implementation challenges in the Singapore context. We have deliberately displayed several functional roles to help readers identify the different ways in which KM challenges may emerge, and give some thought to how they might be addressed. The purpose of this study is to help organizations and managers anticipate and address common, repeated, and damaging but often unacknowledged pitfalls in rolling out a KM project. This purpose drives the subject matter as well as the form in which the case is presented.

The background research for this study comes from two main sources: (1) a survey of public case studies on twenty two KM projects in Singapore from journals, magazines, academic case study projects and conference presentations; and (2) input and insights from Straits Knowledge's survey-based reports (Straits Knowledge, 2002a; 2002b; 2003).

This background research formed the basis of a deep understanding of the context in which KM is implemented in Singapore, and allowed

---

[1]Copyright © Patrick Lambe 2005.

us to identify typical implementation scenarios, as well as commonly perceived challenges and issues. In particular, we found that there was often an over-confidence in technology and process at the expense of a real appreciation of the cultural, leadership and strategy focus issues involved in any KM project. These latter themes come through very strongly in the case study presented here.

The primary material from this case study and those to be published in Lambe (2005) came from a series of fifteen confidential interviews with practising knowledge managers or managers who had been involved in some way with a KM project. The interviews covered public and private sector organizations, government linked corporations, multinationals, small and medium enterprises, and organizations in the educational sector. The interviewees were assured of confidentiality in order to reduce their inhibitions about disclosing information about challenges encountered in their projects. We are profoundly grateful to these interviewees for their knowledge-sharing in support of finding better ways of anticipating and addressing the challenges they encountered.

To mitigate bias, the interview questions did not present or suggest any of the key challenges or barriers previously encountered in our research. The structure of the interviews was typically as follows: (1) we asked the interviewee to give a brief account of the background and rationale behind the KM project being described; (2) we explored the timeline of the project in greater depth, identifying key transition points, both positive and negative; (3) we explored those key transition points in detail, focusing on the challenges identified by the interviewee; and (4) we asked the interviewees what they would have done differently, given their present hindsight and experience.

From the raw material of the interview transcripts, we identified six common themes: each of these is represented as a dominant theme in at least one of the case studies (Lambe, 2005):

- Technology management and project management issues, including integration with existing platforms and systems;
- Knowledge continuity in environments of rapid change, and the need to maintain a very clear focus and set of objectives;
- The resourcing of KM in terms of staffing, time allocation and management support;

- The negative impact of unclear strategic direction and internal politics;
- The impact of having too many stakeholders with divergent agendas in a KM initiative; and
- Issues that emerge when KM is superficially understood by organizational leadership, but is promoted as "politically correct".

Underlying all of these are the problems in KM projects that are caused by poor strategic focus, poor strategic alignment, and poor project planning and resourcing.

Once the themes were identified, they were abstracted from their original contexts, and new scenarios were constructed based on our background research. Our aim in constructing these fictional organizations was to create contexts that would be realistic and recognisably Singaporean, within which the themes we had identified might be expected to play out in the way that we describe them.

It is likely that curious individuals will attempt to "guess" which organization and project are being "represented" here. The case study presented in the following is not in any way intended to represent or identify actual persons or organizations; any resemblance to existing organizations is purely for the purposes of simulating a realistic and recognizable environment. The case was constructed in form of learning activities, known as *decision games*. This form of presentation requires fuller explanation.

11.2. Decision Games

Decision games are a form of presentation pitched somewhere between a case study and a simulation. Like most problem-based case studies, they present you with a well-defined initial context, events which you cannot yourself modify, and a central dilemma to reflect on. Like simulations, they unfold sequentially and invite response and interpretations as you proceed through them. Unlike case studies, they more closely mirror the complex, uncertain and ambiguous unfolding of events in the real world. Unlike simulations, you do not get the chance to systematically explore different, well-defined option routes.

Originally developed as "Tactical Decision Games" by the US Marine Corps for training purposes, the decision game form has been most actively researched and developed for learning and experience exchange purposes by leading decision research company, Klein Associates. Gary Klein, founder of Klein Associates, describes them thus: "Decision games are a centrepiece of a mental conditioning program, simple thought exercises... that capture the essence of a typical, difficult decision. A decision game presents some details leading up to a dilemma, typically charged with lots of uncertainty, and challenges those taking the exercise to come up with a plan of action" (Klein, 2004:35).

In our case, we have taken the decision game to represent not a single decision, but a complex scenario full of uncertainties and ambiguities and competing forces, together with the requirement to chart a clear course of action — characteristics very typical of KM projects in general.

We have presented the decision game in the form of numbered, sequential events. You are put into the position of the knowledge manager responsible for the project, and as you read the events, you are required to evaluate the significance (positive or negative) of the event for your KM project. Your ability to anticipate possible problems, and weak signals of emerging threat or opportunity, immeasurably improves your chances of being able to manage them proactively, rather than reactively. This capacity is what you will be exercising here.

Decision games are powerful problem-based learning exercises, for the following reasons: (1) the sequential presentation of events, many of them ambiguous, better represents the way in which the real world works, than the traditional "tidy" case study format; (2) the challenge to anticipate and "read" weak signals in these events better engages our existing experience, insight and intuition than does a more pre-digested or analytical format; (3) analytical insights and theoretical knowledge from "lessons learned" mean little in a project environment of rapid change, uncertainty, and unpredictable occurrences; and (4) the format is particularly well-adapted to knowledge and experience sharing contexts where people with different levels of applied experience can negotiate their perceptions, intuitions and "readings" of the situation, and thereby get access to other people's experience by proxy.

Decision games therefore form a useful way of testing one's judgement, knowledge and experience while engaging with implementation challenges safely, and if "played" together with a group of peers, they provide a means of accessing other people's intuitions, judgements and experience by proxy.

11.3. How to Use This Case Study

The case study can certainly be read and reflected on by individuals in the traditional way that you would read a normal case study. Analysis of key issues by an expert presented at the end of the chapter will help to focus such reflection.

However, the format can best be utilized by using the decision game features to reflect on each step as it occurs, and to make mental notes of where you think weak or early signals of opportunities and threats are emerging. To identify such signals is not sufficient: you would also need to think through alternative courses of action based on those signals. The evaluation table on the next page will help you map your perceptions of your possibilities as you progress through the case. Once you have reached the conclusion and thought through your answers to the focus questions, it will be worth retracing your steps and re-evaluating what you might have done differently.

The most productive format in which to use the case is in a workshop setting, where you have KM practitioners with diverse ranges and degrees of experience. At each step, use the evaluation table (Table 11.1) to negotiate a common interpretation of your current position (positive, negative or neutral). This negotiation itself will surface important insights based on your colleagues' experience and insights, and start to give you clues about alternative courses of action, and give you a richer knowledge base with which to tackle other KM projects.

In short then, this final method of using the cases is itself a tacit knowledge and experience sharing method that will give knowledge managers a more sophisticated and more highly tuned sensitivity to the possibilities and the threats facing them in their own work.

Table 11.1. Evaluation chart where you indicate each step in your case study — whether you think it is a positive, negative or netural contributor to your desired outcomes.

STEPS

	1	2	3	4	5	6	7	8	9	10	11	12	13	14	15	16	17	18	19	20	21	22	23	24	25	26	27
VERY GOOD																											
GOOD																											
SO-SO																											
NEUTRAL																											
NOT GOOD																											
BAD																											
VERY BAD																											

11.4. The Knowledge Research Institute

The Knowledge Research Institute of Singapore (KRIS) was founded in 2002 with funding from government, private sector technology companies, and its host university, the Nanhua University of Singapore. Its purpose is to promote the adoption of KM in Singapore, and to promote Singapore as a regional knowledge services hub. It has a permanent staff of five people, including its new Director, Dr. Hanifah bte Ismail, a KM expert from Republic University.

KRIS also has a mandate to coordinate the KM research and teaching work conducted in the various universities and polytechnics that fall under the Ministry of Education. Its first task was to establish an online "Knowledge Exchange" portal for the KM community in these institutions. The portal, and the technology behind it, is built into the funding package from the main private sector sponsor, OBM Technologies.

Dr. Hanifah's intention is to create a showpiece knowledge management system that she can demonstrate to the local KM community, as well as visitors from overseas. However, she quickly starts running into problems. Academic KM staff, even in her own host university is reluctant to share insights and research, until it has been formally published through normal academic journals and conferences.

A small debate among some academics at Nanhua about respecting intellectual property rights was quickly squashed by the university, which pointed to its formal IP policy. "It's part of your employment contract," pointed out the President. "It's for everybody's good that you share your knowledge." However, since that debate, contributions have declined in quality.

Dr. Hanifah is also discovering that the research conducted by the Institute is constrained by the major stakeholders. Finally, Dr. Hanifah's efforts to open up her Knowledge Exchange to the broader KM community in the region have met with some resistance. OBM is also a relative newcomer to the KM technology space, its background being in data storage and data mining, and Dr. Hanifah is discovering several user-unfriendly features and limitations in her portal. Is her chance-of-a-lifetime project all going disastrously wrong?

11.5. Sequential Events of Decision Scenario

You are Dr. Hanifah bte Ismail, Director of the Knowledge Research Institute of Singapore (KRIS). Consider the following events, try to interpret what is unfolding, and anticipate what your options for action might be.

1. Your searchable online directory of KM experts, practitioners and solution providers in Singapore is complete, and is now available on your public website. As a last minute touch you have indexed entries by keyword, so that people can search by specialization or KM topic. It looks good!

2. At a meeting with the University President, you are asked why KRIS is not conducting KM projects for the university as a whole. "Shouldn't we be practicing what we preach?" You explain that KRIS's role is to resource the KM community and not to conduct KM projects.

3. Two of the people in your KM directory have emailed you to ask you to take them out of the list: "We are receiving a lot of emails from people asking basic questions about KM. This is just a way of getting free consulting."

4. You are starting a series of free half-day workshops on KM topics. The first workshop "Introduction to KM" attracts over 50 people.

5. You are concerned that the K-Link portal has so little content on KM from your academic members in Nanhua. Most of the contributions are from Republic University and Mercedes Polytechnic. You decide to hold a tea session with the Nanhua KM researchers.

6. After several more emails from the people on your KM directory, you agree to move it to the private, members-only portal. "It's making us targets for spam," says one.

7. Your first major research project is complete. It is a market study of Singapore's role as a regional knowledge services hub, commissioned by your main funding agency, the Knowledge Infrastructure Board (KIB). The results are somewhat disappointing. The findings suggest that while regional market demand is high, most countries look to North America and Europe for expertise in knowledge-based services.

8. While surfing, you discover a link to a new website set up in Singapore by the Learning Organization Community of Knowledge (LOCK). The look and feel is much better than yours, and so is the content! People seem to be engaged in active discussions, posting papers, and the interface is very simple. You ask your webmaster to take a look at it: "Why can't we do something like this?"

9. Your half-day workshops continue to be popular. You now have over 100 people asking for follow-up courses.

10. At your monthly meeting, Professor Khoo, the Chairman of your Executive Committee, asks if you are focussed enough on supporting KM research in Singapore: "I don't see much shared resources and I'm sure your members are producing more than that."

11. The Association for KM Education (AKME), the local professional society for knowledge managers, proposes collaboration by becoming contributing members to your portal: "You should also invite the regional KM societies." You agree that this would give KRIS a much stronger presence.

12. KIB have come back to you on your market study report. "It's too negative," they say. "Please go and collect more data." When you point out that the findings are solid, can stimulate a healthy debate and help clarify Singapore's knowledge services strategy, Clarice Tan, the Deputy Director of Knowledge Services, says, "We already know what our strategy is. Your research is obviously incomplete."

13. Your webmaster has analyzed the LOCK learning organisation website. He says your K-Link system does not have the capability to replicate it: "Ours is a very high-end KM system. They are just using simple web-logging software, and they have no security to speak of. The content management functionality is also pretty thin." "But our collaboration tools are very poor," you say. He promises to talk to OBM about adding collaboration to the portal.

14. At your tea for Nanhua KM researchers, one of the associate professors takes you aside. "Basically the universities are in competition with each other," he says. "And they do not want to let other people know too much about their research areas in case their findings are used before being properly validated. They are much

more comfortable with you using their work once it is published. Why don't you get the Library to help you track down all their past papers?"

15. You receive a letter from OBM Technologies objecting to your proposal to showcase a range of KM technologies from a range of KM vendors in an upcoming conference that you are organizing: "As KRIS's main technology partner we feel that it would be contrary to the spirit of our agreement to promote the products and services of our competitors."

16. Your Executive Committee rejects the proposal to open up K-Link to AKME and other regional professional societies. "It would not be appropriate at this stage," says Professor Khoo. "We do not have anything good enough to show the outside world. Let's get our own house in order first."

17. You receive an email from The Business Times requesting an interview: "We'd like to do a profile on KRIS". You agree to a telephone interview. It goes well.

18. The article in The Business Times comes out. It is a savage attack on your Institute, written by a consistent critic of government spending — not the journalist who interviewed you: "In a time of economic crisis, public money is spent on an institution that has no economic or professional relevance. Despite research showing a strong regional demand for KM-related services, and Singapore's clear lead in this area, KRIS remains an ivory tower refuge, isolated from real-world practice and the business issues of the KM industry here." You suspect the AKME president had a hand in this article. He had seemed disappointed by KRIS's brush-off.

19. Clarice Tan from KIB calls you. She asks you if you had leaked details of the "unfinished" market study to The Business Times. You deny it, angrily. "Well they seem to know a lot of the information in that report. I will remind you that your work with us is confidential. You are not to talk to the media without our express permission."

20. You have been struggling with the issue of the market study. You decide that you cannot in good conscience massage the conclusions any other way. You ask for a meeting with Clarice and tell her so. "Well, we will have to finish it ourselves," she says.

21. The Human Development Secretariat for ASEAN contacts you to ask if you can host a regional seminar on "Knowledge Society and the Development Agenda". You say you will think about it. It is a lot of work, and you feel it might be better handled by the Republic University's School of Development Studies.

22. You ask the Nanhua university librarian if you can host links to the published papers of your academic members on your K-Link Portal. She says it is easier to point them to the full-text databases on the Library portal: "But first they need to be a member of the university, and they can only access them from inside the campus." You remind her that your members are scattered across several institutions, and you only need the KM articles. "I'm sorry, there is nothing I can do," she says. "We are restricted by our license agreements with the publishers."

23. Professor Khoo invites you to lunch. He tells you there have been a number of complaints from the members and from KIB about your work: "They do not feel it is very relevant to what they need. For example, all these free workshops are upsetting the polytechnics and the commercial providers. Maybe you should think about getting more involved in real KM projects. There is plenty of opportunity to do something at Nanhua — my own School of Engineering is ready to try out KM. And you can channel consulting work to our academic members. We all need to make ourselves more relevant to industry." He tells you to take on the ASEAN knowledge society seminar. "It's good for the university."

24. Your webmaster tells you that OBM is still developing its collaboration module: "It should be ready early next year. They have promised to pilot it with us, so we will get a chance to give feedback and ask for additional features."

25. You have had a brainwave. You can re-brand your KM experts directory as "K-Connect", linking them to potential projects and clients. You ask your webmaster to redesign the profile template and send out an email asking them to upgrade their profiles, explaining the purpose.

26. The Nanhua Legal officer calls you. She is concerned that the proposed K-Connect system might involve legal liabilities for the

university: "These people are not our employees. We cannot be held responsible for what they say or do, nor can we suggest that we are endorsing them in any way." She insists that every search results page on K-Connect carries a full disclaimer.

27. You learn that LOCK and AKME have launched a Virtual Knowledge Institute in association with the World Federation of KM Associations. The press release states a combined membership of 350 members in Singapore, "With over 700 virtual members from affiliated societies in the region."

11.6. Focus Questions

- Where did KRIS go wrong?
- What are the strengths and weaknesses (as well as missed opportunities) of the initiative?
- What about the practitioner networks? What was overlooked?
- Are there any (mis)alignment issues facing KIB and KRIS?
- How did Dr. Hanifah handle the project (assess!)?
- What went wrong in terms of K-sharing and IP?
- Imagine you are Dr. Hanifah's KM coach: what would you recommend so as to save this project?
- How can it redefine its mission, and serve the KM community in Singapore?

11.7. Analysis

The initiative that resulted in the foundation of KRIS is very well-intended, and on the face of it, promises to add value to the development of KM in Singapore (and perhaps in the region). The harnessing of support from industry as well as from government and the academic sector was a strong move: these three domains do need to be integrated in order to fully understand the value of KM to an economy.

However, they seem to have missed out the practitioner networks at the start. When the professional societies AKME and LOCK emerge later on and offer collaboration, KRIS no longer appears hospitable to their aims or their needs. In fact, the key issue here is that KRIS has allowed itself to be too tightly constrained by its stakeholder interests: OBM is able to constrain KRIS's ability to work with alternative technology partners, and yet its own technology does not satisfy the Institute's own needs.

The university is able to influence the activities of the Institute against its better judgement, and yet it cannot harness the cooperation or the content of its academic staff. The KIB has a larger agenda for KRIS, and this does not seem to be well aligned with the emerging issues and challenges facing the Director.

Dr. Hanifah generally seems unaware of the strategic issues, and the lack of alignment of stakeholder interests with her own vision. Her lack of experience in the corporate environment means that she very easily alienates the KM and Learning Organization societies, and the commercial providers of KM training, who are upset by her provision of free workshops. A strategic visioning and planning exercise at the beginning of the KM project would have helped to identify some of these issues early on. The lack of involvement of the practitioner networks would also have emerged as a possible blind spot. Even the knowledge-sharing issues had not been identified in advance. Collaboration elements on the portal should have been identified early on as a requirement, given the nature of the project. Similarly, the IP issues around the kind of content they wanted to host should have been clarified at the start.

In the present situation, Dr. Hanifah has a swift recovery job to attempt. On its present course, her Institute risks being hijacked as a vehicle for academic enlargement of consulting activity in the Singapore market. This will likely alienate the principal funding stakeholder KIB even further, and set KRIS in direct opposition to the practitioners' competing portal, which is more likely to succeed.

We suggest that Dr. Hanifah's best course to save her vision for KRIS would be to do what she should have done at the beginning: bring the stakeholders together with the representatives of LOCK and AKME, and negotiate a more open and flexible set of deliverables, based on open collaboration and a commitment to genuine knowledge sharing in support of the Singapore KM market.

References

Klein, G. (2004). *The Power of Intuition*. New York: Currency Doubleday.

Lambe, P. (2005). *Knowledge Management Decision Games* (forthcoming).

Straits Knowledge (2002a). *Knowledge Management in Singapore Organizations*. Survey Report. Singapore.

Straits Knowledge (2002b). *Knowledge-based Leadership in Singapore Organizations*. Survey Report. Singapore.

Straits Knowledge (2003). *Knowledge-based Strategy in Singapore Organizations*. Singapore.

Chapter 12

Creating a KM Platform for Strategic Success: A Case Study of Wipro Technologies, India

RaviShankar Mayasandra N. and Shan Ling Pan

12.1. Introduction

As IT outsourcing vendor organizations in developing countries continue to add to their list of world-wide clients and strengthen the organizational decentralized structures to meet business demands, better management of the dispersed internal knowledge resources is a key concern. Strategic organizational interventions bracketed under the rubric of knowledge management (KM) typically involve the implementation of one or more IT-based systems designated as knowledge management systems (KMS) (Alavi and Leidner, 1999; 2001; Alavi and Tiwana, 2002; Schultze and Boland Jr., 2000). The underlying focus of a KM initiative or a KMS is the creation of a dynamic platform that systematically collates expert knowledge, enabling organizational members to draw on the pooled expertise (Grover and Davenport, 2001; Massey *et al.*, 2002).

It is argued that the response of the organizational constituents to the expectations of organization-wide KM depend on unique embedded structural and socio-cultural contexts in the various organizational units (Davenport *et al.*, 1998; Gold *et al.*, 2001; Mayasandra and Pan, 2004). Particularly so in the case of organizations which have grown into highly decentralized multiple organizational units leading to organizational members closely identifying with various local entities such as work groups, departments, project teams and business units. Hence, there is a possibility that members may find it difficult to appreciate the

259

strategic relevance of organizational interventions like KM. It follows that effective KM implementations ought to have inbuilt organizational mechanisms to handle the likely conflicts arising out of localized differences. Here we attempt to understand the vital issues emerging in IT outsourcing vendor organizations' on-going efforts to create an organization-wide strategic KM infrastructure. In this study, we have considered the challenges surrounding the creation of a strategic KM platform at Wipro Technologies, one of India's premier Information Technology (IT) outsourcing vendor organizations. The study addresses two research questions: 1. How are KM strategies implemented in an IT outsourcing organization? and 2. What are the unique challenges faced by an IT outsourcing organization during the creation of a strategic KM platform?

12.2. A Review of KM Challenges in Organizations

Outsourcing IT requirements to cost-effective locations that are also known for high quality software services and products is an emerging and favored option for many organizations operating from Europe and North America (Barthelemy, 2003; Lacity and Hirschheim, 1993). For organizations taking up the outsourcing jobs, managing its knowledge resources optimally and effectively is a big challenge. Currently, most organizations that offer such outsourcing services employ a host of internal IT-based strategies to better organize and share their vast and often dispersed knowledge resources. However, the structural and socio-cultural differences in the immediate environment of organizations could be extremely complex and it may not be reasonable to always anticipate straightforward consequences of organizational IT interventions (Robey and Boudreau, 1999). One popular IT-based strategy for managing organizational knowledge is KM, which involves the implementation of knowledge management systems (KMS), which are equipped to capture, store and disseminate various forms of organizational knowledge (Alavi and Tiwana, 2002; Massey et al., 2002; Newell et al., 2003).

While KM initiatives promise to channel dispersed knowledge resources towards more effectively meeting business objectives, researchers have also pointed out that realizing benefits from KM processes is contingent upon how unique situations in the immediate organizational environment are handled (Brown and Duguid, 2001; Pentland, 1995). Unique subcultures are seen to represent an opposing force when attempts are made to integrate large enterprises (that hitherto functioned as autonomous powerhouses within the organization) through strategic initiatives like KM (Ghoshal and Gratton, 2002). It follows that the main challenge of a formal KM strategy is seen as the smooth integration of the KMS into the organizational mainstream such that it does not intrude into existing patterns of member behavior.

A well established theory in organizational literature often used to explain the beliefs underlying people's behavior is the organizational identity theory (Dutton and Dukerich, 1991; Brown and Starkey, 2000; Foreman and Whetten, 2002). Gioia and Thomas (1996:372) point out that "organizational identity concerns those features of the organization that members perceive as ostensibly central, enduring and distinctive in character that contribute to how they define the organization and their identification with it". It follows that a sense of positive identification with the organization is bound to result in behaviours that support the management of organizational knowledge. On the other hand, if organizational identity is derived mainly from local factors and contexts, it could potentially prove detrimental to organizational management of knowledge as members may be blinded to the larger interests of the organization. It is pointed out that members may go to extreme lengths to maintain and protect their perceived organizational identities (Brown and Starkey, 2000). In the KM context, how the organization handles such issues is vital and it becomes imperative that a KM strategy implementation reflects and accommodates these difficulties in its ambit.

12.3. Research Methodology

We adopted the case study methodology to understand the major issues surrounding the implementation of the KM initiative at Wipro Technologies. In organizational research, the case study method remains one of the frequently adopted research methods, and the felicity of the method is well documented (Myers, 1994; Orlikowski, 1993). In particular, our study follows the traditions of interpretivist research that underscores and recognizes the difficulties of objectively accessing reality in organizational research (Klein and Myers, 1999). We utilized different sources of evidence. We conducted 41 open-ended interviews with the KM implementation team (consisting of the head of the KM implementation team and the knowledge managers) and with project team members and middle-level managers from 4 different organizational units — V1, V2, V3 and V4.

Typically each interview lasted for an hour and was conducted at 5 different development centre locations of Wipro Technologies in the southern Indian city of Bangalore, which is also the corporate head-quarters of Wipro Technologies. The interviews were conducted in 2 separate phases with each phase lasting about 7 weeks. Most of the interviews were taped with prior permission and transcribed. A few interviews were not taped since the informants were reluctant to share their views on record. The open-ended interviews were typically fol-lowed by more informal discussions (not taped) with organizational members and these guided us towards understanding the often under-stated, but obvious themes that underlay the language and actions used by the informants to air their views about the organization-wide KM initiative. Clarifications regarding those points of the interviews that were unclear were obtained via e-mail correspondence and telephonic discussions.

Following the first phase of data collection, we invited the Head of the KM initiative at Wipro Technologies to our university to present and share Wipro's KM experiences with our research team. During his visit we discussed our initial findings and obtained further inputs about the challenges of implementing an organization-wide KM initia-tive. Other qualitative data that assisted the case analysis included the transcripts of the taped interviews, KM artifacts made available to us, and the notes made during informal discussions.

12.4. Case Description

Wipro Technologies is the global IT services and products division of Wipro Limited, Bangalore, India. Wipro Technologies generated revenues of US$943 million for the financial year ended March 31st 2004 and at present employs more than 30,000 people, from 18 nationalities. Wipro Technologies operates as an autonomous entity headed by a CEO, who reports directly to the Chairman of Wipro Limited. In this paper, all references to the "organization" refer to Wipro Technologies. Wipro Technologies has more than 350 global clients, offering them a host of IT solutions including software application development and maintenance, research and development services, package implementation, systems integration and Business Process Outsourcing (BPO) services. Organized into a number of strategic business units called verticals (defined, based on the industry segment of the customer, e.g. Retail, Manufacturing, etc.) and horizontals (defined, based on the technology focus), Wipro Technologies has software development centers and sales and marketing offices spread across countries in Asia, Europe and North America.

12.5. Organization-Wide KM at Wipro Technologies

Between the years 1998 and 2000, Wipro Technologies more than doubled its employee strength (from 5000 to above 10,000) and with rapid growth and complex projects, demand for access to information increased dramatically. Further, the organization felt it necessary to create a strategic setup to ensure that organizational business units tap into each others' expertise leading to shorter delivery periods for the customers. In September 2000 a top management driven organization-wide KM initiative was initiated and a dedicated full-time knowledge management (KM) implementation team was set-up. At a time when many vendors in the market were promoting and parading KM solutions Wipro took into consideration two important factors — its entire desktop environment was standardized on the Windows 2000 platform and all the mail servers were Microsoft Exchange Servers — and following which, built customized KM applications on Microsoft's basic sharepoint portal server (SPSS) infrastructure for intra-organizational collaboration.

At present, the head of the KM implementation team reports to the CQO (Chief Quality Officer) of Wipro Technologies and holds complete responsibility for implementing KM at Wipro Technologies. Reporting to the Head of the KM team are 12 knowledge managers representing each organizational business unit and responsible for managing the KM initiative in their respective business units. Six of them are full time members of the core organizational KM team while the other six are part-time knowledge managers with additional responsibilities in their own business unit. In addition, a technical team comprising of a project manager and 5 programmers take up the responsibility of developing, implementing and maintaining the KM applications.

The KM initiative, riding on the strong IT capabilities of the organization aims to enhance the ability to access existing information in real time and shorten product and project life cycles. Over the last four years the initiative has evolved gradually and at present revolves around the KM applications accessible through organization-wide knowledge portal called KNet (see Figs. 12.1 and 12.2). In the implementation of the KM initiative at Wipro Technologies, we identified three key recurring and overlapping phases, namely: 1) Planning and Refining the IT-based KM infrastructure; 2) Awareness and Acceptance phase; and 3) Benefits measurement phase. The KM implementation team plans for new IT-based KM applications while refining the existing ones on a continuous basis based on the feedback from the organizational constituencies (Phase 1). The implementation team also employs various metrics that track the participation of organizational members in the KM initiative and in the process attempts to measure the benefits of the organization-wide KM initiative (Phase 3). A programmer from the technical team responsible for the implementation of the KM applications explained:

> "For the KM initiative, we use a KM engagement index and KM effectiveness index. The engagement index involves parameters like the usage of KM applications and contributions to the KM initiative. The effectiveness index involves the measurement of our KM systems against parameters like response to queries and improvements in productivity and quality."

Much of the strategic success of the KM initiative derives from the Awareness and Acceptance phase during which the knowledge managers engage themselves fully in spreading awareness about the KM initiative within their respective business units and strive to get the end

KM initiative (KNet)	KM system	System description
Connecting people to content	Sales support knowledge base	Provides key information to sales personnel
5500 knowledge artifacts are spread across 150 categories and 20 document types.	Technology support KM system (TeckNet)	Captures and allows for sharing of technical knowledge artifacts, which reduces rework and also improves time-to-market
	Reusable components repository	Eliminates redundancies and allows for sharing of components
On an average 400 knowledge artifacts are added every month	Project data bank	Provides instant access to all project information
Connecting people to people	Communities and special interest groups (KNetworks)	Leverages tacit knowledge by getting people to come together and share
	Yellow pages/Find-the-expert (KoNnect)	Profiles employees with regards to their area of expertise making it easier to contact experts
	War rooms	A virtual space, with highly restricted access for top management and middle level managers at different physical locations to collaborate. It is a discussion room set-up that is often accessed even by the CEO when required to take important strategic decisions. The term "War room" highlights it as a place where the key players in the organization often meet and strategize for the business battles and wars confronting Wipro.
KM sustenance programs	KM effectiveness and engagement index	Uses Six Sigma methodologies to gauge engagement and effectiveness of all KM systems
	Rewards and recognition	Attempts to institutionalize the KM initiative across the organization and to motivate employees through virtual cash points, certificates of recognition, etc.

Fig. 12.1. Knowledge management systems (KMS) at Wipro Technologies.

Fig. 12.2. A snapshot of KNet.

users such as software development teams and sales and business personnel to participate in, and contribute to the KM initiative. A knowledge manager responsible for managing the KM initiative in one of the organizational business units V1 said:

"I am putting in a lot of time and effort, trying to brand our KM initiative within the unit. I attend most of the meetings that take place in the vertical and communicate to the middle level managers the scope and reach of our KM initiative. They in turn strongly encourage their team members to have a look at, and utilize the KM set-up."

The most helpful contributions by software developers to the explicit knowledge repositories of KNet are the reusable components that save a lot of time for developers working on other projects. The former head of the KM initiative explained:

"We have a reusable asset framework which now has lots of pieces of code. For example, these pieces could be a whole set of important but basic Java codes. Let's, say it's a code that calculates the time of the day. Now any developer who is building an application needs to display the system time. All he has to do is to go to the repository, take the component and plug it in to his particular application. It's as simple as going to a super-market and picking up what you need from the shelf. Our repositories are so well stocked that developers need not re-write generic codes anymore."

Another often used KM application at Wipro is *Konnect*, which profiles employees with regards to their expertise making it easier for people to establish contact with experts who may be located in some other geographical location. A knowledge manager with business unit V3 noted:

> "If my query is very unique, I can send it as a post card to everybody in the organization and hopefully some one will answer. But the best thing is that this entire thread is automatically captured in the repository, since in the database both the query and the responses are assigned a unique query ID. This feature has been so popular that people are coming to me almost everyday saying how they got a great response to a troublesome problem."

However, one initial difficulty faced by the knowledge managers was due to members being uncomfortable making changes to knowledge sharing habits formulated over a period, or being so occupied with work that they regarded organizational management of knowledge as an overhead. A senior software engineer, who is a part of a 20 member project team in a vertical business unit V2 initially had difficulties in relating to the organization-wide KM initiative:

> "I don't mind sharing my expertise with people from outside my team, and from other business units, but the emotional satisfaction I get out of seeing some one in my own project team benefit from my expertise beats everything. So naturally, I have been guilty of sharing information and exchanging notes mostly with my own team members. Only recently, after our knowledge manager held a few KM sessions and talked about re-usable artifacts available on KNet, have I been active in uploading/downloading stuff on KNet."

The knowledge managers typically go on a KM evangelization drive in their units, which involves talking to middle level project managers to start with and getting their support for the organization's KM efforts. The middle level managers, whom most of the project team members look up to, then encourage their team members to start tapping into the organizational KM platform for their everyday needs and share their expertise with others in the organization. In strategic business unit V3, a senior project-manager heading a 60 member software development team and reputed within the organization as being as a strong votary of the KM initiative said:

> "At least in my team I do not see any resistance to the KM initiative. But what we need to overcome is the indifference, which I am able to do by articulating to my team how we could benefit from the KM initiative. Now for people in my team KNet is a part of their everyday work, whether it is with regards to uploading documents or sharing information or re-using artifacts. So we just need to clearly explain to people how they as individuals can benefit and how their project team and business units benefits from KM."

According to a software engineer in V3:

> "In units where people just don't care or don't see any value in KM, the role of the knowledge manager is critical. She has to do some serious selling of the KM initiative in the unit. Also, whenever heads of the strategic business units and senior project managers drive KM from the top, teams are quite enthusiastic about sharing their know-how and contributing to the KM initiative. In my team, since my manager is very keen on KM, it has become a habit for us to access KNet regularly for our needs. I guess it's a part of the culture of our team."

The Awareness and Acceptance phase also presents another unique challenge since the internal evangelization drive has to accommodate the inherently different nature of relationships that Wipro Technologies has with a few of its client organizations. Project teams in some units do not work on one-off projects; instead they have long-term relationships with the client organization and function as offshore extensions of the client facility. Typically called offshore development centres, Wipro Technologies has a few such arrangements with companies, who interestingly compete with one another in the global markets. In other words, from a KM viewpoint, the onus is on Wipro Technologies to protect the intellectual property of such "competing" companies by making sure that all forms of proprietary knowledge stays within the boundaries of the offshore team working for the particular client organization. A knowledge manager with 2 years of experience in her current KM explained:

> "In our offshore development centres (ODC) here in India we have our people developing software for large client organizations. In many cases, our clients' biggest competitors also happen to be our clients for whom (too) we develop software. So the clients are very particular that our teams working for them don't share vital information outside the team. Of course, we have very strong policies to ensure and protect the intellectual property of our clients."

The former head of the KM initiative elaborated:

> "Yes we do need to be careful about customer sensitive knowledge. To give you an example of how we handle this KM wise, assume that client A and client B are competitors. The Wipro teams working for client A and client B are within their own firewalls. The Client A team can access/contribute only to client A's internal knowledge repositories and are encouraged to do so by the KM team. But they are not allowed access to the client B team's repositories. However, both teams can access/contribute general information to KNet."

The organization encourages members that work on long-term projects with clients to develop a close relationship and identify themselves strongly with the client organization. Further, training sessions are also conducted to acquaint members with the client organization's way of working and the need to contribute to the team-level KM repositories. One of the knowledge managers explained how members from teams that work for competing clients could still make important contributions towards building the organizational knowledge base:

> "The way a telecom switch works is the same irrespective of who the manufacturer is. Now I have seen people unwilling to share even general, but useful insights into the working of a telecom switch because they are within customer firewalls. Now this kind of knowledge, I feel needs to be and could be shared with the rest of the organization."

12.6. Analysis and Lessons Learnt

The field-work conducted in two-phases over a three and a half month period helped us trace the evolution and new developments in the organization on the KM front and provided a processual view of the major issues surrounding Wipro Technologies' efforts to create a strategic KM platform. From the analysis of the interview transcripts, secondary artifacts related to KM and informal discussions with the informants, we learnt three important lessons which we discuss below.

12.7. Aligning KM Strategy with Business Realities

Implementing a successful KM strategy in Wipro's case involves making sure that there is no leakage or flow of knowledge out of a few project teams and at the same time ensuring that there is sharing of organizational knowledge across other units. In this sense, creating a strategic KM infrastructure is a more complex issue when compared to an organization where the term KM obviously gets associated with organization-wide knowledge sharing. From the organization's objective of competing on the strength of its knowledge resources in the global market, the creation and sustenance of isolated client-centric units definitely strengthens the organization's specialized knowledge base. Hence, it is a successful model most likely to be followed by the organization to conduct its business, at least in the near future.

Top-management understands that the creation of client-centric business units is inevitable, even desirable and in-line with business realities. However, the organization also needs to ensure that client-centric business units are not completely isolated from the rest of the organization, in which case such units play only a marginal role in the building of an organizational knowledge strategy. Thus Wipro Technologies is making sure that even the client-centric units participate by contributing general, but useful knowledge to the organization-wide initiative represented by KNet. Further, data from the case suggest that the connection between business benefits and organizational knowledge strategies is not clearly visible in the immediate years following the implementation of a knowledge strategy, particularly in the case of the organization's long-term client relationships.

It appears that in the initial post-implementation stages, KM strategies structurally clash with the organization's model for reaping desired business benefits. In spite of this, we learn from Wipro's KM strategy that it is important for organizations to go ahead with their efforts at creating an organizational KM platform. The idea being that they mitigate and protect the organization against potential disruptions and volatilities in the business environment in the future, and that at such points in the future the KM strategies will indeed begin to clearly demonstrate a clear causal link with business benefits.

12.8. Orchestrating Desired Identity Patterns

The creation of a centralized IT-based KM infrastructure demanded that members in the various organizational units identify themselves strongly with the organization. The idea being that such a strong identification often would lead to active support and contributions to the KM initiative. However, the KM team has realized that the nature of relationships with certain clients makes it impossible for project teams to actively get involved in the creation of an organization-wide knowledge base. The need to share and contribute information in an organization-wide setting often clashes with the proprietary ownership of information by the client organizations.

Qualitative data from the case suggest that the KM team is making conscious efforts to accommodate this situation by encouraging project teams to contribute at least to their team level knowledge repositories. In fact, as noted in the case description, in such cases where proprietary information is involved the organization encourages project teams to develop a close bonding and strong identification with the client organization. In other words, these teams are more prone to operate from ideological positions that reflect their strong identification with the client organization, leading to better management of knowledge locally if not at the organizational level. As a software engineer at business unit V3 commented, "*I don't contribute much to the KM portal because I don't see how what I know will be of use to anybody outside my unit. But as for our own repositories, I do access them a lot.*"

In summary, the creation of an organizational KM platform requires members to respond whole heartedly to ensure its success. However, organizations may be forced to orchestrate dual organizational identity mindsets leading to some pockets of the organization indulging in full-fledged knowledge sharing and others only partial. In a way, it shows that dual organizational identity mindsets, though from a theoretical standpoint undesirable, may actually be imperative to IT outsourcing organizations. In other words, in the process of creating an organizational knowledge base, the organization needs to inculcate an organization-centric focus in some internal constituencies or units while another set of internal constituents need to have a largely client-centric focus.

12.9. Middle Level Managers as Catalysts of Success

It emerged from the case that assuming responsibility for management of organizational knowledge is a tough proposition for software development teams who tend to perceive KM processes as overheads and are more involved with work at the operational level. However, KM managers at Wipro Technologies have been successful in eliciting the support of middle-level managers in promoting KM in their respective business units and project teams. In fact, the extent to which KM has made inroads into the organizational milieu has depended to a large extent on the middle-level managers in the various units.

As noted in the case description, many middle-level managers have been able to generate interest towards KM among members in their project teams and business units, by trying to convey the need to better manage team level knowledge. Judicious use of language (by middle level managers) that helps project team members get rid of the perception of KM as an overhead plays an important role in ensuring that organizational KM gets widespread support. Business units middle level managers such as project leaders, project managers and technical managers who articulated to their subordinates the benefits of KM did exceedingly well in terms of contributing to the KM initiative. In other words, in units and teams where a strong case for KM was made out by their immediate superiors, notwithstanding the inhibitions and restrictions about KM, people actively got involved in the KM initiative. However, it is also to be noted that considerable effort from the knowledge managers is required to get the middle-level managers to buy-in to the KM initiative and evangelize it further in their project teams. This further reiterates the vital role being enacted by the knowledge managers in the KM team.

12.10. Conclusions, Contributions and Future Research

Our case study has attempted to address the major issues surrounding the implementation of an organization-wide KM initiative at Wipro Technologies. It emerged from the case that it is natural for organizational members in IT outsourcing vendor organizations to identify with both the organization and the client organization in everyday organizational life. Further, organizational members may be coaxed to invoke their identification with the client organization, which in the context of strategic initiatives having organizational relevance like KM, presents an interesting situation. It also emerged from the case that in typical organizational units middle level managers play a crucial role in clearly articulating the benefits of organization-wide KM to members in their constituencies and ensuring that end user communities relate better to KM. We also observed that knowledge sharing behaviours among members are also closely linked to the compulsions of the business model adopted by Wipro Technologies. While it is easier to overcome initial resistance to share knowledge among individuals by a conscious internal branding exercise, at the collective level project teams in outsourcing organizations may still choose to and have to share knowledge only within their teams. Even this inclination to share knowledge within project teams, we observe from the case, is a direct consequence of the immediate superiors' belief in the usefulness of sharing knowledge and their ability to communicate the same.

Traditionally, researchers have tried to explain KM behaviours by using concepts of organizational culture and subcultures. In utilizing the concept of identities, this study has attempted to move towards a theoretical explanation that has the potential to offer greater depth when understanding issues of organizational KM implementation. From the managerial viewpoint, a key challenge in organizational KM implementation is to articulate to organizational members very clearly the benefits of the KM initiative. KM implementation teams need to coordinate better with the organizational units and convince middle-level managers to push the initiative in their respective business units and project teams. Further research needs to be conducted to explore other issues of organizational identities that impact and interact with organizational KM strategies.

References

Alavi, M. and D.E. Leidner (1999). Knowledge Management Systems: Issues, Challenges and Benefits. *Communications of the AIS*, 1(7), 2–35.

Alavi, M. and D.E. Leidner (2001). Review: Knowledge Management and Knowledge Management Systems: Conceptual Foundations and Research Issues. *MIS Quarterly*, 25(1), 107–136.

Alavi, M. and A. Tiwana (2002). Knowledge Integration in Virtual Teams: The Potential Role of KMS. *Journal of the American Society for Information Science and Technology*, 53(12), 1029–1037.

Barthelemy, J. (2003). The Hard and Soft Sides of IT Outsourcing Management. *European Management Journal*, 21(5), 539–548.

Brown, J.S. and P. Duguid (2001). Knowledge and Organizations: A Social-Practice Perspective. *Organization Science*, 12(2), 198–213.

Brown, A.D. and K. Starkey (2000). Organizational Identity and Learning: A Psychodynamic Perspective. *The Academy of Management Review*, 25(1), 102–116.

Davenport, T.H., D.W. DeLong and M.C. Beers (1998). Successful Knowledge Management Projects. *Sloan Management Review*, 39(2), 43–57.

Dutton, J.E. and J.M. Dukerich (1991). Keeping an Eye on the Mirror: Image and Identity in Organizational Adaptation. *The Academy of Management Journal*, 34(3), 517–554.

Foreman, P. and D.A. Whetten (2002). Members' Identification with Multiple Identity Organizations. *Organization Science*, 13(6), 618–635.

Ghoshal, S. and L. Gratton (2002). Integrating the Enterprise. *Sloan Management Review*, 44(1), 31–40.

Gioia, D.A. and J.B. Thomas (1996). Identity, Image and Issue Interpretation: Sensemaking during Strategic Change in Academia. *Administrative Science Quarterly*, 41(3), 370–403.

Gold, A.H., A. Malhotra and A.H. Segars (2001). Knowledge Management: An Organizational Capabilities Perspective. *Journal of Management Information Systems*, 18(1), 185–214.

Grover, V. and T.H. Davenport (2001). General Perspectives on Knowledge Management: Fostering a Research Agenda. *Journal of Management Information Systems*, 18(1), 5–21.

Klein, H.K. and M.D. Myers (1999). A Set of Principles for Conducting and Evaluating Interpretive Field Studies in Information Systems. *MIS Quarterly*, 23(1), 67–93.

Lacity, M.C. and R. Hirschheim (1993). The Information Systems Outsourcing Bandwagon. *Sloan Management Review*, 35(1), 73–86.

Massey, A.P., M.M. Montoya-Weiss and T.M. O'Driscoll (2002). Knowledge Management in Pursuit of Performance: Insights from Nortel Networks. *MIS Quarterly*, 26(3), 269–289.

Mayasandra N., R. and S.-L. Pan (2004). Knowledge Management Initiatives in a Global IT Outsourcing Company: A Case Study of Infosys Technologies. *Journal of Information and Knowledge Management*, 3(1), 81–96.

Myers, M.D. (1994). A Disaster for Everyone to See: An Interpretive Analysis of a Failed IS Project. *Accounting, Management and Information Technologies*, 4(4), 185–201.

Newell, S., J.C. Huang, R.D. Galliers and S.-L. Pan (2003). Implementing Enterprise Resource Planning and Knowledge Management Systems in Tandem: Fostering Efficiency and Innovation Complementarity. *Information and Organization*, 13(1), 25–52.

Orlikowski, W.J. (1993). CASE Tools as Organizational Change: Investigating Incremental and Radical Changes in Systems Development. *MIS Quarterly*, 17(3), 309–340.

Pentland, B.T. (1995). Information Systems and Organizational Learning: The Social Epistemology of Organizational Knowledge Systems. *Accounting, Management and Information Technologies*, 5(1), 1–21.

Robey, D. and M.-C. Boudreau (1999). Accounting for the Contradictory Organizational Consequences of Information Technology: Theoretical Directions and Methodological Implications. *Information Systems Research*, 10(2), 167–185.

Schultze, U. and R.J. Boland Jr. (2000). Knowledge Management Technology and the Reproduction of Knowledge Work Practices. *Journal of Strategic Information Systems*, 9(2–3), 193–212.

Part V

Focus on K-sharing Behavior in Organizations

Chapter 13

What Makes Knowledge Sharing in Organizations Tick? — An Empirical Study[1]

Yue Wah Chay, Thomas Menkhoff, Benjamin Loh and
Hans-Dieter Evers

13.1. Introduction

There has been a proliferation of literature on knowledge management with the advent of the knowledge economy (Beck, 1992; Stehr, 1994; Krogh, 2003; Evers and Menkhoff, 2004) as indicated by an increasing body of work in organizational studies, information systems, marketing and the social science disciplines of sociology, psychology, and economics. However, notwithstanding the substantial insights generated about knowledge management issues in contemporary business organizations (Nonaka, 1994; Krogh, 1998; Menkhoff, Chay and Loh, 2004), the development of robust theoretical concepts and models, which could explain why members of organizations do share knowledge, has been slow. It seems that the phenomenon of knowledge sharing, identified as an important component in the management of knowledge workers in organizations, is still something like a black box.

This essay seeks to address this gap by theorizing about knowledge sharing in contemporary organizations based on empirical data collected in a tertiary educational institution in Singapore. The theory

---

[1] This is a longer and revised version of a paper presented at the 38th Annual Hawaii International Conference on System Sciences (HICSS-38), 3–6 January 2005, Hawaii. The original HICSS conference paper was published in the HICSS-38 2005 Conference Proceedings, edited by Ralph H. Sprague.

we propose in this article is rooted in the concept of social capital, and draws together perspectives from the sociology of organizations, economic sociology, social psychology, and the broad umbrella of organizational studies, which encompass literature such as knowledge management, organizational behaviour, and strategic theory of the firm. The key objective of the essay is to identify some of the key factors that influence knowledge sharing behaviour in organizations and to provide plausible theoretical explanations of such behaviours based on empirical data.

13.2. Dimensions of Social Capital

Bourdieu defines social capital as "the aggregate of the actual or potential resources which are linked to possession of a durable network or more or less institutionalized relationships of mutual acquaintance or recognition" (1985:248). This definition focuses on the benefits accruing to individuals by virtue of participation in groups and on the deliberate construction of sociability for the purpose of creating this resource. Bourdieu argues, "the profits which accrue from membership in a group are the basis of the solidarity which makes them possible" (1985:249). The definition implies that social capital is a major aspect of social structure and that it can be put (like other forms of capital) to productive use (Coleman, 1990:302). As Putnam has pointed out, "social capital here refers to features of social organization, such as trust, norms, and networks, that can improve the efficiency of society by facilitating coordinated action" (1993:167).

As a resource, social capital facilitates actions of individuals "who are within the structure" (Coleman, 1990:302) in different ways. Firstly, network ties (Granovetter, 1992) can provide individuals with useful knowledge about opportunities and choices otherwise not available (Lin, 2001). Network ties may prompt an organization and its members on the availability of such knowledge resources. Secondly, these network ties play an important part in influencing decision-making depending upon the strategic location of actors within a network (Burt, 2002; 2004). Thirdly, social credentials of an individual (Lin, 2001) reflect his or her social standing in the network, and other members may seek to acquire the resource of such credentials by forming alliances with such individuals. And finally, social relations are expected to reinforce identity and recognition to gain public acknowledgement of his or her claim to resources (Lin, 2001).

In order to structure the various social and organizational factors that influence knowledge sharing with the help of the social capital concept, this essay adopts three dimensions, namely structural, agency and relational. The following section highlights the different components of these dimensions of social capital, the significance of which will be elaborated upon later in the essay.

Structural dimension. The structural dimension of social capital, in this essay, refers to organizational climate factors that can aid such interactions and networks. Among the most important facets of this dimension are *organizational care* (Krogh, 1998; 2003; Krogh *et al.*, 2001) that examines conditions of low-care and high-care environments in facilitating social exchange, and *recognition and rewards* (Bartol and Srivastava, 2002).

Relational dimension. This essay looks at the relational dimension of social capital though the concept of relational embeddedness, which has been described by Granovetter (1992) as the kind of personal relationships people have developed with one another through a history of interactions. This concept focuses on the building of trust into the relations individuals have that influence their behavior (Putnam, 1993; Fukuyama, 1996; 1999; Cohen and Prusak, 2001). Among the key facets of this dimension are *competence* (Blau, 1964; Schurr and Ozanne, 1985), *integrity* (Hosmer, 1995; Luhmann, 1979) and *open-mindedness* (Tjosvold, Hui and Sun, 2000).

Agency dimension. The agency dimension of social capital examines the role of individual motives in engaging in social interactions that would enable them to acquire the resources available in such interactions (Archer, 1995; 2003; Cicourel, 1973; Rioux and Penner, 2001). This dimension is a relatively new contribution to social capital theory and has yet to be empirically tested. The adoption of motives as a variable in the agency dimension was influenced by Portes (1998:5–6) recommendation to investigate "the motivations of the donors, who

are requested to make these assets available without any immediate return" as a research direction of social capital. Among the key
facets identified to explain motives in this dimension are *prosocial
motives* (Rioux and Penner, 2001), *impression management, altruism* (Jensen, 1998; Conte and Paolucci, 2002), and *shared values*
(Cicourel, 1973).

13.3. Knowledge Sharing Defined

Helmstadter defines knowledge sharing in terms of "voluntary interactions between human actors [through] a framework of shared institutions, including law, ethical norms, behavioral regularities, customs
and so on ... the subject matter of the interactions between the participating actors is knowledge. Such an interaction itself may be called
sharing of knowledge" (2003:11). His definition of knowledge sharing highlights the role of social interactions which lends support to the
theory of social capital where participation in groups and the deliberate
construction of sociability is a prerequisite for the purpose of creating
a resource, in this case knowledge.

However, Helmstadter's definition of "voluntary interactions" is not
unproblematic as it fails to consider issues of politics and power in such
interactions. While knowledge sharing, particularly in the context of
economic organizations, is often encouraged through incentive systems (Bartol and Srivastava, 2002), the corollary also holds when involuntary interactions in the sharing of knowledge are often "enforced"
by appraisals and incentive systems whereby employees who do not
share their knowledge may be penalized and risk retarding their career
advancement in the organization. Studies on knowledge sharing have
thus far been "heavy on notion of negotiation and trust between members of the network and exceptionally light on domination and power-
relations-independent relationships based on reciprocity and mutual
trust, where self interest is sacrificed for the communal good" (Knights,
Murray and Willmott, 1993:978). The writers further argue that such
interactions are often embedded in institutional power relations that
are hierarchical, competitive, coercive and exploitative (see also Aldrich
and Whetten, 1981; Walsham, 1993). This aspect of politics and power

in knowledge sharing will be considered later in this section as one of the conditions whereby involuntary knowledge sharing can occur.

13.4. Tacit and Explicit Knowledge

A definition of knowledge sharing needs further clarification as to what type of knowledge is shared, and it is necessary at this point, to make a slight digression to explain the nature of knowledge itself. Knowledge by its very nature exists in both tacit and explicit forms. Polanyi (1967) is often cited when describing tacit knowledge. Polanyi proposed a concept of tacit knowledge based on three main theses: Firstly, true discovery cannot be accounted for by a set of articulated rules or algorithms; secondly, knowledge is public but is also to a large extent personal and socially constructed; and thirdly, all knowledge originates from tacit knowledge. Therefore, Polanyi argues that tacit knowledge is knowledge that is known but cannot be told. It is the kind of knowledge that cannot be articulated because it has become internalized in the unconscious mind. Explicit knowledge, on the other hand, refers to knowledge that is transmittable in formal, systematic language and can be shared in the form of data, scientific formulae, specifications, manuals and so on (Nonaka, 1994).

In his analysis of knowledge creation, Nonaka (1994; see also Nonaka and Takeuchi, 1995; Nonaka, Konno and Toyama, 2001) examined the concept in terms of a knowledge spiral encompassing four basic patterns of interaction between tacit and explicit knowledge — socialization, externalization, combination, and internalization. In *socialization*, Nonaka uses the term to emphasize the importance of social interaction and joint activities in converting tacit knowledge to explicit knowledge. He argues that since tacit knowledge is context specific and difficult to formalize, transferring tacit knowledge requires sharing the same experience through joint activities such as being together, spending time, or working in the same environment. The next process in his theory of the knowledge spiral is *externalization*, which is the process of articulating tacit knowledge into explicit forms by sharing it through social interaction. Through externalization, tacit knowledge that is unstructured in the individual's mind becomes crystallized through a process of reflection between sharing individuals. Through *combination*, such explicit knowledge becomes more complex and systematic as this level of knowledge is exchanged and combined through documented media such as documents and notations. And finally in *internalization*, explicit knowledge is internalized or reflected by the individual who turns it back into tacit knowledge. This is closely related to the "learning by doing" philosophy where what is read and understood is translated into action.

There is a paucity of research specifically addressing the mechanisms of knowledge sharing between individuals in organizations. Nevertheless, this essay argues that Nonaka's conceptualization of socialization, externalization and combination is of particular importance in explaining the process of knowledge sharing. This is because these processes involve joint social interaction with two or more actors whereby tacit knowledge that resides in an individual's mind is articulated and becomes explicit. This tacit knowledge is further refined and becomes clearer through reflection. Both these processes parallel the basic premise established by Helmstadter's definition of knowledge sharing, which involves the "interactions between human actors [through] a framework of shared institutions ... " (2003:11). This conceptualization of the knowledge sharing process is also attractive as it supports the premise of social capital defined as "the aggregate of the actual or potential resources which are linked to possession of a durable network or more or less institutionalized relationships of mutual acquaintance or recognition" (Bourdieu, 1985:248).

13.5. Conditions for Knowledge Sharing

It is further argued that conditions necessary in allowing individual actors to engage in knowledge sharing through socialization, externalization and combination must be present in order for knowledge to be shared. The following is a review of important knowledge sharing conditions that has been gathered from existing literature, three of which — expected costs of not sharing knowledge, personal compatibility, and opportunistic behavior — are original inclusions based on the critique of Helmstadter's original definition emphasizing "voluntary interaction" whereby knowledge sharing can, indeed, be involuntary in nature and is fraught with issues of power and politics (Knights, Murray and Willmott, 1993).

The first condition is that, in order to facilitate the sharing of knowledge between actors in an organization, there must exist *opportunities* to do so. Ipe (2003) suggests that opportunities to share knowledge in organizations can be both formal and informal in nature. Formal opportunities include, for example, training programmes, structured work teams, and technology-based systems that facilitate the sharing of knowledge. Bartol and Srivastava (2002) refer to such opportunities as "formal channels" while Rulke and Zaheer (2000) call them "purposive learning channels". Informal opportunities include personal relationships and social networks that facilitate the sharing of knowledge (Ipe, 2003).

The second condition is *communication modality*, which looks specifically at the physical proximity of the social space for knowledge sharing to occur. Nohria and Eccles (1992), for example, highlight important differences between face-to-face and electronic-mediated exchanges, and they argue that such exchanges favour the use of face-to-face interactions. They argue further that electronic-mediated exchanges, such as e-mail, require the subsequent use of more face-to-face communication which would undermine the efficiency towards which sharing of knowledge takes place.

The third condition for knowledge sharing to take place through socialization, externalization and combination is the individual's *expectation of the benefits* he or she would accrue when he or she engages in knowledge sharing. This has often been linked to an organization's incentive system. O'Reilly and Pondy (1980) argue that the probability of actors routing information to other actors is positively related to the rewards they expect from sharing the knowledge. This relationship between sharing of knowledge and the expectation of benefits has been further supported by Gupta and Govindarajan (2000) as well as Quinn, Anderson and Finklestein (1996) who studied the incentive systems of organizations and found that significant changes had to be made to these systems to encourage organizational actors to share their knowledge.

The fourth condition of knowledge sharing is the actor's *expectation of the costs* of not sharing knowledge which is based on the formulation of "involuntary interaction" as established earlier and Knights, Murray and Willmott's (1993) argument that knowledge sharing can, indeed, be involuntary in nature and is fraught with issues of power and politics. While individuals may not receive benefits out of knowledge sharing, the costs of not sharing knowledge, e.g. through coercive appraisals and the withdrawal of incentives, may warrant them to involuntarily share their knowledge.

The fifth condition involves the *context compatibility* of those who share knowledge. This condition argues that actors who share certain professional similarities, e.g. work interests, values etc., tend to engage in knowledge sharing. Huang and Wang (2002), for example, found that the selection of team members who were selected based on similar work criteria or exposure to the same training are important factors leading to the sharing and creation of knowledge in organizations.

The sixth condition is that actors are motivated to share knowledge. Davenport, DeLong and Beers (1998) suggest that knowledge is "intimately and inextricably bound with people's egos and occupations" (1998:45). Stenmark (2001) and Thompson, Kruglanski and Spiegel (2000) argue that actors are not likely to share knowledge without strong personal motivation. Motivational factors that influence knowledge sharing between actors can be divided into internal and external factors. Internal factors include the perceived power attached to the knowledge and the reciprocity that results from sharing. External factors include relationship with the recipient and rewards for sharing (Ipe, 2003).

The seventh condition has to do with personal compatibility and liking. This is another original contribution to the literature. Individuals are arguably more likely to share knowledge with another whom they feel comfortable with or share similar personal interests. This is different from the fifth condition, context compatibility, as the former is defined by more personal and intrinsic compatibility factors, while the latter is defined more by professional factors.

The eighth condition of knowledge sharing is opportunism which refers to the possibility that a decision-maker may unconditionally seek his or her self-interests, and that such behavior cannot necessarily be predicted. This argument extends the simple self-interest seeking assumption to include "self-interest seeking with guile", thereby making allowance for strategic behaviour (Williamson, 1975:26). A related line of argument is Goffman's (1969) idea of strategic manipulation of information or misrepresentation of intentions through false or empty threats or promises. The study by Wickramasinghe and Lamb (2002) provides respective insights into the world of healthcare.

13.6. Potential Predictors of Knowledge Sharing

By way of summary, the previous sections established the following arguments. Firstly, knowledge sharing between actors is facilitated through socialization, externalization and/or combination mechanisms in an organization. Secondly, there are several conditions that affect the knowledge resources and motivation to share knowledge through socialization, externalization and/or combination. And thirdly, in reviewing the literature on social capital and knowledge sharing, there is much evidence to support the view that socialization, externalization and/or combination of knowledge are complex social processes that are socially embedded in structural, agency and relational resources and relationships as represented in the concept of social capital.

Considering the social embeddedness of knowledge sharing, this essay suggests that such a theory is likely to be one that is grounded in social relationships. The following section explores this theory by examining the *causal efficacy between the dimensions of social capital and the conditions of knowledge sharing.*

While the focus of the present research considers the impact of each dimension of social capital independently from the other dimensions, it is recognized, however, that these dimensions of social capital may likely be interrelated in important and complex ways. For example, particular structural configurations, such as those with strong communication channels and reward systems, have consistently been shown to be associated with the relational aspect of work group trust (Bartol and Srivastava, 2002).

We argue that social capital can facilitate the sharing of knowledge by affecting the necessary conditions for such a process. To explore this proposition, this essay now examines the ways in which each of the three dimensions of social capital — structural, agency and relational — influences the eight conditions of knowledge sharing highlighted earlier.

13.6.1. *Hypothesis Development*

13.6.1.1. Structural dimension of social capital as driver of knowledge sharing

Organizational care. According to Krogh, care is a social norm in human relationships and institutions "which involves the dimensions of trust, active empathy, access to help, lenience in judgment, and the extent to which the former four dimensions are shared in the community" (2003:382). In caring for another, Krogh, Ichiko and Nonaka suggest that a care provider, such as a fellow colleague or senior management in the organization, may provide support and valuable knowledge for the purpose of task execution or to integrate a person into the organization and network and so on. This type of support characterizes an organization as one possessing high-care (2001:38). In a low-care organizational climate, on the contrary, there is a low propensity to help and care is not a shared value in the organization's culture. Thus, we hypothesized the following:

H_1: *Organizational care is positively related to knowledge sharing.*

Recognition and rewards. Bartol and Srivastava (2002) as well as Thompson, Kruglanski and Spiegel (2000) suggest that rewards and incentives are central to the motivation of an individual to pursue resources through strategic linkages or alliances. In the context of knowledge sharing, Davenport, Delong and Beers suggest that knowledge is "intimately and inextricably bound with people's egos and occupations" (1998:45). According to O'Reilly and Pondy (1980), the probability of actors routing information to other actors is positively related to the rewards they expect from sharing the knowledge. These two different perspectives suggest that the sharing of knowledge may likely be influenced by the desire to obtain recognition or the pursuit of strategic alliances through opportunistic motives. We proposed the following hypothesis:

H₂: Rewards and recognition are positively related to knowledge sharing.

13.6.1.2. Agency dimension of social capital as driver of knowledge sharing

Prosocial motives. The concept of prosocial motives is more commonly used as a psychometric variable in the field of psychology and has been used in recent years in the study of organizational citizenship behavior (Rioux and Penner, 2001). We argue that prosocial motives of an individual may have important relevance to explain why individuals may pursue resources available in interactions characterized by social capital. Prosocial motives, in this case, are defined by the sociability and the propensity of individuals to relate to another because of personal compatibility or liking, and may volunteer knowledge to help another as a result of this compatibility. Based on this formulation, we proposed the following hypothesis:

H₃: Individual prosocial motives are positively related to knowledge sharing.

Impression Management. The formulation of this variable is a response to Portes' (1998) suggestion to investigate the motives behind individuals to volunteer information or resources in a social capital transaction. Impression management is postulated here to be influenced by the expected costs of not sharing knowledge, e.g. withdrawal of incentives, that may lead the individual to share his knowledge to "keep up appearances". We hypothesized that:

H₄: Impression management influences opportunistic behavior and is positively related to knowledge sharing.

13.6.1.3. Relational dimension of social capital as driver of knowledge sharing

Competence. It has been argued by Blau (1964) as well as Schurr and Ozanne (1985) that the ability to perform work tasks, also known as *proficiency or competence*, builds trust with the colleagues the individual interacts with in an organization. This is based on the assumption that ability fulfils some measure of trust on the particular individual in successfully completing a given task. In terms of knowledge sharing, it denotes an ability to relay trustworthy information to the work group. In order to understand the influence of ability as a facet of trust in social capital, we hypothesized the following:

H_5: *Competence will be positively related to knowledge sharing.*

Open-mindedness. Tjosvold, Hui and Sun (2000) suggest that open-mindedness integrates people in a community and confers harmony and trust that new ideas and practices will not be discounted but accepted. In the context of knowledge sharing, we hypothesized the following:

H_6: *Open-mindedness is positively related to knowledge sharing.*

13.7. Method

13.7.1. *Sample*

In understanding the social and organizational factors that influence knowledge sharing, a model of knowledge sharing was developed based on the work of Nahapiet and Ghoshal (1998). The model is presented in Fig. 13.1.

To assess the various social capital dimensions, several standard scales were identified, analyzed and used to measure knowledge sharing, organizational concern, open-mindedness and so forth. In 2003, an online survey was developed and subsequently administered in a tertiary educational institution (academic staff, administrators and students) in Singapore. A total of 262 persons responded to the survey, which assessed various demographic variables and traits as well as the three social capital dimensions highlighted above. 42% of the respondents were male (N = 110) with 74.4% (N = 195) of Chinese ethnicity. Indians made up 11.1% (N = 29), Malays 3.8% (N = 10) with the remaining 10.1% belonging to other ethnic races. 81.3% (N = 209) of the sample was involved in education with the remaining respondents

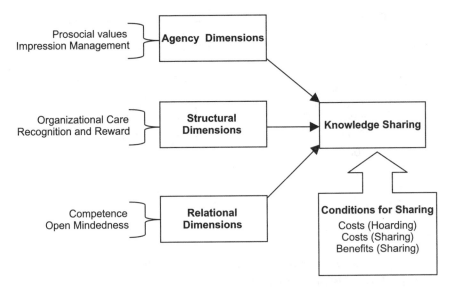

Fig. 13.1. A model of the antecedents of knowledge sharing.

Table 13.1. Sample distribution by organization.

		Frequency	Percent	Valid Percent	Cumulative Percent
Valid	1 HEI*	213	81.3	81.9	81.9
	2 Banks	4	1.5	1.5	83.5
	3 Consulting Firm	3	1.1	1.2	84.6
	4 IT	6	2.3	2.3	86.9
	5 Others	30	11.5	11.5	98.5
	6 Not Reported	4	1.5	1.5	100.0
	Total	260	99.2	100.0	
Missing	9	2	.8		
Total		262	100.0		

* HEI = Higher educational institution.

drawn from private sector companies in banking and finance, IT, and service industries. The academic community of respondents comprised 30.9% students, 40.8% administrative staff, and 10.3% faculty members (see Tables 13.1 and 13.2).

Table 13.2. Sample distribution — Higher educational institution.

		Frequency	Percent	Valid Percent	Cumulative Percent
Valid	1 Students	81	30.9	30.9	30.9
	2 Admin Staff	107	40.8	40.8	71.8
	2 Faculty	27	10.3	10.3	82.1
	4 Others	47	17.9	17.9	100.0
	Total	262	100.0	100.0	

13.7.2. *Measures*

The outcome measure was *knowledge sharing*.

Knowledge Sharing: A 5-item measure adapted from Liebowitz (1999) was used to measure knowledge sharing orientation. Response options ranged from (1) "strongly disagree" to (5) "strongly agree". Sample items are "Ideas and best practices are shared routinely" and "It is part of the culture of this organization to share knowledge". The scale's alpha reliability in this study is .93.

Organizational concern and *recognition and rewards* were the main organizational climate variables assessed (structural dimension).

Organizational Concern: A 4-item scale developed by Rioux and Penner (2001) was used to measure the extent to which staff valued the organization. Sample items are "I care about this company" and "The organization values my contributions". Response options ranged from (1) "strongly disagree" to (5) "strongly agree". The scale's alpha reliability in this study is .91.

Reward and Recognition: The authors developed this 4-item scale. Sample items are "Our appraisal/staff evaluation system encourages knowledge sharing" and "People who share knowledge are given due recognition in this organization". Response options ranged from (1) "strongly disagree" to (5) "strongly agree". The scale's alpha reliability in this study is .92.

Prosocial motives and *impression management* were the main motivational factors assessed (agency dimension).

Pro-Social Motives: A 6-item measure adapted from Rioux and Penner (2001) was used to measure prosocial motives and altruistic behaviors. Response options ranged from (1) "strongly disagree" to (5) "strongly agree" for each of the items. Sample items are "People here always put themselves first", and "I want to help my colleagues in any way I can". The alpha reliability in this study is .95.

Impression Management: We constructed a 4-item measure based on insights gained by Goffman (1969) and Portes (1998). Sample items are "I want to avoid looking bad in front of others as if I did not contribute", and "I want to avoid being blacklisted by my boss". The alpha reliability in this study is .89.

Competency and *open-mindedness* were the main trust-related factors assessed (relational dimension).

Competence: This 4-item scale was adapted from Gefen (2000). It measures the competency and knowledge of co-workers. Sample items include "My colleagues are competent in what they do at work", and "My colleagues are knowledgeable about their job". The scale's alpha reliability in this study is .95.

Open-mindedness: A 4-item scale adapted from Payne and Pheysey (1971) was used. Response options ranged from (1) "not at all likely" to (5) "extremely likely" for one of the items and, (1) "strongly disagree" to (5) "strongly agree" for the other three items. Sample items are "One of the most important values emphasized in my workgroup is open-mindedness" and "My co-workers speak out openly". The scale's alpha reliability in this study is .76.

Other variables included *costs of hoarding knowledge* as well as *costs and benefits of knowledge sharing*.

Costs of Knowledge Hoarding: We constructed a 4-item measure. Sample items are "I might be excluded from information within the organization if I do not engage in knowledge sharing" and "It will be very difficult to create new knowledge if I do not exchange knowledge with others". Response options ranged from (1) "strongly disagree" to (5) "strongly agree". The alpha reliability in this study is .85.

Costs of Knowledge Sharing: We constructed a 4-item measure. Sample items are "Sharing knowledge in this organization may lead to criticism and ridicule" and "Sharing knowledge in this organization is like 'pointing a gun at your face' and may imply all kinds of disadvantages". Response options ranged from (1) "strongly disagree" to (5) "strongly agree". The alpha reliability in this study is .93.

Benefits of Knowledge Sharing: the authors constructed a 4-item measure. Sample items are "Knowledge sharing makes innovation easier", and "I make more informed decisions with the inputs of my colleagues". Response options ranged from (1) "strongly disagree" to (5) "strongly agree". The alpha reliability in this study is .95.

13.8. Analysis

Controls. Three demographic variables, age, full-time work experience and gender were employed as control variables. Gender was coded (0) "male" and (1) "female."

Hierarchical regression analysis was used to examine the predictors of knowledge sharing. Explanatory (independent) variables were entered into the regression in a specified order as a means of determining their individual and joint contributions to explaining the outcome variable.

13.9. Results

The means, standard deviations and intercorrelations of measures of knowledge sharing and the various social capital dimensions are given in Tables 13.3 and 13.4.

The results of the correlation analysis are consistent with the proposed hypotheses, indicating support for each of structural, agency, and relational dimensions of social capital as drivers of knowledge sharing. Furthermore, costs of sharing was negatively related to sharing; when costs of sharing was high, knowledge sharing was low.

Results of multiple regression analyses carried out to determine whether structural, agency and relational factors predicted knowledge sharing are presented in Table 13.4 (Regression Model, Predictors of

Table 13.3. Means, standard deviations and
Pearson intercorrelations of major variables in the study.

Measure	M	SD	1	2	3	4	5	6	7	8	9	10	11	12	13
1. Knowledge Sharing	3.05	.83	(0.93)												
2. Gender	.54	.50	.19*	(−)											
3. Age	30.78	10.74	−.17*	−.13	(−)										
4. Work Experience	8.13	9.20	−.18*	−.05	.71**	(−)									
5. Organizational Care	3.65	.77	.55**	.10	.07	.03	(0.91)								
6. Reward & Recognition	2.85	.89	.69**	.08	−.19*	−.23**	.46**	(0.92)							
7. Impression Management	3.24	.82	.36**	.09	−.19*	−.23**	.38**	.38**	(0.89)						
8. Competence	3.69	.81	.49**	.13	.09	.01	.74**	.45**	.35**	(0.95)					
9. Open-mindedness	3.12	.72	.70**	.14	−.12	−.16*	.61**	.72**	.42**	.62**	(0.76)				
10. Pro-Social Motives	3.66	.71	.41**	.16*	.06	−.01	.74**	.30**	.37**	.59**	.48**	(0.95)			
11. Costs of Hoarding	3.18	.69	.62**	.12	−.05	−.07	.52**	.56**	.43**	.44**	.53**	.53**	(0.85)		
12. Benefits of Sharing	3.90	.82	.45**	.09	.04	−.04	.71**	.33**	.41**	.71**	.48**	.71**	.58**	(0.95)	
13. Costs of Sharing	2.83	.83	−.05	.03	.15	.14	.14	−.04	.27**	.09	.02	.31**	.33**	.25**	(0.93)

*Correlation is significant at the 0.05 level (2-tailed).

**Correlation is significant at the 0.01 level (2-tailed).

†Cronbach's Alpha reliability value shown in brackets.

Table 13.4. Regression model of the predictors of knowledge sharing (N = 148).

Variable	Model 1	Model 2	Model 3	Model 4[1]
Intercept	3.05***	3.05***	3.05***	3.03***
Age	−.01	−.01	−.01	−.01
Work Experience	−.01	−.01	.01	.01
Gender	.29*	.13	.12	.12
Organizational Concern		.18	.12	.16
Reward and Recognition		.32***	.20***	.16*
Impression Management		−.05	−.04	.01
Competence		−.05	−.07	−.03
Open-mindedness		.42***	.38***	.42***
Pro-social Motives		−.03	−.07	−.04
Costs of Hoarding			.34***	.33***
Knowledge Expected Benefits of Knowledge Sharing			.06	−.03
Expected Costs of Knowledge Sharing			.20***	−.18***
Reward & Recognition				−.20***
Competence Reward				.12*
Recognition and Costs of Knowledge Hoarding				
F	3.357**	25.098***	24.140***	22.773***
R^2	.065	.647	.701	.721
ΔR^2	.065	.582	.054	.020

*$p < .05$.
**$p < .025$.
***$p < .01$.

[1] The ß values are the unstandardized coefficients from the final regression equation, each term being corrected for all other terms.

Knowledge Sharing) and Fig. 13.2 (Relation between Knowledge Sharing and Reward and Recognition for High and Low Competence).

As Table 13.4 indicates, reward and recognition, open-mindedness and cost concerns with regard to both knowledge hoarding and sharing turned out to be the strongest predictors of knowledge sharing rather than pro-social motives or organizational concern.

Table 13.4 includes two interaction terms, over and above the main effect model. The results from this table are used to graph the

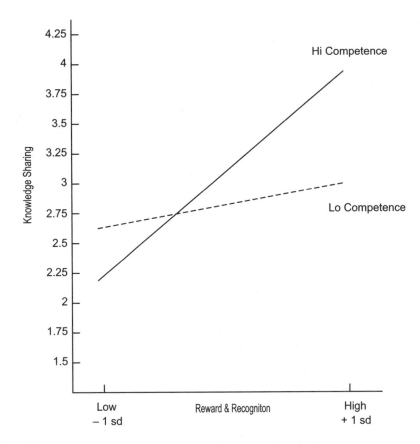

Fig. 13.2. Relation between knowledge sharing and reward and recognition for high and low competence.

presentation of the interaction between rewards and recognition and competence (see Fig. 13.2).

Figure 13.2 shows relation between knowledge sharing and reward-recognition for high and low competence individuals. It graphically presents the joint influence of reward-recognition and competence on

knowledge sharing. For low competence individuals (1 SD below mean), knowledge sharing remained relatively consistent irrespective of the level of reward-recognition. In contrast, this effect was very marked for high competence (1 SD above mean) individuals. The line representing high competence individuals shows that knowledge sharing is strongly and positively related to competence; knowledge sharing is lowest when they perceive that reward-recognition is low.

In short, individuals who are highly competent in their work abilities are less likely to share what they know when they perceive there are few rewards or when their sharing is not recognized by the organization. Individuals who are low on competency, relative to their colleagues, tend to share their knowledge regardless of whether there are organizational incentives to do so.

13.10. Discussion and Conclusions

The conceptual view of knowledge sharing presented here in this essay is a social one. It has been argued that social capital facilitates the sharing of knowledge by affecting the conditions necessary for such a process. The essay examined the ways in which each of the dimensions of social capital — structural, agency and relational — influence knowledge sharing.

The findings suggest that contemporary organizations, which engage in knowledge-intensive and knowledge-generating activities, need to institute an environment conducive to the development of all three dimensions of social capital in order for effective knowledge sharing to take place. Particular emphasis needs to be put on organizational climate variables such as recognition and rewards, which turned out to be very critical predictors of knowledge sharing.

As the study's findings show, the structural dimension of social capital matters and so does the relational dimension. The criticality of open-mindedness as another predictor of knowledge sharing implies that organizations need to implement proper recruitment and screening processes so as to attract a particular type of person who has the required demographic traits, which may make sharing easier. The plausible assumption that personal compatibility predicts knowledge sharing will have to be examined in the context of another study. Voluntary interactions between human actors aimed at exchanging information and experiences often occur when people are comfortable with each other, e.g. due to social similarities.

The study also shows that organizational members consider the possible costs of knowledge sharing and hoarding very carefully before they act. Prosocial motives or altruism do not matter much in the context of our sample which might be a function of the fact that many of the respondents were highly qualified knowledge workers who are known to have a unique orientation (e.g. they are loyal to their own profession but not necessarily to their employer). Individuals who are highly competent in their work abilities turned out to be less likely to share what they know (in contrast to individuals who are low on competency) when they perceive that there are few rewards or when sharing is not recognized by the organization.

Overall, the findings provide evidence for the importance of an effective performance management system if an organization wants to successfully manage the transition from a "knowledge is power culture" to a high-performing organization where knowledge sharing is seen as a key enabler of improved business performance and value innovation.

Some limitations were observed in the development of the framework. Firstly, the impact of each dimension of social capital had been considered independently from the other dimensions. It was noted that these dimensions of social capital might likely be interrelated in important and complex ways. As the primary objective of the analysis was to focus on the independent effects of those dimensions to the conditions of knowledge sharing, the richness of the exploration was limited. Future research, therefore, should consider the interrelationships of these dimensions as intervening explanatory factors that could further uncover the mechanisms and dynamics of why knowledge sharing takes place.

Secondly, the different facets chosen to represent the dimensions of social capital are by no means exhaustive. Various other facets such as network ties, norms, and obligations dominant in the social capital literature could have been used as well. However, as this essay attempts to relate social capital robustly with knowledge sharing, the choice of social capital variables was limited to the most relevant. An inclusion of more of such variables would have also meant that the medium of an essay or journal publication, which stresses a tight word limit, would have been unsuitable for such an exposition.

As the research was confined to just one organization, the findings (although they are highly plausible) can not be generalized. More research covering different types of organizations and sectors are necessary to further support the study approach.

Nevertheless, it is believed that this essay has made an important theoretical-empirical contribution to the rapidly progressing field of KM and the development of a stronger theoretical base. This is important since the topic of knowledge sharing is often discussed from the viewpoint of practitioners who stress more on attributes and formulas for effective knowledge sharing rather than theory-driven explanations.

There are several possible avenues where future research on the theory of knowledge sharing can embark on. More attention should be given to the agency dimension of knowledge sharing which, following Archer's (2003) concept of the *internal conversations* of private individuals, could examine how different reflexivities can influence the individual's decision-making in participating in resource-based knowledge sharing activities that could benefit their career or life trajectories. This would entail examining the tacit-dimension of knowledge and how such knowledge is explicated and structured to explain decisions that are subsequently made. This essay points towards a psychometric tool and questionnaire, the Tacit Knowledge Inventory for Managers, by occupational psychologists Richard Wagner and Robert Sternberg (Yale University) as a reference for such a research direction.

Furthermore, it would add an interesting angle to compare the theory of knowledge sharing in different organizational settings, such as the military where a top-down hierarchical structure may elicit different knowledge sharing dynamics, and a flat-structured business organization. Different national and cultural settings may also produce different observations. The research possibilities are rich and worthy to be explored further.

References

Aldrich, H. and D. Whetten (1981). Organization-sets, Action-sets and Networks: Making the Most of Simplicity. In *Handbook of Organizational Design*, P.C. Nystrom and W.H. Starbuck (eds.), pp. 385–408. Oxford: Oxford University Press.

Archer, M.S. (1995). *Realist Social Theory: The Morphogenetic Approach*. Cambridge and New York: Cambridge University Press.

Archer, M.S. (2003). *Structure, Agency, and the Internal Conversation*. Cambridge and New York: Cambridge University Press.

Bartol, K.M. and A. Srivastava (2002). Encouraging Knowledge Sharing: The Role of Organizational Reward Systems. *Journal of Leadership and Organizational Studies*, 9(1), 64–76.

Beck, U. (1992). *Risk Society: Towards a New Modernity*. London and Newbury Park, CA: Sage Publications.

Blau, P. (1964). *Exchange and Power in Social Life*. New York: Wiley.

Bourdieu, P. (1985). The Forms of Capital. In *Handbook of Theory and Research for the Sociology of Education*, J.G. Richardson (ed.), pp. 241–258. New York: Greenwood.

Bourdieu, P. and L.J.D. Wacquant (1992). *An Invitation to Reflexive Sociology*. Chicago: University of Chicago Press.

Brown, P. and H. Lauder (2000). Human Capital, Social Capital, and Collective Intelligence. In *Social Capital: Critical Perspectives*, S. Baron, J. Field and T. Schuller (eds.), pp. 226–242. Oxford and New York: Oxford University Press.

Burt, R. (2002). The Social Capital of Structural Holes. In *The New Economic Sociology: Developments in an Emerging Field*, M.F. Guillen *et al.* (eds.), pp. 148–190. New York: Russell Sage Foundation.

Burt, R. (2004). Structural Holes and Good Ideas. *American Journal of Sociology*, 110(2), 349–399.

Cicourel, A.V. (1973). *Cognitive Sociology: Language and Meaning in Social Interaction*. Harmondsworth: Penguin.

Cohen, D. and L. Prusak (2001). *In Good Company: How Social Capital Makes Organizations Work*. Boston: Harvard Business School Press.

Cohen, W.M. and D.A. Levinthal (1990). Absorptive Capacity: A New Perspective on Learning and Innovation. *Administrative Science Quarterly*, 35(1), 28–152.

Coleman, J.S. (1990). *Foundations of Social Theory*. Cambridge, MA and London: Belknap.

Conte, R. and M. Paolucci (2002). *Reputation in Artificial Societies: Social Beliefs for Social Order*. Boston: Kluwer Academic Press.

Davenport, T.H., D.W. DeLong and M.C. Beers (1998). Successful Knowledge Management Projects. *Sloan Management Review*, 39(2), 43–57.

Evers, H.-D. and T. Menkhoff (2004). Reflections about the Role of Expert Knowledge and Consultants in an Emerging Knowledge Economy. *Human Systems Management*, 23(4), 137–149.

Fukuyama, F. (1996). *Trust: The Social Virtues and the Creation of Prosperity*. London: Penguin.

Fukuyama, F. (1999). *The Great Disruption: Human Nature and the Reconstitution of Social Order*. London: Profile.

Gabbay, S.M. and R. Leenders (2001). Social Capital of Organizations: From Social Structure to the Management of Corporate Social Capital. In *Social Capital of Organizations*, S.M. Gabbay and R. Leenders (eds.), pp. 1–20. Oxford.

Gefen, D. (2000). Lessons Learnt from the Successful Adoption of an ERP: The Central Role of Trust. In *Decision Making: Recent Developments and Worldwide Applications*, S.H. Zanakis, G. Doukidis and C. Zopounidis (eds.), pp. 17–30. Dordrecht and Boston, MA: Kluwer Academic Publishers.

Giddens, A. (1979). *Central Problems in Social Theory*. London: Macmillan.

Goffman, E. (1969). *The Presentation of Self in Everyday Life*. London: Allen Lane.

Gupta, A.K. and V. Govindarajan (2000). Knowledge Management's Social Dimension: Lessons from Nucor Steel. *Sloan Management Review*, 42(1), 71–80.

Granovetter, M.S. (1985). Economic Action and Social Structure: The Problem of Embeddedness. *American Journal of Sociology*, 91(3), 481–510.

Granovetter, M.S. (1992). Problems of Explanation in Economic Sociology. In *Networks and Organizations: Structure, Form and Action*, N. Nohria and R. Eccles (eds.), pp. 25–56. Boston: Harvard Business School Press.

Granovetter, M.S. (2002). A Theoretical Agenda for Economic Sociology. In *The New Economic Sociology: Developments in an Emerging Field*, M.F. Guillen *et al.* (eds.), pp. 35–60. New York: Russell Sage Foundation.

Guterman, J. (2002). Out of Sight, Out of Mind. *Harvard Management Communication Letter*, 5(9), 3–4.

Hansen, M.T. (1999). The Search-Transfer Problem: The Role of Weak Ties in Sharing Knowledge Across Organizational Sub-Units. *Administrative Science Quarterly*, 44(1), 82–111.

Helmstadter, E. (2003). The Institutional Economics of Knowledge Sharing: Basic Issues. In *The Economics of Knowledge Sharing: A New Institutional Approach*, E. Helmstadter (ed.), pp. 11–38. Cheltenham and Northampton, MA: Edward Elgar.

Hosmer, L.T. (1995). Trust: The Connecting Link Between Organizational Theory and Philosophical Ethics. *Academy of Management Review*, 20(2), 379–403.

Huang, J.C. and S.F. Wang (2002). Knowledge Conversion Abilities and Knowledge Creation and Innovation: A New Perspective on Team Composition. In *Proceedings of the Third European Conference on Organizational Knowledge, Learning, and Capabilities, 5–6 April 2002, Athens, Greece*. Athens: Athens Laboratory of Business Administration. Available online: http://www.alba.edu.gr/OKLC2002/Proceedings/track3.html.

Ipe, M. (2003). Knowledge Sharing in Organizations: A Conceptual Framework. *Human Resource Development Review*, 2(4), 337–359.

Jensen, M.C. (1998). *Foundations of Organizational Strategy*. Harvard, MA: Harvard University Press.

Knights, D., F. Murray and H. Willmott (1993). Networking as Knowledge Work: A Study of Strategic Inter-organizational Development in the Financial Services

Industry. *Journal of Management Studies*, 30(6), 975–995.

Krogh, G.V. (1998). Care in Knowledge Creation. *California Management Review*, 40(3), 133–153.

Krogh, G.V. (2003). Knowledge Sharing and the Communal Resource. In *The Blackwell Handbook of Organizational Learning and Knowledge Management*, M. Easterby-Smith and M.A. Lyles (eds.), pp. 372–392. Malden, MA and Oxford: Blackwell Publishing.

Krogh, G.V., K. Ichijo and I. Nonaka (2001). Bringing Care into Knowledge Development of Business Organizations. In *Knowledge Emergence: Social, Technical, and Evolutionary Dimensions of Knowledge Creation*, I. Nonaka and T. Nishiguchi (eds.), pp. 30–52. Oxford and New York: Oxford University Press.

Liebowitz, J. (ed.) (1999). *Knowledge Management Handbook*. Boca Raton, FL: CRC Press.

Liebowitz, J. (2000). *Building Organizational Intelligence*. Boca Raton, FL: CRC Press.

Lin, N. (2001). Building a Network Theory of Social Capital. In *Social Capital: Theory and Research*, N. Lin, K. Cook and R.S. Burt (eds.), pp. 3–29. New York: Aldine De Gruyter.

Luhmann, N. (1979). *Trust and Power*. London: John Wiley and Sons.

Menkhoff, T., Y.W. Chay and B. Loh (2004). Notes from an "Intelligent Island": Towards Strategic Knowledge Management in Singapore's Small Business Sector. *International Quarterly for Asian Studies*, 35(1–2), 85–99.

Nahapiet, J. and S. Ghoshal (1998). Social Capital, Intellectual Capital, and the Organizational Advantage. *Academy of Management Review*, 23(2), 242–266.

Nohria, N. and R. Eccles (1992). Face-to-Face: Making Network Organizations Work. In *Networks and Organizations: Structure, Form and Action*, N. Nohria and R. Eccles (eds.), pp. 288–308. Boston: Harvard Business School Press.

Nonaka, I. (1994). A Dynamic Theory of Organizational Knowledge Creation. *Organizational Science*, 5(1), 14–37.

Nonaka, I., N. Konno and R. Toyama (2001). Emergence of "Ba": A Conceptual Framework for the Continuous and Self-Transcending Process of Knowledge Creation. In *Knowledge Emergence: Social, Technical, and Evolutionary Dimensions of Knowledge Creation*, I. Nonaka and T. Nishiguchi (eds.), pp. 13–29. Oxford and New York: Oxford University Press.

Nonaka, I. and H. Takeuchi (1995). *The Knowledge Creating Company: How Japanese Companies Create the Dynamics of Innovation*. New York: Oxford University Press.

O'Reilly, C. and L. Pondy (1980). Organizational Communications. In *Organizational Behavior*, S. Kerr (ed.). Columbus: Grid.

Payne, R.L. and D.C. Pheysey (1971). G. G. Stern's Organizational Climate Index: A Reconceptualization and Application to Business Organizations. *Organizational Behavior and Human Performance*, 6, 77–98.

Polanyi, M. (1967). *The Tacit Dimension*. London: Routledge and Kegan Paul.

Portes, A. (1998). Social Capital: Its Origins and Applications in Modern Sociology. *Annual Review of Sociology*, 24, 1–24.

Pritchard, R.D. and B.W. Karasick (1973). The Effects of Organizational Climate on Managerial Job Performance and Job Satisfaction. *Organizational Behavior and Human Performances*, 9, 126–146.

Putnam, R.D. (1993). *Making Democracy Work*. Princeton, NJ: Princeton University Press.

Putnam, R.D. (1995). Bowling Alone: America's Declining Social Capital. *Journal of Democracy*, 6(1), 65–78.

Quinn, J.B., P. Anderson and S. Finklestein (1996). Leveraging Intellect. *Academy of Management Executive*, 10(3), 7–27.

Rioux, S. and L.A. Penner (2001). The Causes of Organizational Citizenship Behavior: A Motivational Analysis. *Journal of Applied Psychology*, 86(6), 1303–1314.

Rulke, D.L. and S. Zaheer (2000). Shared and Unshared Transactive Knowledge in Complex Organizations: An Exploratory Study. In *Organizational Cognition: Computation and Interpretation*, Z. Shapira and T. Lant (eds.), pp. 83–100. Mahwah, NJ: Lawrence Erlbaum.

Schurr, P.H. and J.L. Ozanne (1985). Influences on Exchange Processes: Buyers' Preconceptions of a Seller's Trustworthiness and Bargaining Toughness. *Journal of Consumer Research*, 11(4), 939–953.

Stehr, N. (1994). *Knowledge Societies*. Thousand Oaks, CA: Sage Publications.

Stenmark, D. (2001). Leaveraging Tacit Organizational Knowledge. *Journal of Management Information Systems*, 17(3), 9–24.

Szulanski, G. and R. Cappetta (2003). Stickiness: Conceptualizing, Measuring, and Predicting Difficulties in the Transfer of Knowledge Within Organizations. In *The Blackwell Handbook of Organizational Learning and Knowledge Management*, M. Easterby-Smith and M.A. Lyles (eds.), pp. 513–534. Malden, MA and Oxford: Blackwell.

Thompson, E.P., A.W. Kruglanski and S. Spiegel (2000). Attitudes as Knowledge Structures and Persuasion as a Specific Case of Subjective Knowledge Acquisition. In *Why We Evaluate: Functions of Attitudes*, G.R. Maio and J.M. Olson (eds.), pp. 59–95. Mahwah, NJ and London: Lawrence Erlbaum Associates.

Tjosvold, D., C. Hui and H. Sun (2000). Social Face and Open-mindedness: Constructive Conflict in Asia. In *Asian Management Matters: Regional Relevance and Global Impact*, C.M. Lau *et al.* (eds.). London: Imperial College Press.

Walsham, G. (1993). *Interpreting Information Systems in Organizations*. Chichester: John Wiley and Sons.

Wickramasinghe, N. and R. Lamb (2002). Enterprise-wide Systems Enabling Physicians to Manage Care. *International Journal of Healthcare Technology and Management*, 4(3–4), 288–302.

Williamson, O.E. (1975). *Markets and Hierarchies: Analysis and Antitrust Implications*. New York: The Free Press.

Chapter 14

The Moderating Effects of Friendship Ties and Dispositional Factors on Inducement and Knowledge Sharing Among Employees

Ho-Beng Chia, Dishan Kamdar, Glenn J. Nosworthy and Yue Wah Chay

"New knowledge is created when people transfer and share what they know, internalize it and apply what they learned. The value and worth of individual, group and corporate intellectual assets grow exponentially when shared and increases in value with use. Human inertia is the biggest obstacle to knowledge management efforts." (Wah, 1999)

14.1. Introduction

Knowledge is often seen as know-how, rich in information, encompassing data, facts and a host of entities including intelligence. Knowledge and its management has, in the last few years, attracted considerable research attention spawning multi-disciplinary approaches including technology, strategy, decision science, economics and psychology.

The theme Wah has clearly explicated underscores the important role that knowledge sharing plays in the knowledge management process. Similarly, Malhotra (1997) suggested that "knowledge management does not reside in the collection of information". According to him, unless interventions are made to facilitate sharing of knowledge in the firm, the whole knowledge management cycle will be futile.

Knowledge sharing is an important element in knowledge management and refers to the dissemination of job-relevant information to coworkers in a firm (Cummings, 2001). Knowledge sharing is

305

especially important today because knowledge is supplanting land, labor, and capital as the primary source of competitive advantage, and as such, the ability to create new knowledge as well as to share existing knowledge becomes crucial for organizational success (Lesser, 2000; Weiss, 1999). However, employees may consider knowledge to be a commodity that gives them personal competitive advantage over their coworkers in the pursuit of organizational rewards. If this is the case, organizations will not be able to establish a knowledge-sharing environment simply by fiat.

In order to craft interventions that facilitate desired behavior in this domain, we need to understand the motives and contingencies associated with knowledge hoarding and knowledge sharing. Previous research on knowledge management has focused almost exclusively on the informational infrastructure such as communications media, databases, directories, and search engines. In contrast, there has been relatively little consideration of the human part of the equation, particularly the motivational factors that drive individuals to communicate, share, learn, and use knowledge. For instance, in several in-depth interviews conducted by the authors, human resource practitioners from prominent companies had varied opinions as to how knowledge sharing can be achieved. Some believe that knowledge sharing requires having strong ties through strong organizational culture and group cohesiveness, others believe that knowledge sharing has to be explicitly appraised or rewarded by providing performance bonus before it will be forthcoming. Others believed that certain personal orientation/motives would suffice in promoting knowledge sharing, as some individuals may be predisposed to share with others.

Similarly, researchers have demonstrated that extra-role behaviors (ERB) are partially influenced by dispositional factors (Chia *et al.*, 2002; Organ and Ryan, 1995), and that they can also be induced through rewards systems (Lesser, 2000; Weiss, 1999). Extra-role behaviors have also been examined within the framework of exchange relationships (e.g. Deluga, 1998; Hui, Law and Chen, 1999). However, the role of these factors in the sharing of knowledge within organizations has not been investigated.

The present study, therefore, examined how these elements might affect employees' intention or willingness to share knowledge that would otherwise give them a personal competitive advantage. This study conceives knowledge sharing as a subset of extra-role behavior (Zellars, Tepper and Giacalone, 2001) in the sense that it is discretionary and promotes overall organizational effectiveness. Specifically, we examined the relative and interaction effects of appraisal, performance bonus, closeness of ties and personal orientations (specifically, impression management and Machiavellianism) on the willingness to share knowledge with employees in one's work unit.

14.2. Sharing Knowledge

Knowledge is one of the most important resources in today's competitive world (Drucker, 1997). According to Quinn, Anderson and Finkelstein (1996), intellectual capital generates the bulk of added value in both service and manufacturing industries. With the apparent significance of knowledge/information, the importance of distributing information to co-workers and the prevention of information hoarding becomes especially vital for an organization's overall competitive advantage. Hence, the fundamental premise of knowledge management today lies in the ability to facilitate information sharing through the use of information technology. Investing substantial capital in information technology, without creating a culture of sharing knowledge/information will do little to benefit the firm in the long run.

Given the importance of sharing knowledge, prominent organizations such as the World Bank, McKinsey and Company, Ernest and Young and Accenture are devoting huge amounts of capital to devise elaborate ways to codify, store and provide access to both explicit and tacit knowledge (see Wah, 1999; Hansen, Nohria and Tierney, 1999; Pascarella, 1997 and Smith, 2001). Employees may often have access to vital knowledge that may improve individual and, subsequently, firm performance; however, they may decide to hoard such information for personal competitive advantage over co-workers. Such proprietary knowledge may be learned through experience; know-how based on practice or may be acquired from exclusive sources (Smith, 2001). For example, if an employee in a manufacturing unit has figured out a way to improve work process efficiency, he/she may not share this "innovation" with others but instead use it to improve personal productivity relative to co-workers. Doing this may improve the employee's likelihood of a promotion or reward, but from the organizational standpoint it represents a major opportunity cost. If the individual had shared his/her "innovation" with co-workers, it could lead to substantial costs savings and thereby increase the competitiveness of the firm.

In addition to loss of opportunity, information hoarding may also lead to soured relationships among employees. If coworkers find out that an individual has withheld value-added knowledge for personal/selfish gain, relationships may become strained. This may indirectly affect unit performance through reduced teamwork effort and group cohesion and may eventually affect firm productivity and efficiency. Hence, organizations have to recognize, nourish and appropriately reward the sharing of information/knowledge to enable the exchange, flow and use of knowledge (Smith, 2001).

14.3. Knowledge Sharing in "Strong Situations"

As previously noted, researchers have found that certain dispositional factors predict extra-role behaviors. For instance, it has been demonstrated that individuals who are high on conscientiousness or agreeableness tend to exhibit more extra-role behavior than others (Podsakoff et al., 2000). A meta-analysis reported by Organ and Ryan (1995) revealed that various personality factors such as conscientiousness, agreeableness, positive affectivity and negative affectivity predict organizational citizenship behavior (OCB). Researchers have also found strong positive correlations between locus of control and citizenship behaviors (Motowildo and Van Scotter, 1994; Funderberg and Levy, 1997). Lepine and Van Dyne (2001), Hogan et al. (1998) and Hui, Law and Chen (1999) found neuroticism to be negatively correlated with co-operative behavior. Several other researchers have also found positive links between extroversion and citizenship behaviors (Lepine and Van Dyne, 2001; McManus and Kelly, 1999; Miller, Griffin and Hart, 1999).

Most of these studies have not, however, examined person-situation interactions with respect to these various extra-role behaviors. While these studies have been centered on the relative importance of employee attributes like personality (see Podsakoff *et al.*, 2000 for a review), there has been a general lack of research concentration that has been devoted to the role of situational forces and its potential interaction with dispositional factors. According to researchers (Shoda, Mischel and Wright, 1989; Mischel and Shoda, 1995; West, 1983), dispositional factors play a reduced role in explaining behavior in "strong situations." Strong situations are characterized by rules, norms and expectations regarding appropriate or desired behavior. In contrast, "weak situations" are those in which there are few demands or pressures determining how an individual behaves. As noted by Van Dyne *et al.* (2000:5), "personality has more predictive power in weak situations (situations that do not have compelling external incentives)." They further assert: "In strong situations, well recognized and widely accepted guidelines for interaction reduces inter-individual variability ... Most individuals in strong situations construe the situation in the same way and tend to conform to the norms and expectations; hence, personality constructs generally have little predictive power in a strong situation."

In the present study, we look at: (i) how organizational control systems specifically appraise employees to share acquired proprietary knowledge, or the absence of such appraisals and (ii) different types of performance bonuses (i.e., bonus pegged to team performance, individual performance or the absence of such bonus) affect knowledge sharing intentions. In "strong" situations where employees are specifically appraised for sharing information with co-workers and/or rewarded on team performance, we can expect less variance in sharing intent, and personality factors should be relatively weaker predictors of knowledge sharing intent. For instance, in such situations, those who would otherwise not share will do so because of the inducements and hence they will be equally likely to share knowledge with those who are predisposed to be helpful (e.g. conscientiousness).

H_{1a}: *Appraisal for knowledge sharing will increase willingness/ intent to share proprietary knowledge.*

H_{1b}: *Performance bonus will increase willingness/intent to share proprietary knowledge; specifically, employees will be most likely to share proprietary knowledge when team based performance bonus are provided, followed by individual based performance bonus, then by no bonus.*

As stated in H_{1b} above, we expect more sharing of information when bonuses are pegged to team performance than when there is no bonus or when bonus is pegged to individual performance. Individual based performance bonus may actually pose impediments in creating a knowledge sharing culture as employees "rather hoard" value-adding information to achieve personal competitive gains. However, we can expect employees to share more under individual based performance bonus than when no bonus is given. This is because there may be a possibility that the information/knowledge recipient may reciprocate the goodwill in some way or another so that it may directly or indirectly improve the knowledge transferer's performance at the moment or in the near future. This may in turn improve the knowledge transferer's chances of reaping better individual performance. For instance, the information recipient may reciprocate by rendering favors, or by providing advice or help that may improve the knowledge transferer's performance. On the contrary, in the absence of any performance bonus, employees may not be motivated to share knowledge, as any potential direct or indirect performance advantage gained via sharing will not be rewarded by the organization.

14.4. Closeness of Ties

In addition to situational factors, the strength/closeness of ties among employees may also explain substantial variance in sharing intentions. Closeness of ties are often studied by social network researchers in relation to the concept of social capital (Seibert, Kraimer and Linden, 2001). According to Johnson (2001) and Lesser (2000), social capital is the value created by fostering connections between individuals. Employees generally seek to form close ties with one another so that this relational bond may be of mutual benefit, both directly and indirectly. These relational bonds may also play an important role in creating a knowledge sharing culture in an organization (Frenzen and Nakamoto, 1993; Granovetter, 1973; 1982; Hansen, 1999; Uzzi, 1999).

Strength of ties researchers argue that information sharing among employees relies on two factors: the employees' relational embeddedness in their social network and the knowledge redundancy among employees (Granovetter, 1973; Frenzen and Nakamoto, 1993; Brown and Reingen, 1987; Hansen, 1999; Krackhardt, 1992; Uzzi, 1999; Burt, 1992; Sabel, 1993). Rindfleisch and Moorman (2001) have suggested that employees are more likely to transmit information or share proprietary knowledge with people with whom they have higher levels of relational embededness (Frenzen and Nakamoto, 1993; Brown and Reingen, 1987), higher levels of frequent contact (Hansen, 1999) and emotional closeness (Krackhardt, 1992). In an organizational setting, a coworker who is a close friend will be an example of someone with whom one would have established high levels of relational embededdness, has recurrent contacts with, feels emotional attachment, reciprocity and indebtedness (Granovetter, 1973; Marsden and Campbell, 1984) and shares a similar cognitive structure (Granitz and Ward, 2001; Sirsi, Ward and Reingen, 1996; Kameda *et al.*, 1997). Hence, we can expect employees to be most willing to share sensitive proprietary information with those with whom they form strong ties, e.g. close friends in organization/work group (Rindfleisch and Moorman, 2001).

In addition to relational embeddedness, knowledge redundancy among employees also affects sharing intentions with others in the organization. Employees will also tend to share knowledge more with others they feel are otherwise unlikely to be aware of or have access to that knowledge. For example, in addition to the arguments made above, Granovetter (1973) also suggested that distant and infrequent relationships are effective for knowledge sharing because they provide access to novel information by bridging otherwise disconnected groups of individuals in the organization. According to Hansen (1999), strong ties, in contrast are likely to lead to redundant knowledge because they tend to occur among a small group of actors who generally have equal access to information. Hence knowledge sharing may also be enhanced by a low degree of redundancy among employee's knowledge structure (Rindfleisch and Moorman, 2001).

Given the arguments made in the above paragraphs, in the event that employees are performing similar tasks, we can expect individuals to more likely share proprietary information with close fiends than with coworkers in their work unit/division. Conversely, we hypothesize that:

H_2: *When employees are performing similar tasks, individuals will generally be more likely to share valuable information with close friends in the organization than with co-workers.*

14.4.1. *Closeness of Ties and Rewards*

The presence of valued rewards strongly encourages desired behaviors. However, if organizations wish to increase knowledge sharing, the more specific and relevant the inducements to knowledge sharing, the stronger the effects are likely to be (Locke, 1968; Locke and Latham, 1990). While various researchers have suggested that inducements serve as strong motivators, very few have explored the motivational impact of different types of inducements from the "strength of ties perspective". As suggested in hypotheses H_{1a} and H_{1b}, the presence of appraisals and bonus will encourage knowledge sharing. However, companies must realize that the more specific and relevant the goals are, the more likely that the desired behavior will be elicited. For instance, appraisals transmit a clear signal that knowledge sharing is desired and will be rewarded. In contrast, performance bonuses indicate that performance is needed but does not specify how that performance can be attained. The development of closer ties among colleagues in the absence of appraisals may be least likely to achieve knowledge sharing because the intervention relies on social exchange. Nevertheless, the intervention does not specify that knowledge is a currency of reciprocity, and co-workers have the option to use other currencies in their social exchanges. By providing appraisals for knowledge sharing, the organization cues employees into recognizing that knowledge sharing is a legitimate currency for social exchange. Therefore, the use of appraisals jointly with developing close ties may be an effective strategy to promote knowledge sharing. In contrast, the use of performance bonuses may not provide much additive effect when ties are strong as it will not provide a clear indication that knowledge sharing is desired and will be rewarded. Consequently, we hypothesize that:

H_3: *The use of appraisal jointly with developing close ties may be a more effective strategy to promote knowledge sharing than the use of performance bonus in conjunction with developing close ties.*

14.5. Personal Orientation and Motives

Various researchers have also established that individual orientations and motives can play an important role in discretionary organizational behavior (Chia *et al.*, 2002; Rioux and Penner, 2001; Bolino, 1999). Consideration of motives is important for more than just definitional reasons. For instance, rewarding knowledge sharing becomes even more problematic when some employees may be engaging in the behavior out of pure self-interest rather than a genuine concern for co-workers or the organization. More importantly, understanding knowledge sharing requires us to consider the situational parameters that encourage or discourage it, and therefore the motives underlying it. In other words, if we would like to elicit or predict knowledge sharing, we need to understand how these behaviors serve the needs of the individual and how the situation can be engineered to meet these needs. Thus, the inclusion of motives in our analysis of knowledge sharing would help us predict these behaviors across a variety of situations and would improve predictive validity within situations.

One such motive is impression management. Impression managers are mainly concerned with constructing and maintaining a positive public image and have a concomitant desire to avoid looking bad in the eyes of their coworkers and supervisors (Rosenfeld, Giacalone, and Riourdon, 1995; Schlenker, 1980). This motive is purely egoistic in nature and not associated with any kinds of personal or work related values, but rather with impression management. In Rioux and Penner (2001)'s article, the authors articulated that various researchers have recently noted that engaging in extra-role behaviors like OCB might be quite impression enhancing and self-serving (e.g. Eastman, 1994; Fandt and Ferris, 1990; Ferris *et al.*, 1994; Bolino, 1999) and some scholars have identified tactics that people use to enhance their images at work (Jones and Pitmann, 1982; Tedeschi and Melburg, 1984). Furthermore, Wayne and Green (1993) noted that impression management behaviors correlated positively (r = 0.49) with extra-role behaviors like OCB.

Impression managers are more concerned with the opportunity for image building that a situation presents rather than immediate tangible rewards (Bolino, 1999; Turnley and Bolino, 2001). While they are self-interested in the long-term, impression managers may strive to appear selfless in specific situations, as they wish to be seen as altruistic and helpful. Consequently, in situations where inducements are obvious, impression managers may actually decline to share personally valuable information with coworkers because they will not receive "image credit" for doing so and may even be regarded as instrumental. Often referred to as faking, impression managers consciously distort responses/refuse to help when tangible rewards are present, in an attempt to present a favorable image (Paulhus, 1984; 1991). In other words, they will not want to sacrifice the competitive advantage they derive from the knowledge because there is no image-related benefit in doing so. This would be consistent with recent research that suggests that impression managers are less likely to engage in pro-social behaviors that are associated with tangible rewards (Chia *et al.*, 2002). On the other hand, when dealing with people with whom they have a well-established relationship (family, close friends, etc.), impression managers should be less concerned with image construction and should be more willing to share valuable information. In these covenantal-exchange relationships, they should act more like true altruists and should not be sensitive to external reward contingencies. We thus offer the following hypotheses:

H_{4a}: *Impression management will be positively related to the intention to share information with coworkers when information sharing is not explicitly recognized in the perfor-appraisal system and negatively related when knowledge sharing is appraised.*

H_{4b}: *Impression management will interact with performance appraisal when coworkers are the potential recipients of shared knowledge; there will be no interaction when potential recipients are friends in the organization.*

Another personal orientation that has not received much research attention in the domain of extra-role behaviors is Machavellianism. This trait had been drawn from the political doctrine of Niccolo Machiavelli, which denies the relevance of morality in political affairs and holds that craft and deceit are justified in pursuing and maintaining political power (The American Heritage 2000.) Even today, the word is used in the English language meaning of or relating to Machiavelli or his political theory, characterized by political cunning, duplicity, or bad faith (Encyclopedia Britannica 1992). Over the past years, researchers have identified various factors relating to Machaivellianism, such as age (Gable and Topol, 1988; Vitell, Lumpkin and Rawwas, 1991; Shirley, 1995), ethnicity (Mobley, 1982; Cristie and Geis, 1970), gender (Gable and Topol, 1991; Burton and Hegarty, 1999), birth order (Randall and Randall, 1990; Boone and Kutz, 1988; Leman, 1985), equity sensitivity (King and Miles, 1994; Mudrack, Mason and Stepanski, 1999), occupational choice (Shirley, 1995), leadership (Drory and Gluskinos, 1980), task orientation and task effectiveness (Jones and White, 1983), managerial work attitudes and perceptions (Hollon, 1983), career (Corzine, Buntzman and Busch, 1988), student corporate social responsibility orientation (Burton and Hegarthy, 1999), ethics (Nelson and Gilbertson, 1991; Rayburn and Rayburn, 1996; Singhapakdi, 1993), marketing performance (Hunt and Chonko, 1984), social mobility (Touhey, 1993), altruism (Barber, 1994), locus of control (Mudrack, 1990), culture (Cyriac and Dharmaraj, 1994) and sales performance (Ricks and Fraedrich, 1999).

Despite the proliferation of inquiry in the Machiavellianism trait, there has been no research, to our knowledge, that has been devoted to understanding Machiavellianism from the perspective of knowledge sharing. Furthermore, the relationship between performance appraisals and Machiavellinism has not been widely researched. Machiavellians can be distinguished from impression managers. Machiavellians tend to employ manipulative strategies in dealing with others in order to achieve personal objectives (Cristie and Geis, 1970). They often use clever but often-dishonest methods that deceive people so that they get what they want, especially power or control (Barber, 1994; Watson and Morris, 1994). Those high on Machiavellianism approach people and situations in terms of strategic self-interest and are relatively unaffected by considerations of loyalty and interpersonal attachment (Mudrack, Mason and Stepanski, 1999; Robinson and Shaver, 1973). According to Mudrack *et al.* (1999:540) "Machiavellians, like entitleds, are takers and may use any means necessary to get what they want ... They may even lie, cheat, steal and bend rules for personal gains". They are generally not altruistic or empathic; they disregard, or are oblivious to the interests of those around them, and tend to be cynical about the motives of others (Allsopp, Eysenck and Eysenck, 1991; Barnett and Thompson, 1985; Pandey and Singh, 1987; Mudrack, 1993; Butler, 1991; Gurtman, 1992). Hence, we can expect that individuals high on Machiavellianism will be more concerned with tangible rewards associated with helping others and relatively less concerned with their self-image. Furthermore, their approach to others should not be contingent on familiarity or the closeness of their relationships. We consequently hypothesize that:

> H_5: *Machiavellianism will be positively related to the intention to share information with both coworkers and close-friends when information sharing is appraised.*

We make no hypothesis for Machiavellians under no appraisal condition because their behaviors will be dependent on how they perceive the relative value of withholding information versus sharing knowledge. One might argue that it is apparent that Machiavellians would rather decline to share/hoard information with others when no externally induced benefits are provided. However, we feel that their behavior under such "weak situations" is not as simple as it looks. It may be the case that Machiavellians, being social strategists and manipulators themselves, may also possibly share information when not appraised, in pursuit of reaching some hidden agendas such as improving chances to move ahead in career, as a means of controlling how they are being perceived, as a means to fool others who are gullible, to flatter important people, to pretend to be good and kind, etc. Hence we cannot make conclusive predictions about their sharing intentions in such situations.

14.6. Scenario Methodology

There has been an assumption that OCB and other scales that tap extra-role behaviors will actually capture the behavioral-intent of respondents. Questions that ask respondents to rate "how often do you help other employees;" "how often do you go out of your way to help new coworkers feel at ease" or "how frequently do you adjust your work schedules to accommodate other employees' request for time off," do not actually fully capture respondents' willingness to volunteer to perform that extra role behavior. Another methodology, that does not appear to have gained wide currency among extra-role behavior researchers, despite its popularity in other research areas, for instance, evaluating managerial salary raise decisions (Sherer, Schwab and Heneman, 1987), managerial decision making about employee discipline (Klass and Wheeler, 1990), studying social desirability (Rossi and Madden, 1985), determining important tasks within jobs (Sanchez and Levine, 1989), examining relationships between attitudes and leadership styles (Adams and Richards, 1985), job evaluation (Davis and Sauser, 1991), use with the employment interview (Graves and Karren, 1992) and goal importance and goal setting process (Hollenbeck and Williams, 1987), is the use of written scenarios. By having participants indicate how they would respond in specified situations, researchers can more readily identify the situational factors and constraints relating to extra-role behavior. Using experimental manipulations, this vignette-based approach can also help identify motives that individuals may not be aware of or may be reluctant to admit to. In other words, the use of written scenarios in knowledge sharing research might help us better understand this class of behaviors as well as the function it serves for the individuals who engage in them. Vignette based procedure is designed to statistically describe the information processing strategies of individuals (Hobson and Gibson, 1983). Used in a variety of settings (Slovic, Fischoff and Lichtenstein, 1977), vignette design is one of the most reliable methodologies used in research involving human judgment (Mazen, 1990) and decision rules, deriving a linear model of the judgmental process. As it is hard or nearly impossible to observe/record the decision process, coupled with the reported difficulty decision makers have using multiple criteria, (Parasumaran, Berry and Zeithaml, 1985; 1988), plus the need to control for self reporting biases, vignettee based design seems to be the ideal methodological choice. The main advantage of using this methodology is that influences on judgments are derived from actual decisions made by individuals rather than from self-reported reasons for selecting alternatives (Donnelly and Bownas, 1984). Furthermore, the use of a variety of research methodologies within a stream of research will help validate the results (Whitfield and Strauss, 2000). The use of multi-methods also help avoid criticism that the results are an artifact of the dominant research methodology (Hall and Rist, 1999; Lyon, Lumpkin and Dess, 2000). According to Cavanagh and Fritzsche (1985), employing the scenario method allows the researchers to reflect the multi-dimensional issues of the real world, hence creating more valid and reliable results (Alexander and Becker, 1978). Hence, in this study we used a vignette based experimental approach instead of a cross sectional approach to study knowledge sharing.

14.6.1. *Method*

14.6.1.1. Sample

A sample of 295 employees (Indian nationals) from a division of a fortune 500 company located in India participated in this study. We chose a single division within the company with a large employee base because we wanted to develop realistic scenarios that were as close to those available at the workplace. In addition, we also required that all respondents in this study were performing similar tasks as posited in our hypothesis. Every third employee was approached and they agreed to participate. English was the working language in this division. Ninety-two percent of the respondents were males. The mean age was 33.32 years ($SD = 7.44$), and 92% of the respondents had at least a Bachelor's degree. This reflects the high level of educational requirements needed in the refinery. Eighty percent of the participants were married; the average tenure in the company was 6.24 years ($SD = 5.63$); and the average number of years of working experience was 9.06 years ($SD = 6.29$).

14.6.2. *Procedure*

The study has a 2 × 3 (between subjects) × 2 (within subjects) factorial design. The 2 between-subjects factors represent the tangible incentive conditions to which participants will be randomly assigned. Conditions in the first factor are no bonus, individual-based inducements, or team-based bonus; and conditions in the second factor pertain to specifically appraising knowledge sharing vs. not appraising knowledge sharing. The 2-level within-subjects factor is the potential recipient of the knowledge: coworkers who are considered "close friends" and other co-workers in one's unit. Participants were randomly assigned to one of six possible experimental conditions contained in a set of 3 written scenarios. In designing the scenarios for this study, we made sure that they were relevant, familiar and generalizable (Weber, 1992; Granitz and Ward, 2001; Cavanagh and Fritzsche, 1985) so that it created greater realism (Fredrickson, 1986) and thus more realistic responses (Granitz and Ward, 2001).

These scenarios describe opportunities to share acquired information and knowledge with other coworkers. Participants responded to each of the three scenarios and the responses were aggregated across the scenarios. In addition to the scenario responses, participants also completed a number of measures including the constructs impression management and Machiavellianism. Participants were assured of strict confidentiality of their responses and were told that their identities and responses will not be disclosed to their employer. Questionnaires were completed in the researcher's presence and any questions that the respondents had were clarified immediately.

14.6.3. *Treatment Conditions and Dependent Variables*

Participants were presented with three scenarios that described opportunities to share acquired programs and information that will enable refinery engineers to design their projects faster and more efficiently (please refer to Appendix 14.1 for examples of the scenarios). Embedded in the scenarios was the treatment stimulus that stated whether the company appraised knowledge sharing and the type of performance bonus, if any. After reading each of the three scenarios, participants responded to 2 questions.

The first was "How likely is it that you would share this idea with most of your coworkers in your division?" The second was "How likely is it that you would share this idea with only coworkers you are close friends with in the division?" The response alternatives ranged from (1) "Very unlikely" to (7) "Very likely." The responses were collapsed across the three scenarios to arrive at a composite measure of sharing intent. The Cronbach's alphas for the 2 dependent variables were high ($\alpha = .94$ and $.92$ for sharing with coworkers and close friends respectively). In other words, the 3 scenarios may be considered akin to items, albeit in greater detail, measuring a simple construct.

Although the use of written vignettes has been widespread in such areas as employee selection and appraisal (e.g., Moore, 1984; Rose, 1978), this method has not been used by extra-role behavior researchers. Some writers have criticized the use of "paper people" in organizational research and have questioned the method's ability to achieve realism, spontaneity and subject involvement (Granitz and Ward, 2001; Aronson, Brewer and Carlsmith, 1985; Campbell and Stanley, 1963; Freedman, Carlsmith and Sears, 1970; Mathison, 1988; Sawyer, 1975). However, Murphy et al. (1986) found that "paper people" designs resulted in larger effect sizes than behavioral observations and suggests that the stronger effect sizes were the results of less ambiguity and contamination. Thus the use of vignettes makes the measurement more precise and valid for the things we want to measure.

Woehr and Lance (1991) found that videotapes, behavioral observations and scripts that contain "noise" could yield equivalent effects size. This finding, further reassures the use of vignettes. Experimental design eliminates contaminants and allows for more control and precision, hence achieving greater validity. According to Casella (2000), the use of vignettes allows researchers to make a more valid comparison of the responses in standardized context with greater amount of background information and details. Cleveland (1991) found that raters gave very comparable ratings to actual and hypothetical job applicants. She argued that the use of "paper people" could be appropriate when the processes involved in a research setting are similar to the actual processes in an applied setting. Accordingly, we created scripted scenarios containing knowledge sharing information as well as information on job related behaviors. The intent was to better simulate reality by imbedding the manipulated behaviors among the noise behaviors.

The scenarios and the manipulations and questionnaires had been pre-tested to ensure validity: pre-tests participants ($N = 15$) were asked to indicate the extent to which the scenarios depicted the intended manipulations and how realistic the scenarios were for the type of work that they do, and the meaning and clarity of the questionnaires. The pre-tests indicated that the subjects generally agreed that the vignettes portrayed the variables being manipulated, that the scenarios were realistic, and questionnaires comprehensible.

14.6.4. *Motive and Orientation Measures*

Impression management motive was measured with a 10-item subscale from Rioux and Penner's motives scale (2001). The entire scale was used for analysis (Cronbach's alpha = .82). Machiavellianism was assessed using a 20-item scale (Christie and Geis, 1970). This scale is frequently used and established, evident from the high internal reliability found in the present study (Cronbach's alpha for the entire scale was .92.) All the items described above were measured on a 7-point response scale. Options ranged from 1 (Very Strongly Disagree) to 7 (Very Strongly Agree).

14.7. Confirmatory Factor Analysis (CFA)

We conducted confirmatory factor analysis to isolate the degree of measurement error and assess whether the items measuring the independent variables captured the proposed underlying dimensions. The structural equation modeling software AMOS was used for assessing the fit of the measurement model. The overall model fit was evaluated using multiple goodness-of-fit measures. There are a number of goodness-of-fit measures developed to assess overall model fit. Generally, there are three types of measures: (1) absolute fit measures, e.g. Goodness-of-Fit-Index (GFI), Root Mean Square Error of Approximation (RMSEA, p value); (2) incremental fit measures, e.g. Comparative Fit Index (CFI), Tucker-Lewis coefficient (TLI); and (3) parsimonious fit measures (Normalized Chi-Square: χ^2/df). The application of a combination of measures from the 3 types to assess the goodness-of-fit of a model is encouraged. This is because the practice of using a combination of measures will enable "the researcher to gain a consensus across the types of measures as to the acceptability of the proposed model" (Hair *et al.*, 1998, p. 611). A value greater than 0.90 is considered an acceptable fit for GFI, CFI and TLI (Hair *et al.*, 1998). A RMSEA value of about 0.05 or less indicates a close fit to the model (Brownw and Cudeck, 1993). The recommended value for the normalized chi square is between 1 and 2, and a p value higher than 0.05 indicates that the model fits the population.

Results of the CFA analysis for the independent variables showed that the 2 factor measurement model (impression management and Machiavellianism) had a very good fit to the observed covariance matrix (GFI = 0.93, RMSEA = 0.02, CFI = 0.99, TLI = 0.99, $\chi^2/df = 1.11$, p = .09). This indicated that the measures depict the proposed underlying dimensions and can be clearly distinguished from one another.

14.7.1. *Results*

Table 14.1 shows the means, standard deviations and intercorrelations of the major variables in the study. The reliabilities of all the variables were above the cut-off level of .07. There was no multicollinearity amongst variables.

A repeated measures ANOVA was employed to test hypotheses $H_{1a} - H_3$. The between subject factors were type of performance bonus (none, individual based, and team based) and appraisals (no appraisals vs. appraisals). The within subject factor was the closeness of ties, operationalized as beneficiary (close friends versus co-workers). The dependent variable was the intention to share information.

Table 14.2 shows the results of the ANOVA analysis. Except for the main effect of beneficiary, all other main 2-way interaction, and 3-way interaction effects were highly significant ($p \leq .001$). Hence,

Table 14.1. Pearson's correlation, Cronbach's Alpha, means, and standard deviation of major variables.

$N = 295$	α	M	SD	1	2	3
1 Sharing with coworkers	.94	3.94	1.63			
2 Sharing with close friends	.92	4.08	1.68	.47**		
3 Impression Management	.84	3.78	1.02	−.26**	−.20**	
4 Machiavellianism	.91	4.10	0.94	.34**	−.02	.07

$+p \le .1.$
$*p \le 0.05.$
$**p \le 0.01.$
$***p \le 0.001.$
Note: All tests are 2-tailed.

Table 14.2. Repeated measures ANOVA: Intention to share information.

Source	SS	df	MS	F	η^2
Between Subject Effect					
Appraisal (A)	651.50	1	651.50	1116.99***	.79
Bonus (B)	251.69	2	125.84	215.76***	.60
A × B	22.60	2	11.30	19.37***	.12
Error	168.56	289	0.58		
Within Subject Effect					
Closeness of Ties (CT)	1.66	1	1.66	1.74	.01
CT × A	12.78	1	12.78	13.44***	.04
CT × B	73.66	2	36.83	38.75***	.21
CT × A × B	35.02	2	17.51	18.40***	.11
Error	274.73	289	0.95		

$*** p \le 0.001.$

friendship ties do not predict sharing of information. Hypothesis H_2 was not supported.

The effect size of appraisal ($\eta^2 = .79$) for sharing was larger than that of bonuses ($\eta^2 = .60$) even though both show strong inducement for sharing knowledge. The mean score (μ) for intention to share knowledge increased from 2.97 to 5.07 when knowledge sharing was appraised. In the no bonus condition, intention to share was 3.15 (μ) compared to 4.20 (μ) in the individual performance bonus condition,

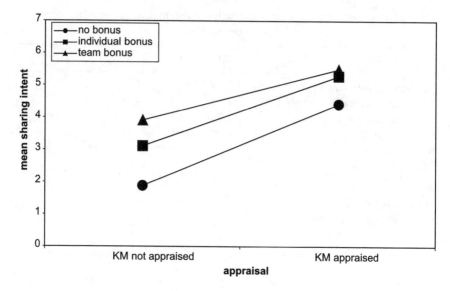

Fig. 14.1. Two-way interaction effects between appraisal and bonus on sharing intent.

and 4.71 (μ) in the team bonus conditions, supporting hypotheses H_{1a} and H_{1b}.

Figure 14.1 presents the results of the 2-way interaction ($\eta^2 = .12$) and shows that in the absence of appraisals, bonus types yields significantly stronger effects than when appraisal for performance is present.

The 3-way interaction among beneficiary, bonuses and appraisals ($\eta^2 = .11$), presented graphically in Fig. 14.2, shows that with close friends, the bonus factor does not significantly increase sharing intent if they are already appraised for sharing although sharing intent significantly increases when appraisal is absent. However, the intention to share with ordinary co-workers is also significantly increased by the additive effects of both appraisal and bonuses (see Fig. 14.3). Hence hypothesis 3 is supported.

Hypotheses $H_{4a} - H_5$ were tested using a series of hierarchical regression analyses. Following Cohen and Cohen's (1983) and Aiken and West's (1991) recommendations, all continuous independent variables were centered. This was carried out by subtracting mean values of each independent variable. The adjusted variables each have a mean of zero but their sample distribution remains unchanged (Mehra, Kilduff and

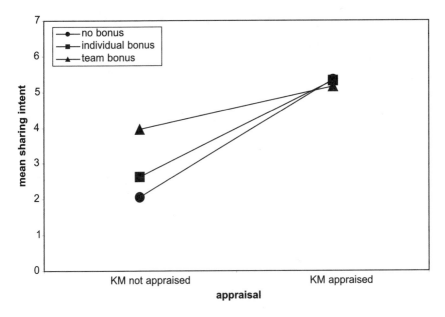

Fig. 14.2. Three-way interaction effects between appraisal, bonus and sharing information with close friends.

Brass, 2001). We, however, did not center the dummy variables in the analysis, as recommended by Aiken and West (1991:130).

Separate analyses were performed for each person (impression management, Machiavellianism) and categorical (appraisal versus none) variable and for each dependent variable (intention to share with co-workers; and with close-friends). The person variable was entered first followed by the categorical variable for the treatment conditions (appraisal versus none) and finally by the interaction term. The moderator hypothesis is supported if the interaction term is significant and in the anticipated directions (Baron and Kenny, 1986; Lee, Pillutla and Law, 2000). The results are shown in Tables 14.3 and 14.4.

Effects for the appraisal factors for all four analyses (impression management with co-workers — $\Delta F\,(1\,292) = 108.39$; impression management with close friends — $\Delta F\,(1\,292) = 375.43$; Machiavellianism with co-workers — $\Delta F\,(1\,292) = 150.99$; Machiavellianism with close friends — $\Delta F\,(1\,292) = 395.41$; all ΔR^2 were significant at $p \leq .001$. This further confirms hypothesis H_{1a}.

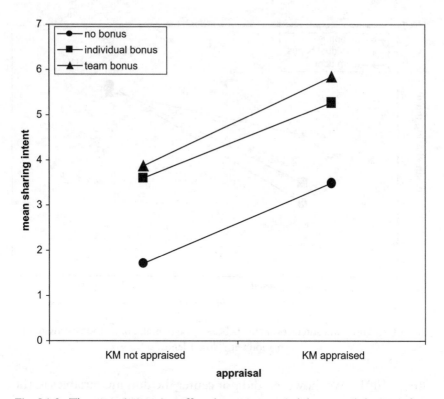

Fig. 14.3. Three-way interaction effects between appraisal, bonus and sharing information with coworkers.

Significant interaction effects between appraisal factor and each of the person variables were found for sharing with co-workers: impression management, $\Delta F(1\,291) = 23.77$, $p \leq .001$; Machiavellinism, $\Delta F(1\,291) = 24.54$, $p \leq .001$. However, on both predictors, no significant interaction effects were found for sharing with close friends. Hypothesis H_{4b} was supported. The beta coefficients are shown in Table 14.5 and the interaction effects are illustrated graphically in Figs. 14.4 and 14.5.

The presence of appraisals was a strong inducement to share knowledge whether the beneficiaries are co-workers or close friends. However, as predicted in hypothesis H_{4a}, impression management is positively related to knowledge sharing when it is not appraised and negatively related to knowledge sharing when it is ($\beta = -.29, p \leq .001$).

Table 14.3. Interaction effects between appraisal and person variables (centered on their means) on sharing intentions with co-workers.

	R^2	Adj. R^2	SE	ΔR^2	Change Statistics ΔF	DF
Model						
Impression Management (IM)	.08	.08	1.53	.08	25.49***	1 293
IM and Appraisal (APR)	.33	.32	1.31	.25	108.39***	1 292
IM, APR, and (IM × APR)	.38	.37	1.26	.05	23.77***	1 291
Model						
Machiavellianism (MAC)	.15	.15	1.47	.15	53.41***	1 293
MAC and APR	.44	.44	1.20	.29	150.99***	1 292
MAC, APR, and (MAC × APR)	.49	.48	1.15	.04	24.54***	1 291

***$p < 0.001$.

Table 14.4. Interaction effects between appraisal and person variables (centered on their means) on sharing intentions with close friends.

	R^2	Adj. R^2	SE	ΔR^2	Change Statistics ΔF	DF
Model						
IM	.03	.03	1.56	.03	9.69**	1,293
IM and APR	.58	.57	1.03	.55	375.43***	1,292
IM, APR, and (IM × APR)	.58	.57	1.04	.00	.17	1,291
Model						
MAC	.00	.00	1.59	.00	.01	1,293
MAC and APR	.58	.57	1.04	.58	395.41***	1,292
MAC, APR, and (MAC × APR)	.58	.57	1.04	.00	.14	1,291

***$p < 0.001$.

Machiavellianism had no significant effect on knowledge sharing when the beneficiaries are close friends. In contrast, when dealing with co-workers who were not close friends, Machiavellianism had a strong effect on knowledge sharing.

Unexpectedly, those low on Machiavellianism were unmotivated while those high on Machiavellianism seemed overly motivated by the

328 H.-B. Chia et al.

Table 14.5. Standardized beta for regression of appraisal condition, predictors, and interaction terms on sharing intention.

	Impression Management		Machiavellianism	
	Co-worker	Close Friend	Co-worker	Close Friend
Appraisal	.50***	.77***	.54***	.76***
Predictor	.06	.07	.14*	−.06
Appraisal × Predictor	−.29***	−.02	.30***	.02
$F(3\ 291)$	59.39	132.18	91.65	131.47
R^2	.38	.58	.49	.58
Adj R^2	.37	.57	.48	.57
Adj. R^2	.37	.57	.48	.57

***$p \leq 0.001$.

appraisal of knowledge sharing ($\beta = .30$, $p \leq .001$). Hypothesis H_5 was partially supported.

14.7.2. Discussion

One of the most important contributions of the present study is that it clarifies the relative effects of situational factors, friendship ties and personal orientation not previously identified as antecedents of knowledge management, or more importantly knowledge sharing. This study went beyond existing conceptualizations of knowledge sharing, providing a more diverse set of behaviors (using a vignette-based experimental design) representing a richer, more comprehensive conceptualization of extra-role behavior that is not found in other empirical research on ERB or OCB. The results of this study clearly demonstrate the vital role that situational factors, and inducements in particular, play in motivating sharing of knowledge among coworkers. A much higher degree of sharing was found in "strong situations" or situations that included tangible inducements (both direct and indirect in form of appraisals or performance bonuses respectively) for sharing. The results suggest that if organizations wish to increase knowledge sharing, the more specific and relevant the inducements to knowledge sharing, the stronger the effect is likely

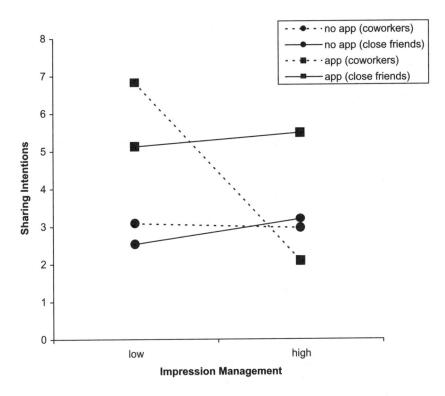

Fig. 14.4. Interaction effects of appraisal and impression management on sharing intentions.

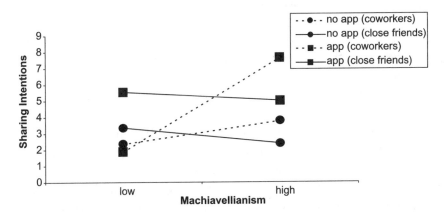

Fig. 14.5. Interaction effects of appraisal and Machiavellianism on sharing intentions.

to be. The strength of this effect is, however, declining in the order — appraisal for knowledge sharing, performance bonuses, and closeness of ties. Overall, the results suggest that employing the two interventions (appraisals and performance bonus) simultaneously can be effective because both have sizable additive effects. However, the results support the use of appraisal jointly with developing close ties as an effective strategy to promote knowledge sharing. In addition, this combination may be a substitute for performance bonuses in achieving knowledge sharing. In contrast, bonuses provided no additive effects when ties are strong. This finding has vital implications for human resource managers, practitioners as well as academics.

However, it is prudent to note that in the absence of inducements, friendship ties do not predict sharing intentions. We offer a post hoc rationale for this finding. As stated in the literature, strength of ties researchers attribute sharing intentions to be reliant on knowledge redundancy among employees and relational embeddedness in the emloyees' social network. If we assume both of these factors to have an equal effect on sharing intentions, then it is most likely that employees would share proprietary information with close friends in their division. This relation would only hold true if all employees in that particular division performed similar tasks — high levels of knowledge redundancy among coworkers and close friends in that division, and have access to almost similar information. The sample of the present study consists of engineers from the instrumentation division of a refinery. An interview with the chairperson of this division revealed that all employees performed almost exactly similar tasks, and were divided into teams to handle different projects. The chairperson also informed us that all employees work under a common "shed" and are rotated frequently, approximately every 20 days, to work with different teams on different projects. Interviews with employees and managers in this division further revealed that employees in this division lived in very close proximity with one another at their quarters (3 adjacent buildings) and met very frequently on occasions such as birthdays, festivals and other non-company social gatherings. Hence, it may be probable that employees form a close network with most coworkers in their division and as a result, would generally not make a distinction to share with either close friends or co-workers.

Another plausible reason for this finding could be that the knowledge redundancy among coworkers is given a heavier priority than relational embededdness when employees decide with whom they wish to share proprietary information. In the context of the sample used in this study, if employees put greater weight on knowledge redundancy, then it is probable that they would be "equally likely" to share proprietary information with most co-workers in their division without giving preference to close friends who perform similar tasks. Despite these post-hoc rationales, additional future research is warranted to further explore this issue.

The results of this study also clearly demonstrate that while situational variables can have strong effects on knowledge sharing, person variables also act as important moderators. The relationship between recognizing knowledge sharing in the performance appraisal system and employees' willingness to share personally valuable information was moderated by certain dispositional factors.

Machiavellians appeared to respond in a straightforwardly self-interested manner, sharing knowledge more freely when doing so was recognized in the appraisal process. However, impression managers find themselves in a more difficult position. They are caught in the dilemma of wanting to pursue their material self-interests but without appearing instrumental. This concern for a positive public image moderates their response to systems that are clearly and obviously designed to link self-interest with desired behaviors. For example, there is evidence that people use humility and modesty, e.g. not affected by the self-interest outcomes of the sharing act, to ingratiate themselves to others (Baumeister and Jones, 1978; Langston and Cantor, 1989; Schlenker and Leary, 1982; Stires and Jones, 1969). As Giacalone and Rosenfeld (1989) pointed out, the purpose of such forms of self-deception is to mask the desire to look good. Hence the respondents were cautious ingratiators, trying to prevent the detection and the avoidance of the attribution that one is a deliberate manipulator. They would not want to take any risk that makes them look "intentional ingratiators" whose sincerity is often discounted. Hence impression management was negatively related to knowledge sharing with co-workers who were not close friends when knowledge sharing was formally appraised, but was positively related when knowledge sharing was not appraised.

Besides the person-situation interaction, the relationship with potential recipients of shared knowledge appears to affect knowledge sharing intentions. When the potential recipient is a close friend, impression managers appear to be less concerned with their image and actually act in a way that is more self-interested. Presumably, the close relationship is accompanied by acceptance, so impression managers can let down their guard and act more instrumentally. With close friends, they do not have to be concerned about constructing a positive image, so they benefit most by "hoarding" valuable information. In contrast, by sharing with coworkers they can benefit in terms of image construction and preservation and such benefits may outweigh the job-specific advantage provided the knowledge; however, appraising for knowledge sharing seems to "deter" impression managers from sharing valuable information because observers might attribute their sharing to instrumental motives. On the other hand, sharing knowledge when doing so is not appraised increases the chances of being seen as altruistic or committed to the job and organization. Our manipulation checks revealed that impression managers perceived sharing information with coworkers who are not close friends when appraised to be negatively related to benefits in terms of reputation ($r = -0.58$; $p \leq 0.01$) and in terms of monetary rewards ($r = -0.48$; $p \leq 0.01$).

Machiavellians behave differently from impression managers because they are focused more on tangible rewards and are less concerned with their public image with persons that cannot provide tangible rewards. They have a tendency to exploit the efforts of others, to be free riders, and to be highly instrumental (Mudrack, Mason and Stepanski, 1999). However, even such generalizations have their limits. Our results most clearly show this instrumentality when the potential recipients of valuable knowledge are not close friends. For subjects at the 80th percentile (high MACH), their sharing intentions increased significantly, from μ (mean) $= 3.26$ to $\mu = 5.61$, in the no appraisal condition to when appraised (please refer to Fig. 14.2).

Unexpectedly, they were also somewhat more willing to share than their low-MACH counterparts when not appraised. The goal of a Machiavellian is to obtain rewards, e.g. promotion, pay raise, better career prospects, etc., without undue consideration of empathy, altruism, or well-being of others. They were very much more likely to share knowledge with coworkers when appraised (note the steep positive gradient, Fig. 14.2), probably in expectation of the positive consequences that would accrue in the event that they share. Our manipulation check showed that MACHs perceived sharing information when appraised to be positively related to benefits in terms of reputation ($r = 0.52$; $p \leq 0.01$) and in terms of monetary rewards ($r = 0.58$; $p \leq 0.01$). Unexpectedly, their willingness to share more than low MACHs in non-appraisal condition could be driven by other forms of self-interest, e.g. to create reciprocal obligations on the coworkers to reap future benefits via reputation building. Our manipulative check revealed that Machiavellians perceived sharing to yield reputation benefits when not appraised ($r = 0.18$, $p \leq 0.01$). However, with close friends, Machiavellianism is not related to the willingness to share knowledge when specifically appraised. In other words, Machiavellians behave instrumentally only when personal relationships are relatively weak, but they treat their friends much as non-Machiavellians would.

One final contribution of note is a methodological one. Most previous studies have relied on self-report or other-report ratings of extra-role behaviors. This study, by contrast, used a policy capturing approach that is more common in disciplines such as social psychology. Our findings demonstrate that we can develop a better understanding of extra-role behaviors if we go beyond simple ratings to measure behavioral intentions or actual behavior. Self-report ratings are subject to error such as socially desirable responding; other-report ratings may be influenced or limited by the target person's efforts at impression management, the rater's affect toward the person, or constraints on the rater's opportunity to observe the person. By using scenarios in a between-subjects design, we can study ERB free from these sources of error and can better examine the situational determinants of such behaviors. Consequently, a wider use of this approach in ERB research is recommended.

14.8. Managerial Implications

Within the context of managing organizational behavior, the results from this study have potential practical implications. Firstly, although scholars, practitioners and researchers claim that knowledge management is vital for survival in the 21st century, successful implementation of KM infrastructure without facilitating/motivating employees to share knowledge with each other may be futile. As Wah (1999) rightly noted, "*Human inertia is the biggest obstacle to knowledge management efforts*". Our study shows that knowledge sharing will not be forthcoming without the presence of inducements. Organizations should broaden their appraisals and performance criterion to include knowledge sharing endeavors as part of employees' performance evaluation and criteria for promotion. In addition, managers should also concurrently use team-based performance bonus to facilitate optimum outcome for establishing a knowledge sharing culture. Alternatively, we recommend that management could save resources in the following ways — money devoted to performance bonus could be used to encourage KS, at the same time achieving higher levels of knowledge sharing by fostering close ties among colleagues; through strong organizational culture and group cohesiveness; job rotation, as well as appraising KS. This strategy could free up resources which could be put to better use by channeling them to other vital functions such as training.

Secondly, while rewarding employees for knowledge sharing, managers should match an individual's personal orientation to inducements. This study brings to light an ominous difference between impression management and Machiavellianism. While clear and obvious tangible rewards appeal to Machiavellians, it deterred impression managers. When dealing with people whom they have not established a close relationship, impression managers tend to protect the image they are building and avoid situations where they can be seen as instrumental. Hence, these impression managers should be rewarded indirectly with image building opportunities, for example, opportunities for public recognition such as "best employee of the month" or public commendations for service beyond the call of duty. Also, if managers need employees to share information across divisions/functional groups, then it would be most appropriate to hire impression managers for such roles as they make good boundary spanners. For Machiavellians, managers should link tangible rewards directly to sharing behaviors. Alternatively, managers could structure work in teams in concert with creating a strong organizational culture that promotes group cohesiveness, as Machiavellians were found to be not-affected by tangible rewards when sharing with close friends.

14.9. Limitations

While many interesting findings and conclusions have resulted in this research, it is prudent to note some shortcomings which place our optimism regarding knowledge sharing into better perspective. This study was conducted on an Indian sample, and there is always the possibility that the findings may reflect something specific to the Indian culture. Using Hofstede's (1980) proposition, we explored possible implications of Indian culture along the four dimensions of collectivism, power distance, uncertainty avoidance, and masculinity. India was ranked close to America, Britain and Canada along the dimensions of masculinity and uncertainty avoidance. Indians are ranked highest in terms of power distance while Americans fall on the lower end of this dimension. Indians are considered to be semi-collectivists, i.e., they fall midway on the collectivism scale while Americans and Britons are considered to be less collectivistic but more individualistic in nature. Hence, our findings may not be generalizable with respect to an American, British, or non-Asian population. Thus, future studies should seek to replicate the results in other cultures. Secondly, this study only studied one type of tangible inducement. Other types of inducements may not interact in the same way with the person variables that this study has conducted.

14.10. Directions for Future Research

Despite its limitations, the present study has shown that self-interest (inducements) embedded in situational variables is an important dimension that should be further explored. Because of the sparse research on the relationship between self-interest and other variables like impression management, Machiavellianism and sharing intentions, future research should further explore these relationships. The contribution of the present study lies in initiating some new directions in explaining these important behaviors. It was found that extrinsic rewards could greatly increase sharing intent. Future research might also investigate how little the extrinsic rewards need to be to elicit knowledge sharing. If a little goes a long way, the potential benefits should far outdistance the costs and everyone is likely to benefit.

Also, future research should explore the relationship between impression management and knowledge sharing using more exhaustive impression management scales such as self-monitoring scale (Snyder, 1974), balanced inventory of desirable response (BIRD) (Paulhus, 1991), self-presentation scale (Roth, Snyder and Pace, 1986), and measure of ingratiatory behaviors in organizations settings scale (MIBOS) (Kumar and Beyerlein, 1991). This will further substantiate the findings from the present study.

Although one of the core themes of this research was the importance of impression management and Machiavellianism, the scenarios did not include any manipulation of the extent to which supervisors or anyone else would be able to observe and record the respondent's knowledge sharing activities. Hence future research should include such manipulation to ascertain supervisor's ability to observe and record their subordinate's sharing endeavors.

Future research could also look at the generalizability of the present findings under different "information shelf life" conditions. It could be the case that "length of period over which a proprietary information may be useful" may moderate the relationships found in this study. Further, this study examined employees sharing intention with close friends and coworkers in one's work unit/division. Future research could serve as an extension to this study by including sharing of information with coworkers outside one's immediate work unit.

Finally, as we already noted, future research on extra-role behaviors should use scenarios rather than relying on self and other report ratings. Although scenarios are a fairly infrequent though fruitful methodology in the ERB domain, this study showed that such a methodology could better examine the situational determinants of ERB as it is less affected by social desirability and impression enhancing errors. Hence the methodological "advance" of using scenarios in this study turned out to be quite useful and is therefore recommended for future ERB research.

References

Adams, J. and J. Richards (1985). A Policy-capturing Approach to Examine Relationships Between Attitudes and Leadership Style. *Psychological Reports*, 57, 1274–1289.

Aiken, L.S. and S.G. West (1991). *Multiple Regression: Testing and Interpreting Interactions*. Thousand Oaks, CA: Sage.

Alexander, C.S. and H.J. Becker (1978). The Use of Vignettes in Survey Research. *Public Opinion Quarterly*, 42(1), 93–104.

Allsopp, J., H.J. Eysensk and S.B.G. Eysenck (1991). Machiavellianism as a Component in Psychoticism and Extraversion. *Personality and Individual Differences*, 12, 29–41.

Aronson, E., M.B. Brewer and J.M. Carlsmith (1985). Experimentation and Social Psychology. *The Handbook of Social Psychology*, 1, 441–486.

Barber, N. (1994). Machiavellianism and Altruism: Effect of Relatedness of Target Person on Machiavellianism and Helping Attitudes. *Psychological Reports*, 75, 403–422.

Barnett, M.A. and S. Thompson (1985). The Role of Perspective Taking and Empathy in Children's Machiavellinism, Prosocial Behavior and Motive for Helping. *Journal of Genetic Psychology*, 146, 295–305.

Baron, R.M. and D.A. Kenny (1986). The Mediator Moderator Variable Distinction in Social Psychological Research: Conceptual, Strategic and Statistical Considerations. *Journal of Personality and Social Psychology*, 51, 173–182.

Baumeister, R.F. and E.E. Jones (1978). When Self-presenting is Constrained by the Target's Knowledge: Consistency and Compensation. *Journal of Personality and Social Psychology*, 36, 608–618.

Brown, J.J. and P.H. Reingen (1987). Social Ties and Word of Mouth Referral Behavior. *Journal of Consumer Research*, 14, 350–362.

Browne, M.W. and R. Cudeck (1993). Alternative Ways of Assessing Model Fit. In *Testing Structural Equations Models*, K.A. Bollen and J.S. Long (eds.), pp. 136–62. Newbury Park, California: Sage.

Bolino, M.C. (1999). Citizenship and Impression Management: Good Soldiers or Good Actors? *Academy of Management Review*, 24, 82–98.

Boon, L. and D. Kurtz (1988). Selling and Sales Management in Action: Birth Order and the Sales Profession. *Journal of Personnel Selling and Sales Management*, 8, 53–55.

Burt, R.S. (1992). *Structural Holes: The Social Structure of Competition*. Harvard University Press.

Burton, B.K. and W.H. Hegarthy (1999). Some Determinants of Student Corporate Social Responsibility Orientation. *Business and Society*, 38(2), 118–205.

Butler, J.K. (1991). Toward Understanding and Measuring Conditions of Trust: Evolution of a Condition of Trust Inventory. *Journal of Management*, 17, 643–663.

Byrne, B.M. (2001). Structural Equation Modeling with AMOS: Basic Concepts, Applications, and Programming. Mahwah, NJ: Lawrence Erlbaum.

Campbell, D.T. and J.C. Stanley (1963). *Experimental and Quasi-Experimental Designs for Research*. Chicago, IL: Band McNally.

Casella, G. (2000). Vignettes for the Year 2000: Theory and Methods. *Journal of the American Statistical Association*, 95, 1269.

Cavanagh, G.E. and D.J. Fritzsche (1985). Using Vignettes in Business Ethics Research. In *Research in Corporate Social Performance and Policy*.

Chia, H.B., G.J. Nosworthy, D. Kamdar and Y.W. Chay (2002). Person-by-Situation Effects on Organizational Citizenship Behavior: Same Incentive, Different Self-Interests. Unpublished manuscript.

Christie, R. and F. Geis (1970). *Studies in Machiavellianism*. New York: Academic Press.

Cleveland, J.N. (1991). Using Hypothetical and Actual Applicants in Assessing Person-Organization Fit: A Methodological Note. *Journal of Applied Social Psychology*, 21, 1004–1011.

Cohen, J. and P. Cohen (1975). *Applied Multiple Regression/Correlation Analysis for the Behavioral Sciences*. Hillsdale, NJ: Erlbaum.

Corzine, J.B., G. Buntzman and E.T. Busch (1988). Machiavellian and Careers at Pleateau. *Psychological Reports*, 63, 243–246.

Costa, P.T., Jr. and R.R. McCrae (1989). *The NEO-PI/NEO-FFI Manual Supplement*. Odessa, FL: Psychological Assessment Resources, Inc.

Cummings, J.N. (2001). Work Groups and Knowledge Sharing in a Global Organization. Paper presented at the Academy of Management Conference.

Cyriac, K. and R. Dharmaraj (1994). Machiavellianism in Indian Management. *Journal of Business Ethics*, 13(4), 281–294.

Davis, K.R. and W.I. Sauser (1991). Effects of Alternate Weighing Methods in a Policy Capturing Approach to Job Evaluation: A Review and Empirical Investigation. *Personnel Journal*, 44, 85–127.

Deluga, R.J. (1998). Leader-member Exchange Quality and Effectiveness Ratings: The Role of Subordinate-supervisor Conscientiousness Similarity. *Group and Organization Management*, 23, 189–216.

Donnelly, L.F. and D.A. Bownas (1984). Policy Capturing: An Approach to Understanding Personnel Decision-making Processes. *Public Personnel Management Journal*, 13, 81–89.

Drory, A. and U.M. Gluskinos (1980). Machiavellianism and Leadership. *Journal of Applied Psychology*, 65, 81–86.

Drucker, P.F. (1997). The Future That Has Already Happened. *Harvard Business Review*, 75(5), 20–24.

Eastman, K.K. (1994). In the Eyes of the Beholder: An Attributional Approach to Ingratiation and Organizational Citizenship Behavior. *Academy of Management Journal*, 37, 379–391.

Fandt, P.M. and G.R. Ferris (1990). The Management of Information and Impressions: When Employees Behave Opportunistically. *Organizational Behavior and Human Decision Processes*, 45, 140–158.

Ferris, G.R., T.A. Judge, K.M. Rowland and D.E. Fitzgibbons (1994). Subordinate Influence and the Performance Evaluation Process: Test of a Model. *Organizational Behavior and Human Decision Processes*, 58, 101–135.

Frenzen, J. and K. Nakamoto (1993). Structure, Cooperation and the Flow of Market Information. *Journal of Consumer Research*, 20, 360–375.

Folger, R. (1993). Justice, Motivation, and Performance Beyond Role Requirements. *Employee Responsibility and Rights Journal*, 6, 239–248.

Fredrickson, J.W. (1986). An Exploratory Approach to Measuring Perceptions of Strategic Decision Making Process Constructs. *Strategic Management Journal*, 7, 473–483.

Freedman, J.J., J.M. Carlsmith and D. Sears (1970). *Social Psychology*. Englewood Cliffs, NJ: Prentice-Hall.

Funderberg, S.A. and P.E. Levy (1997). The Influence of Individual and Contextual Variables on 360-degree Feedback System Attitudes. *Group and Organization Management*, 22, 210–235.

Gabel, M. and M.T. Topol (1988). Machiavellianism and the Department Store Executive. *Journal of Retailing*, 64(1), 68–85.

Gabel, M. and M.T. Topol (1991). Machiavellian Managers: Do They Perform Better? *Journal of Business Psychology*, 5, 355–367.

Galbraith, J.R. (1994). *Competing with Flexible Lateral Organizations* (2nd Ed.). Reading, MA: Addison-Wesley.

Giacolone, R.A. and P. Rosenfeld (1989). *Impression Management in the Organization*. Hillsdale, NJ: L. Erlbaum Associates.

Granitz, N.A. and J.C. Ward (2001). Actual and Perceived Sharing of Ethical Reasoning and Moral Intent Among In-group and Out-group Members. *Journal of Business Ethics*, 33(4), 299–322.

Graves, L.N. and R.J. Karren (1992). Interviewer Decision Processes and Effectiveness: An Experimental Policy-capturing Investigation. *Personnel Psychology*, 45, 313–340.

Granovetter, M. (1973). The Strength of Weak Ties. *American Journal of Sociology*, 78(6), 360–380.

Greenberg, J. (1993). Justice and Organizational Citizenship: A Commentary on the State of Science. *Employee Responsibility and Rights Journal,* 6, 249–256.

Gurtman, M.B. (1992). Trust, Distrust, and Interpersonal Problems: A Circumplex Analysis. *Journal of Personality and Social Psychology,* 62, 989–1002.

Hair, J.F., R.E. Anderson, R.L. Tatham and C.B. William (1998). *Multivariate Data Analysis,* 5th Ed. New Jersey: Prentice Hall International, Inc.

Hall, A.L. and R.C. Rist (1999). Integrating Multiple Qualitative Research Methods (or avoiding the precariousness of a one-legged stool). *Psychology and Management,* 16, 291–304.

Hansen, M.T. (1999). The Search-transfer Problem: The Role of Weak Ties in Sharing Knowledge Across Organizational Subunits. *Administrative Science Quarterly,* 44, 82–111.

Hansen, M.T., N. Nohria and T. Tierney (1999). What's Your Strategy for Managing Knowledge? *Harvard Business Review,* March-April, 106–116.

Higgins, E.T. and J.A. Bargh (1987). Social Cognition and Social Perception. *Annual Review of Psychology,* 38, 369–425.

Hobson, C.J. and F.W. Gibson (1983). Policy Capturing as an Approach to Understanding and Improving Performance Appraisal: A Review of the Literature. *Academy of Management Review,* 8, 640–649.

Hofstede, G. (1980). *Culture's consequences: International Differences in Work-related Values.* Beverly Hills, CA: Sage.

Hogan, J., S.L. Rybicki, S.J. Motowildo and W.C. Borman (1998). Relations Between Contextual Performance, Personality and Occupational Advancement. *Human Performance,* 11, 189–207.

Hollenbeck, J.R. and C.R. Williams (1987). Goal Importance, Self-focus, and the Goal-setting Process. *Journal of Applied Psychology,* 72, 204–211.

Hollon, C.J. (1983). Machiavellianism and Managerial Work Attitudes and Perceptions. *Psychological Reports,* 52, 432–434.

Howard, A. (1995). A Framework for Work Change. In *The Changing Nature of Work,* A. Howard (ed.), pp. 3–44. San Francisco: Jossey-Bass.

Hui, C., K.S. Law and Z.X. Chen (1999). A Structural Equation Model of the Effects of Negative Affectivity, Leader-member Exchange, and Perceived Job Mobility on In-role and Extra-role Performance: A Chinese Case. *Organizational Behavior and Human Decision Processes,* 77, 3–21.

Hunt, S.D. and L.B. Chonko (1984). Marketing and Machiavellianism. *Journal of Marketing,* 48, 30–42.

Johnson, D. (2001). Society: Investing in Human Relations. *The Futurist,* 35(4), 9–11.

Jones, E.E. and K.E. Davis (1965). From Acts to Dispositions. In *Advances in Experimental Psychology,* L. Berkowitz (ed.), pp. 220–265. New York: Academic Press.

Jones, E.E. and T.S. Pittman (1982). *Towards a General Theory of Self-presentation.* In *Psychological Perspectives on the Self,* J. Suls (ed.), pp. 231–263. Hillsdale, NJ: Lawrence Erlbaum Associates.

Jones, R.E. and C.S. White (1983). Relationships Between Machiavellianism, Task Orientation and Team Effectiveness. *Psychological Reports*, 53, 859–866.

Kameda, T., Y. Ohtsubo and T. Masanori (1997). Centrality in Sosiocognitive Networks and Social Influence: An Illustration in a Group Decision Making Context. *Journal of Personality and Social Psychology*, 73(2), 296–309.

King, W.C., Jr. and E.W. Miles (1994). The Measurement of Equity Sensitivity. *Journal of Occupational and Organizational Psychology*, 67, 133–142.

Klass, S.B. and H.N. Wheeler (1990). Managerial Decision Making About Employee Discipline: A Policy-capturing Approach. *Personnel Psychology*, 43, 117–134.

Krackhardt, D. (1992). The Strength of Strong Ties: The Importance of Philos in Organizations. In *Networks and Organizations: Structure, Form and Action*, pp. 216–239. Harvard Business School Press.

Kumar, K. and M. Beyerlein (1991). Construction and Validation of an Instrument for Measuring Ingratiatory Behaviors in Organizational Settings. *Journal of Applied Psychology*, 76, 619–627.

Langston, C.A. and N. Cantor (1989). Social Anxiety and Social Constraint: When Making Friends is Hard. *Journal of Personality and Social Psychology*, 56, 649–661.

Lepine, J. and L. Van Dyne (2001). Voice and Cooperative Behavior as Contrasting Forms of Contextual Performance: Evidence of Differential Relationships with Big Five Personality Characteristics and Cognitive Ability. *Journal of Applied Psychology*, 86, 325–336.

Lee, C., M. Pillutla and K.S. Law (2000). Power-distance, Gender and Organizational Justice. *Journal of Management*, 26, 685–704.

Leman, K. (1985). *The Birth Order Book*. New York: Dell publishing company.

Lesser, L.L. (2000). *Knowledge and Social Capital: Foundations and Applications*. Butterworth-Heinemann Publications.

Locke, E.A. (1968). Toward a Theory of Task Motivation and Incentives. *Organizational Behavior and Human Performance*, 3, 157–189.

Locke, E.A. and G.P. Latham (1990). *A Theory of Goal Setting and Task Performance*. New Jersey: Prentice Hall.

Lyon, D.W., G.T. Lumpkin and G.G. Dess (2000). Enhancing Entrepreneual Orientation Research: Operationalizing and Measuring a Key Strategic Decision Making Process. *Journal of Management*, 26, 1055–1085.

Malhotra, Y. (1997). Knowledge Management in Inquiring Organizations. Paper presented at the 3rd Americas Conference on Information System, Indianapolis.

Marsden, P.V. and K.E. Campbell (1984). Measuring Tie Strength. *Social Forces*, 63, 482–501.

Mathison, D.L. (1988). Business Ethics Cases and Decision Models: A Call for Relevancy in the Classroom. *Journal of Business Ethics*, 7(2), 77–82.

Mazen, A.M. (1990). The Moderating Role of Social Desirability, Age, and Experience in Human Judgment: Just how Indirect is Policy Capturing? *Organizational Behavior and Human Decision Processes*, 45, 19–40.

McManus, M.A. and M.C. Kelly (1999). Personality Measures and Biodata: Evidence Regarding Their Incremental Predictive Value in the Life Insurance Industry. *Personnel Psychology*, 52, 137–148.

Mehra, A., M Kilduff and D.J. Brass (2001). The Social Networks of High and Low Self-monitors: Implications for Workplace Performance. *Administrative Science Quarterly*, 46(1), 121–146.

Michael, R.J. and R.L. Gayle (1996). Relationship Between Type Machiavellinism and Type A Personality and Ethical Orientation. *Journal of Business Ethics*, 15, 209–219.

Miller, R.L., M.A. Griffin and P.M. Hart (1999). Personality and Organizational Health: The Role of Conscientiousness. *Work and Stress*, 13, 7–19.

Mischel, W. (1977). The Interaction of Person and Situation. In *Personality at the Crossroads: Current Issues in International Psychology*, I.D. Magnusson and N.S. Endler (eds.). Hillsdale, NJ: Erlbaum.

Mischel, W. (1968). *Personality and Assessment*. New York: Wiley.

Mischel, W. and Y. Shoda (1995). A Cognitive-affective System Theory of Personality: Reconceptualizing Situations, Dispositions, Dynamics, and Invariance in Personality Structure. *Psychological Review*, 102, 246–268.

Mobley, W.H. (1982). Supervisor and Employee Race and Sex Effects on Performance Appraisals: A Field Study of Adverse Impact and Generalizability. *Academy of Management Journal*, 25, 598–606.

Mohrman, S.A. and S.G. Cohen (1995). When People Get Out of the Box: New Relationships, New Systems. In *The Changing Nature of Work*, A. Howard (ed.), pp. 365–410. San Francisco: Jossey-Bass.

Moore, D.P. (1984). Evaluating In-role and Out-of-role Performers. *Academy of Management Journal*, 27, 603–618.

Motowildo, S.J. and J.R. Van Scotter (1994). Evidence that Task Performance should be Distinguished from Contextual Performance. *Journal of Applied Psychology*, 79, 475–480.

Mudrack, P.E. (1990). Machiavellianism and Locus of Control: A Meta-analytic Review. *Journal of Social Psychology*, 130, 125–126.

Mudrack, P.E. (1993). An Investigation into the Acceptability of Workplace Behaviors of a Dubious Ethical Nature. *Journal of Business Ethics*, 12, 517–524.

Mudrack, P.E., E.S. Mason and K.M. Stepanski (1999). Equity Sensitivity and Business Ethics. *Journal of Occupational and Organizational Psychology*, 72, 539–560.

Murphy, K.R., B.M. Herr, M.C. Lockhart and E. Maguire (1986). Evaluating the Performance of Paper People. *Journal of Applied Psychology*, 71, 654–661.

Nelson, G. and D. Gilbertson (1991). Machiavellianism Revisited. *Journal of Business Ethics*, 10, 633–639.

Nonaka, I. (1991). The Knowledge Creating Company. *Harvard Business Review*, November-December, 96–104.

Nonaka, I. (1994). A Dynamic Theory of Organizational Knowledge Creation. *Organization Science*, 5(1).

Organ, D.W. and K. Ryan (1995). A Meta-analytic Review of Attitudinal and Dispositional Predictors of Organizational Citizenship Behavior. *Personnel Psychology*, 48, 775–802.

Pandey, J. and P. Singh (1987). Effects of Machivellianism, Other-enhancement, and Power Position on Affect, Power Feeling and Evaluation of the Ingratiator. *Journal of Psychology*, 121, 287–300.

Parasumaran, A., L.L. Berry and V.A. Zeithaml (1985). A Conceptual Model of Service Quality. *Journal of Marketing*, 49, 41–50.

Parasumaran, A., L.L. Berry and V.A. Zeithaml (1988). A Multiple Item Scale for Measuring Consumer Perceptions of Service. *Journal of Retailing*, 64, 12–40.

Pascarella, P. (1997). Harnessing Knowledge. *Management Review*, October, 37–40.

Paulhus, D.L. (1984). Two-component Model of Social Desirable Responding. *Journal of Personality and Social Psychology*, 46, 598–609.

Paulhus, D.L. (1991). Measurement and Control of Response Bias. In *Measures of Personality and Social Psychological Attitudes*, D. Paulhus (ed.), pp. 17–59. New York: Academic Press.

Podsakoff, P.M., S.B. MacKenzie, J.B. Paine and D.G. Bachrach (2000). Organizational Citizenship Behaviors: A Critical Review of the Theoretical and Empirical Literature and Suggestions for Future Research. *Journal of Management*, 26, 513–563.

Polanyi, M. (1967). *The Tacit Dimension*. New York: Doubleday.

Quinn, J.B., P. Anderson and S. Finkelstein (1996). Leveraging Intellect. *Academy of Management Executive*, 10(3), 7–27.

Randall, J. and C. Randall (1990). Review of Salesperson Selection Technique and Criteria: A Managerial Approach. *International Journal of Research in Marketing*, 7, 81–95.

Rayburn, J.M. and L.G. Rayburn (1996). Relationship Between Machiavellianism and Type A Personality and Ethical-orientation. *Journal of Business Ethics*, 18, 209–219.

Ricks, J. and J. Fraedrich (1999). The Paradox of Machiavellianism: Machiavellianism May Make for Productive Sales but Poor Management Reviews. *Journal of Business Ethics*, 20(3), 197–205.

Rindfleisch, A. and C. Moorman (2001). The Acquisition and Utilization of Information in New Product Alliances: A Strength of Ties Perspective. *Journal of Marketing*, 65(2), 1–18.

Rioux, S. and L.A. Penner (2001). The Causes of Organizational Citizenship Behavior: A Motivational Analysis. *Journal of Applied Psychology*, 86(6), 1306–1314.

Robinson, J.P. and R. Shaver (1973). *Measurement of Social Psychological Attitudes*. Ann Arbor, MI: Institute for Social Research.

Rose, G.L. (1978). Sex Effects on Effort Attributions in Managerial Performance Evaluation. *Organizational Behavior and Human Performance*, 21, 367–378.

Rosenfeld, P.R., R.A. Giacalone and C.A. Riordan (1995). *Impression Management in Organizations: Theory, Measurement and Practice*. New York: Routledge.

Rossi, A.L. and J.M. Madden (1985). A Note on Policy Capturing as a Method for Studying Social Desirability. *Bulletin of the Psychonomic Society*, 23, 465–466.

Roth, D.L., C.R. Snyder and L.M. Pace (1986). Dimensions of Favorable Self-Presentation. *Journal of Personality and Social Psychology*, 51, 867–874.

Sabel, C.E. (1993). Studied Trust: Building New Forms of Cooperation in a Volatile Economy. *Human Relations*, 46(9), 133–170.

Sanchez, J.I. and E.L. Levine (1989). Determining Important Tasks Within Jobs: A Policy-capturing Approach. *Journal of Applied Psychology*, 74, 336–342.

Sawyer, A. (1975). Demand Artifacts in Laboratory Experiments in Consumer Research. *Journal of Consumer Research*, 1(4), 20–30.

Schlenker, B.R. (1980). *Impression Management: The Self-concept, Social Identity, and Interpersonal Relations*. Monterey, CA: Brooks/Cole.

Schlenker, B.R. and M.R. Leary (1982). Audiences' Reactions to Self–enhancing, Self-denigrating and Accurate Self-presentations. *Journal of experimental Social Psychology*, 18, 89–104.

Seibert, S.E., M.L. Kraimer and R.C. Linder (2001). A Social Capital Theory of Career Success. *Academy of Management Journal*, 44(2), 219–237.

Sheerer, P.D., D.P. Schwab and H.G. Heneman (1987). Managerial Salary Raise Decisions: A Policy-capturing Approach. *Personnel Psychology*, 40, 27–38.

Shirley, M. (1995). Machiavellian Characteristics Among Nurses. *Nursing Management*, 26(5), 58–68.

Shoda, Y., W. Mischel and J.C. Wright (1989). Intuitive Interactionism in Person Perception: Effects of Situation-behavior Relations on Disposition Judgments. *Journal of Applied Psychology*, 56, 41–53.

Singhapakdi, A. (1993). Ethical Perception of Marketers: The Interaction Effects of Machiavellianism and Organizational Ethical Culture. *Journal of Business Ethics*, 12, 407–418.

Sirsi, A.K., J.C. Ward and P.H. Reingen (1996). Microcultural Analysis of Variation in Sharing in Causal Reasoning About Behavior. *Journal of Consumer Research*, 22(4), 345–372.

Slovic, P., B. Fischoff and S. Lichtenstein (1977). Behavioral Decision Theory. *Annual Review of Psychology*, 28, 1–39.

Smith, E.A. (2001). The Role of Tacit and Explicit Knowledge in the Workplace. *Journal of Knowledge Management*, 5(4), 311–321.

Smith, E.A. (1995). *Creating Productive Organizations: Developing Your Workforce*, Boca Raton, FL: St. Lucie Press.

Snyder, M. (1994). Traits and Motives in the Psychology of Personality. *Psychological Inquiry*, 5, 162–166.

Snyder, M. (1974). Self-monitoring of Expressive Behavior. *Journal of Personality and Social Psychology*, 30, 526–537.

Stires, L.K. and E.E. Jones (1969). Modesty versus Self-enhancement as Alternative Forms of Ingratiation. *Journal of Experimental Social Psychology*, 5, 172–188.

Tedeschi, J.T. and V. Melburg (1984). Impression Management and Influence in the Organization. In *Research in the Sociology of Organizations*, 3, 31–48 S.B. Bacharach and E.J. Lawler (eds.). Greewwich, CT: JAI Press.

Touhey, J.C. (1993). Intelligence, Machiavellianism and Social Mobility. *British Journal of the Society of Clinical Psychologists*, 12, 34–37.

Turnley, W.H. and M.C. Bolino (2001). Achieving Desired Images While Avoiding Undesired Images: Exploring the Role of Self-monitoring in Impression Management. *Journal of Applied Psychology*, 86, 351–360.

Uzzi, B. (1999). Embeddedness in the Making of Financial Capital: How Social Relations and Networks Benefit Firms Seeking Financing. *American Sociological Review*, 64, 481–505.

Van Dyne, L., L. Cummings and J. McLean Parks (1995). Extra-role Behaviors: In Pursuit of Construct and Definitional Clarity. In *Research in Organizational Behavior*, 17, 215–285, L.L. Cummings and B.M. Staw (eds.). Greenwich, CT: JAI Press.

Van Dyne, L., D. VandeWalle, T. Kostova, M.E. Lathlam and L.L. Cummings (2000). Collectivism, Propensity to Trust, and Self Esteem as Predictors of Organizational Citizenship in a Non-work Setting. *Journal of Organizational Behavior*, 21, 3–23.

Vittel, S., J. Lumpkin and M. Rawwas (1991). Consumer Ethics. *Journal of Business Ethics*, 10(5), 365–376.

Wah, L. (1999). Making Knowledge Stick. *Management Review*, May, 24–29.

Watson, P.J. and R.J. Morris (1994). Communal Orientation and Individualism: Factors and Correlations with Values, Social Adjustments, and Self Esteem. *Journal of Psychology*, 128, 289–297.

Wayne, S.J. and S.A. Green (1993). The Effects of Leader Member Exchange on Employee Citizenship and Impression Management Behavior. *Human Relations*, 46, 431–440.

Whitfield, K. and G. Strauss (2000). Methods Matter: Changes in Industrial Relations Research and Their Implications. *British Journal of Industrial Relations*, 38, 141–151.

Weber, J. (1992). Scenarios in Business Ethics Research: Review, Critical Assessment and Recommendations. *Business Ethics Quarterly*, 2, 137–160.

Weiss, L. (1999). The Anatomy of Knowledge Sharing in Professional Organizational Service Firms. *Organization Development Journal*, 17, 61–73.

West, S.G. (1983). Personality and Prediction: An Introduction. *Journal of Personality*, 51, 275–285.

Woehr, D.J. and C.E. Lance (1991). Paper People versus Direct Observation: An Empirical Examination of Laboratory Methodologies. *Journal of Organizational Behavior*, 12, 387–397.

Zellars, K.L., B.T. Tepper and R.A. Giacalone (2001). Paper presented at the Academy of Management Conference.

Appendix 14.1. Examples of Scenarios and Manipulations

1. Your close friend is the Vice President of a major software design firm that specializes in developing software programs for the oil industry. One day, he tells you that his firm has just developed a new programme that will enable refinery engineers to design their projects more efficiently and at less than half the average time taken. This programme will go on the market in eight months time, and it is certain that your company will purchase it then. In the meantime, however, he is willing to pass on a fully-functional trial version of the programme to you free of charge.
2. You were reading through a technical journal that you subscribed to and found an article describing a program available for free at the Internet. This program would update a software package that you and your colleagues are currently using on a daily basis. With this updated program, you will be able to produce process designs faster and more efficiently than your present rate.
3. One day out of your own personal interest, you attended a self-funded 2-day "software course" in designing process control systems using the latest software. In this course you meet up with someone from an American refinery who shares his work process and experiences with you. After exchanging ideas and interacting with him, you realize that certain aspects of your personal work procedures can be done more efficiently, and this will drastically reduce paper loads and save you lots of time.

Appraisal and No Bonus Condition Included the Following Paragraph

In your company, the performance appraisal system assesses employees' willingness to share knowledge/information. Employees are paid a fixed salary and there are no bonuses for individual or team performance.

Appraisal and Individual Based Bonus Condition Included the Following Paragraph

In your company, the performance appraisal system assesses employees' willingness to share knowledge/information. Employees are paid a fixed salary and bonuses are tied to individual performance.

Appraisal and Team Based Bonus Condition Included the Following Paragraph

In your company, the performance appraisal system assesses employees' willingness to share knowledge/information. Employees are paid a fixed salary and bonuses are tied to team performance.

No Appraisal and No Bonus Condition Included the Following Paragraph

In your company, the performance appraisal system does not specifically assess employees' willingness to share knowledge/information. Employees are paid a fixed salary and there are no bonuses for individual or team performance.

No Appraisal and Individual Based Bonus Condition Included the Following Paragraph

In your company, the performance appraisal system does not specifically assess employees' willingness to share knowledge/information. Employees are paid a fixed salary and bonuses are tied to individual performance.

Appendix 14.1 (Continued)

No Appraisal and Team Based Bonus Condition Included the Following Paragraph

In your company, the performance appraisal system does not specifically assess employees' willingness to share knowledge/information. Employees are paid a fixed salary and bonuses are tied to team performance.

Index